Withdrawn
Withdrawn
Withdrawn

Russian Research Center Studies, 4

CHINESE COMMUNISM AND THE RISE OF MAO

The Russian Research Center of Harvard University is supported by a grant from the Carnegie Corporation. The Center carries out interdisciplinary study of Russian institutions and behavior and related subjects.

chinese communism

AND THE RISE OF

mao

BENJAMIN I. SCHWARTZ *Isadore 1916 —*

HARVARD UNIVERSITY PRESS
CAMBRIDGE · MASSACHUSETTS

TO MY BELOVED WIFE, BERNICE

PREFACE

Some eight years have elapsed since this book was written. During that time, the Chinese Communist Party has firmly established its power on the mainland of China, and world-wide interest in all aspects of Chinese Communism has grown immensely. Much work has been done on the history and origins of the movement and many new facts have been brought to light. The Chinese Communist Party has itself elaborated a new orthodox account of its own history, which differs in some marked respects from pervious orthodox accounts (as illustrated in the writings of Hu Hua, Hu Ch'iao-mu, and others) and has brought to light new documentation.

In view of these developments, a re-examination of some of the interpretations brought forth in the book is perhaps warranted. While there are many issues which are certainly open to further discussion, I shall concern myself in this brief preface only with questions which seem fundamental.

As indicated in the introduction, my main concerns in writing this book were first with the history of the internal political relations of the Chinese Communist movement and the history of the relations of the movement as a whole to the Kremlin and second with the closely related question of the evolution of Marxist-Leninist ideology within the Chinese environment — the question of the evolving relations between ideology and actuality. Behind this concern there lay an even larger question — What role if any has ideology played in the history of Communism? In dealing with the latter question, I was not exclusively concerned with Chinese affairs as such. I was also fascinated by the enormous claims made for Marxist-Leninist doctrine as a master science providing its chosen initiates not only with the key to the past but with an infallible science for navigating in the treacherous waters of current social and political events. The self-image of the ideal Communist leader (at least until recently) was of the man whose environment provided him with few perplexities or surprises. He was the intellectual master of all he surveyed. At any given point of time he could make an infallibly correct socio-historic analysis of the current situation and his policy decisions were squarely based on these analyses. The fact that the doctrine was often called a "method" rather than a "dogma" changed nothing in this image. One of the purposes of the book was to examine these enormous claims within the context of the Chinese experience.

If we turn our attention to the first of these concerns — the concern with the inner political history of the movement — accumulating evidence has now made it clear that the statement on page 185 that "the complete victory of the Mao-Chu leadership within the Chinese movement can be said to have been achieved during the 1932–33 period when the Central Committee moved its headquarters from Shanghai to Juichin" stands subject to correction. It is now clear that Mao did not achieve full ascendancy within the movement until the Tsunyi Conference of 1935. It is also clear that certain members of the Central Committee group such as Po Ku (not, however, Wang Ming) managed to wield considerable power within the Soviet areas after 1933 and that there may have even been a temporary decline of Mao's power during the period 1933–1935. The whole story of the complicated factional disputes of the 1933–1935 period remains to be unraveled. It is possible to conceive of many reasons why the members of the "28 Bolshevik" group were able to maintain positions of power within the Soviet areas. They still enjoyed the high prestige of their party positions and presumably the full backing of Moscow and of local Kremlin agents such as the mysterious General Li Teh. They may also have been able to link up quite effectively with elements within the Soviet areas and Red Army high command who were by no means fully reconciled to Mao's ascendancy.

But while this revision of the factual record must be made, I would, nevertheless, maintain the essential correctness of the analysis of the basic factors involved. Indeed the new evidence, it seems to me, in some ways lends added support to this analysis. The assertion that there was a deep conflict between the Central Committee group and the Mao leadership has now received further support from many sources. The assumption that in the end the Central Committee group lost out because it had no firm base of power within the Soviet areas has by no means been weakened. The contention "that the gravitation of power into the hands of Mao Tse-tung and Chu Teh was the result of circumstances and power relations existing within the Chinese Communist movement rather than of any decision made in Moscow" has, it seems to me, been strengthened rather than weakened by the new evidence which has since become available. Finally, the Chinese Communists themselves now insist that one of the basic issues of ideology (to the extent that ideology was involved) between the Central Committee group and the Mao leadership was the question of whether the strength of the Red Army was to be used to preserve the rural bases or as an instrument to recapture the movement's urban bases.

On the question of the evolution of ideology, I would not be inclined to modify any of the basic propositions set forth in the book. Since this book was published, many have insisted that Lenin himself opened the door to the possibility of a complete divorce of a Communist Party from its supposed class basis, the industrial proletariat. But while Lenin may have opened the door, it was Mao who was forced by Chinese circumstances to march through it.

Nothing that has happened since the thirties would lead me to modify the view that Communist doctrine has undergone a steady process of decomposition rather than a process of "extension and enrichment." As these lines are being written, much of the ideology is in flux not only in China but also in other parts of the Communist world. This does not mean that nothing remains. The concept of a Leninist party, the Stalinist model of economic development, the underlying Hegelian faith that "History is on our side" probably still exercise a deep and tenacious hold on those in power. But the overweening claims of Marxism-Leninism as a master science infallibly guiding its initiates from the present into the future enjoys less empirical support than ever. Instead, it seems quite clear that this socio-political philosophy is as much buffeted, twisted, and shaped by unforeseen contingencies and unexpected possibilities as political philosophies which make far less sweeping claims.

May 10, 1958   BENJAMIN I. SCHWARTZ

ACKNOWLEDGMENTS

It would be impossible to list here the names of all those who have helped in the preparation of this study with their valuable suggestions and bibliographical leads.

However, I should particularly like to thank Professor John K. Fairbank wno has been my teacher and guide ever since I first decided upon the bold venture of specializing in Far Eastern studies. My obligations to him really cannot be measured.

I should also like to thank Professor Clyde Kluckhohn, Director of the Russian Research Center, for furthering the publication of this volume and for offering me much valuable guidance.

For bibliographical aid, I owe a special debt to Mrs. Mary Wright and the staff of the Hoover Library at Stanford University who made available to me that library's precious collection of Chinese sources, as well as a debt to Dr. Arthur W. Hummel of the Library of Congress who called to my attention certain valuable documents available only at that library.

CONTENTS

INTRODUCTION

It is the purpose of this study to investigate the history of the Chinese Communist movement, within a limited period, in terms of its doctrinal frame of reference and of its internal political relations. It is thus *not* its primary purpose to consider the movement in terms of the "objective" social and political conditions which have encouraged its growth, or in terms of its effect on the masses. Nor does it deal in any detail with those elements of China's traditional culture which may have facilitated the movement's growth. It need hardly be added that none of these aspects can be considered in isolation from the other. One cannot, of course, understand the tensions which have developed in China between Marxist-Leninist dogma and reality, or the political relations among various groups within the party and between the party and Moscow without reference to China's objective conditions or its cultural heritage. While bearing this fact in mind, however, we feel that we are justified in focusing our attention on an area which has been particularly neglected hitherto.

We are aware that there are those who might be inclined to doubt the value of such an investigation. To those who dwell on the presumably Olympian heights of sociological, economic, geopolitical, and historic abstraction, everything which has happened in China may seem to have flowed inexorably from the "objective situation." To such people the ideological presuppositions of the leaders of the Communist movement may seem to be so much froth on the surface of reality, while the details of their political relations may seem to be so much small talk not worthy of the scholar.

It would, of course, be sheer folly to deny the transcendent importance of objective conditions. All political action must be carried on with reference to the tasks imposed by the objective situation. I do, however, emphatically reject that type of animism which maintains that "situations" automatically create their own results. *The manner in which the tasks are met or not met* is determined quite as much by the ideas, intentions, and ambitions of those who finally assume the responsibility for meeting them, as by any other factor. The fact that in China the Communists, with their own peculiar presuppositions, have inherited the responsibility for meeting these tasks will, I think, be a factor of paramount importance in determining the shape of future objective situations.

Furthermore, it is not our purpose to consider doctrine *in vacuo*, but to treat doctrine as molded and twisted by living men, operating in concrete situations and animated by a variety of motives. What emerges in China will certainly not be the simple result of the present doctrines and intentions of the Communist leaders. It is more likely to be the result of the tension between such doctrines and intentions and the situation in which these leaders are involved. To ignore the doctrines of the leaders, however, is to ignore one of the determining factors in this tension.

Paradoxically, one of the prices often paid by those who have a supercilious disdain for ideological matters, who refuse to consider any but the "objective" factors, is a peculiar naïveté with regard to ideological claims. Precisely because of their refusal to consider matters of doctrine they are often inclined to accept at face value ideological pronouncements which are simply empty ritual phrases. It is only by a study of the tension between doctrine and behavior that one can learn to distinguish between what has become dead letter and what is still living faith.

It may further be objected, however, that in concentrating on the thoughts and intentions of a handful of leaders we are ignoring the fact that what we are witnessing in China is a sweeping popular movement, an elemental upsurge of the masses, and that the leaders are merely the agents of the needs and aspirations of these masses. Now, while we are firmly convinced that the Communist movement in China has risen to power on the crest of a popular movement, this does not mean that the Communist leadership is, as it were, the mystic embodiment of the popular will, or that all its acts are the expression of the aspirations of the people. Within the Communist dispensation, in particular, there is every reason to suppose that basic historic decisions will be made by the political leaders and not by the surging masses.

There are two oversimplified views to be avoided, I think, in considering the relations of the small groups of the intellectually and politically articulate to the masses in such lands as China. There is, on the one hand, the inclination to think that because these groups have come to think in a foreign idiom, they are therefore entirely cut off from the masses and have no relation to them. To those who hold such views it must be pointed out that these men cannot completely escape from the environment from which they have sprung or the situation in which they are involved, even when they look abroad for solutions.

On the other hand, there is also the inclination to think that the voice of the westernized intellectual-politician in Asia is simply the voice of the masses made articulate. This view ignores the extent to which the thought of these intellectuals has been colored by their commitment to foreign philosophies as well as by their own ambitions. We would therefore suggest that, in general, the relations of these groups to the masses are not simple but paradoxical. They are involved in a common situation with the masses and yet, to a considerable extent, alienated from them.

Applying this generalization to the Chinese Communist movement, there can be little doubt that the present Communist leaders in China have risen to power by addressing themselves to the immediate felt needs of China's peasant millions. To leap, however, from this fact to the conclusion that they are the embodiment of the aspirations of the Chinese people and that they will automatically continue to express the needs and aspirations of the masses is to construct a myth designed to sanction in advance all their future activities. The needs of the masses have a time dimension. Lenin may have been in complete harmony with the felt needs of the masses when he proclaimed the motto of land and peace. Was he then in harmony with their felt needs at the time of the Kronstadt uprising?

As for the aspirations of the masses beyond their physical and economic needs, how can they be known unless we go into the Chinese village and live with its inhabitants? It may of course be that beyond their desire to escape from their present wretchedness the masses are simply confused about the type of life which they wish to live. Whatever may be the case, it behooves us to approach this whole question in a spirit of humble agnosticism. If by the phrase "the aspirations of the masses" we simply mean that their political leaders know what is best for them, that the leaders will succeed in making their own aspirations those of the masses, then let us say so and not indulge in sentimental rhetoric. We know that the masses wish to escape from their present wretchedness. In the absence of knowledge, however, we have no right to say that the masses of China wish to reproduce the pattern of either Detroit or Magnitogorsk in China. We are, however, in a somewhat better position to study the ambitions and aspirations of their leaders.

I would therefore suggest that in China we have witnessed not only an elemental upsurge of the masses, but also the rise of a vigorous new ruling group to power. These are two related but separate facts.

To some it may appear that this study concerns itself overmuch with the hairsplitting details of the Marxist-Leninist *scolastique*. In the first place, it should be observed that this doctrinaire hairsplitting is the atmosphere in which the Chinese Communist leaders live and the air which they breathe. Unless we form some acquaintance with it, we cut ourselves off from an understanding of their mental world.

More important, however, it is only by grappling with the details of doctrine that we can attempt to judge what elements of doctrine are still the mainsprings of action and what elements have already become dead verbiage designed to conceal the decay of doctrine.

In general, it is our view that in spite of its seeming "successes," Marxism has in its movement eastward — into situations for which its original premises made little provision — undergone a slow but steady process of decomposition. This process had already gone some distance with Lenin, himself, and might have gone still further if he had lived longer. Elements which are organically inseparable in the original doctrine had already been torn asunder and isolated from each other with Lenin. With Stalin, of course, this process has gone still further, and it has been one of the aims of this study to show how the process has been carried forward yet another step by the experience of the Chinese Communist Party.

At every step, to be sure, the process has been inhibited and counterbalanced by a tremendous "will to orthodoxy" (closely related to the power interests of the groups involved). Whenever circumstances have finally led to a course of action not provided for by previous doctrine, every attempt is made to prove that such action was actually contemplated in advance and new rationalizations are then devised to fit new experiences into an elaborate façade designed to prove an unerring consistency and unfailing foresight. On the other hand, so long as political action seems to be in harmony with orthodox tenets, such tenets are considered inviolate and not open to question.

It is the conclusion of this study that the political strategy of Mao Tse-tung was not planned in advance in Moscow, and even ran counter to tenets of orthodoxy which were still considered sacrosanct and inviolate in Moscow at the time when this strategy was first crystallized; that it was only the force of circumstance which finally led Moscow to provide a façade of rationalization for this new experience.

If this conclusion is true, what bearing does it have on the immensely complex question of the relations of the Kremlin to the Chinese Communist Party? If the Maoist strategy was not planned in advance in Moscow, if the Mao leadership was not directly chosen by Moscow, these are historic factors which must bear some weight in the consideration of this question. However, it must be emphasized that relations between Moscow and the Chinese Communist Party are quite as likely to be determined by a whole range of factors operating in the present and in the future as by factors inherited from the past.

On the other hand, this conclusion does bear much more directly on the enormous claims made for Marxism-Leninism as a sort of magical science enabling its self-chosen high priests in the Kremlin to plan their grandiose global strategy well in advance, allowing no room for unexpected contingency. An immense effort is currently being made by orthodox Stalinist historiography to present the Chinese Communist success as the result of Stalin's own prescience and masterly planning. It is strange to note that this myth has been accepted and even insisted upon by many who regard themselves as the Kremlin's bitterest foes. It is our own conviction, however, that Communist success no less than Communist failure is often unplanned in advance.

To underestimate the cleverness of the Soviet leaders or their single-minded pursuit of their objectives, would be sheer folly. On the other hand, to accept their own image of themselves as super-human "social engineers" operating on the basis of an infallible historic science is equally dangerous. We should not underestimate the attractiveness of such an image to large segments of modern humanity desperately looking for straws to cling to, and we must remember that such an image has a paralytic effect on those opposing the Kremlin and discourages belief in the possibility of maneuvering against it in a world still full of incalculable contingencies.

I THE ORIGINS OF MARXISM-LENINISM IN CHINA

In view of the rapid spread of Marxism-Leninism in China after 1919, it is curious to observe what little attention Marxism itself attracted there during the years preceding the Russian revolution. It is curious because the small group of westernized Chinese intelligentsia was at this time exposing itself to every variety of doctrine from the West, and theories which in their western context seem far removed from each other in time made their appearance in China with a strange air of contemporaneity.

If we peruse the pages of the *Hsin Ch'ing-nien* review, the undisputed organ of the advanced intelligentsia after 1915, we find discussions of Adam Smith, Nietzsche, John Stuart Mill, Tolstoy, Thomas Henry Huxley, Darwin, Spencer, Rousseau, Montesquieu, Kropotkin, and a host of secondary figures.[1] We will search in vain, however, for discussions of Marx. This neglect cannot be explained by sheer ignorance [2] nor yet by any fear of "radicalism" for, in its recoil from Chinese tradition and from the past in general, this group of intellectuals was predisposed to adopt the most "modern" and extreme solutions which the West had to offer.

In attempting to account for this omission I would suggest that to the Chinese intelligentsia, immersed as they were in their own situation — the Chinese situation — Marxism in its pre-Leninist form must have seemed most irrelevant.[3] For before the appearance of the Leninist argument, with its tortured interpretations and glaring omissions, it had seemed clear to all that Marx had expected capitalism to break at its most highly developed point,[4] at the sector in which there already existed "all the productive forces which could be developed in the bosom of the old society." [5] Hence, the Marxist movement in Europe kept its eyes firmly fixed on the industrialized West. There is no hint in Marx's scattered discussions of the world's "backward areas" that these areas were to play a leading role in the imminent transformation from capitalism to socialism. In the period of primitive accumulation these areas had provided a field for ruthless exploitation by commercial capital. In the period of industrial capitalism we gather that capitalism would soon bring these areas into the orbit of "civilization" and remake them in its own image.[6] The central drama would be enacted, however, in capitalism's original home and not in the backward areas. This, in sum, was the attitude of the pre-Leninist Marxist movement. None of the innovations and flexibilities introduced by Lenin in his attempt to adapt Marxism to Russian realities were as yet widely known. There was as yet no hint that a small proletariat, well organized and led by professional revolutionaries, could initiate the world revolution in a "backward area." There was no hint of the strategic role of "backward nations" in the world revolution or of the possibility envisioned by Trotsky of "carrying out pre-socialist tasks by socialist methods." In short, pre-Leninist Marxism had no message immediately relevant to the situation in which the Chinese intelligentsia found themselves.

In tracing the origins of Marxism-Leninism in China, I can think of no better method than that of following in some detail the intellectual development of Li Ta-chao and Ch'en Tu-hsiu during the years immediately preceding the founding of the Chinese Communist Party. Not only were these men the actual founders of the Communist Party and the sponsors of Marxism-Leninism in China, but they were also among the few undisputed leaders of the whole westernized intelligentsia. Their relationship to their students at Peking University — the students of the May Fourth Movement — can hardly be understood in terms of the occidental student-professor relationship. It was much closer in spirit to the traditional Chinese sage-disciple relationship. It is, therefore, no exaggeration to say that in their reactions to the events of their day, they epitomized, to some extent, the experience of a whole segment of the advanced intelligentsia.

Ch'en Tu-hsiu,[7] the founder of the *Hsin Ch'ing-nien* review, had in the years preceding 1919 committed himself to a fairly consistent philosophy resting on the twin pillars of "democracy and science." On its negative side, this philosophy had involved a total rejection of traditional Chinese culture in all its manifestations — Buddhist,

Taoist, and Confucian. Buddhism and Taoism by their radically antiworldly bias had paralyzed the energies of China for centuries. Confucianism on its side had suffocated the individual in a network of family and social obligations.[8] The final result had been passivity, stagnation, and impotence in the face of the challenge from the West. The answer to this challenge could be found only in the West itself. How was one to account for the bursting vitality of the West, its spiritual and physical dynamism? What did the West have that the East lacks? The answer in Ch'en's view was quite clear — democracy and science. It is perhaps worth noting here that, as a rebel against Chinese tradition, as a fervent "modernist," Ch'en was little inclined to seek the secret of the West in anything preceding the eighteenth century. In this he accurately mirrored the mentality of the whole advanced intelligentsia.

What then was Ch'en's conception of democracy? Essentially it was the concept of Manchester liberalism. By removing the fetters which tradition had placed on the individual, by granting him the liberty to pursue his enlightened self-interest, and by securing this liberty in law, democracy had set free the energies of the individual.[9] Ch'en was well aware of the fact that much of the achievement of the modern West lay in the realm of productive economic activity and he was convinced that the removal of the fetters of Confucianism and the liberation of the energies of the individual could produce similar results in China. It is to be noted here that the type of individualism which he espoused was not the nihilistic individualism of the romantics, but the economically motivated individualism of Manchester liberalism. It was, in a sense, a socially motivated individualism for, in his view, the liberation of the individual would revitalize Chinese society. One cannot help but feel that still lurking silently in the background was the old Confucian feeling that the individual must justify himself by his service to the social order.

Ch'en's conception of the role of science reminds one above all of the Russian nihilists. Like them, he saw in science a weapon, a corrosive to be used in dissolving traditional society. He did, of course, appreciate the dynamic role of science in conquering nature, but he was particularly conscious of it as a weapon against "superstitions." As in the case of the nihilists, his readings had led him to identify science with certain extremely crude forms of naturalism.[10] By stridently proclaiming on the authority of science that the material atom was the only ultimate reality, he was quickly able to dispose of the whole basis of the "religion of rites," as well as of the mysticism of Buddhism and Taoism.

Such, in brief, was the philosophic program with which Ch'en Tu-hsiu hoped to transform Chinese society. It rested on an extremely roseate view of the contemporary West and was suffused with the optimistic faith that the sheer process of enlightenment and the transplantation of democratic political forms would perform similar miracles on Chinese soil.

Li Ta-chao [11] was a man of fundamentally different temper. While Ch'en Tu-hsiu concerned himself by predilection with concrete social and literary problems, Li Ta-chao was eminently a man of metaphysical bent. During his years as professor of history at Peking, he had evolved a vague and yet significant "system" which seems a strange amalgam of Chinese and Western elements. One can find here echoes of Buddha and Ch'ü Yuan,[12] of Emerson and Hegel. The outlines of this system are to be found in two essays entitled "Youth" (*Ch'ing-ch'un*)[13] and "Now" (*Chin*),[14] written at different times and yet illustrating the same fundamental theme.

Reality, Li tells us, is an eternal inexhaustible flux without beginning and without end, and with no limits in space. Considered as an absolute this process of reality is one. There is, however, a sphere of the relative in which reality appears to be divided into numerous discrete phenomena (*wan wu*, or "ten thousand things" of traditional Chinese philosophy). The human individual is, of course, part of the relative world of phenomena and hence is just as transient as all other phenomena. Nevertheless, his "ego" is part of the absolute reality and as such eternal. "The ego" is the universe and the universe is the "ego." [15] There is here a hint that this absolute reality is absolute spirit, although it is nowhere specifically stated. Running through this process is a principle of duality whereby each phenomenon has its counterphenomenon. "There is life and death, prosperity and decline, Yin and Yang, fortune and misfortune, youth and old age, health and debility." [16]

Thus far, Li's philosophy was well within the bounds of an extremely ancient Chinese way of thought. One can find here, in spite of the frequent use of western philosophic terminology, echoes of Ch'ü Yuan, Buddhism, and Taoism. It was at this point, however, that Li diverged sharply from the past, and Emerson's glowing optimism and western theories of "progressive evolution" began to assert themselves. While the above view of reality had always borne with it pessimistic implications, always leading to the conviction that man's mortal life is futile, in Li's mind it became associated with a fervent optimism.

While the world of phenomena may seem to be a meaningless flux, while youth and age, life and death seem to follow each other with meaningless repetitiousness, at its heart the universe is eternally young. "The universe is eternal, hence youth is eternal, hence I am eternal." [17] This eternal youthfulness transcends all changes in the phenomenal world. "It is the pivot about which the universe revolves." [18]

Another unexpected feature was Li's concept of time. Philosophies which speak in terms of "eternal flux," of "ceaseless change," generally deny the existence of the present instant. Li, however, stated "some philosophies aver that only the past and the future exist. Others say that actually only the present exists. I am inclined to find reason in the latter view." [19] "The past finds its final resting place in the present while the present is the origin of the future." [20] It is in the present that the youthful spirit of the universe constantly realizes itself anew. The human spirit as part of the world spirit also has the power of regenerating itself in the present and of shaking off the dead incubus of the past. The optimistic flavor of this philosophy was further heightened by Li's acceptance of the creed of progressive evolution. Not only does the universe have the power of self-renewal but of self-renewal on an ever higher plane — in evermore refulgent "nows."

In spite of the Emersonian inspiration [21] of much of this thought it is rather significant that Li did not exalt the individual. For Emerson, the world spirit finds its realization in the life of the individual. For Li, the individual finds his significance only in the world spirit. It is important to note in this connection that Li was a professor of history and that he had some knowledge of German philosophy of history. He had thus developed a bias in favor of impersonal historic forces as opposed to the role of the individual. Traditional Chinese thought and Hegel both prepared him for the easy acceptance of this aspect of Marxist thought.

In spite of the metaphysical cast of Li's mind, however, we soon find that, like Ch'en Tu-hsiu, he was moved by a more immediate preoccupation than the search for philosophic truth — namely, the plight of China. Essentially, Li's whole philosophy was his defiant reply to the charge that China was a dead civilization with no further possibilities of development. The Chinese nation, like mankind in general, could slough off the incubus of the past and experience a new youth in the present. "Our nation has gone through an extremely long history and the accumulated dust of the past is heavily weighing it down. By fettering its life it has brought our nation to a state of extreme decay . . . What we must prove to the world is not that the old China is not dead, but that a new youthful China is in the process of being born." [22]

How was this rebirth to be brought about? On this point Li was vague. He did not commit himself to a whole social program as did Ch'en. He did not look to the individual or to specific socio-economic programs to bring about the rebirth, but to the historic process itself. China, in his view, was now part of the world historic process and all the upheavals and wars which distinguish the modern world must certainly be the birth pangs of a tremendous global rebirth, in which China must participate. Thus, instead of committing himself to specific solutions, he looked to the future with an air of eager anticipation.

Comparing Ch'en Tu-hsiu and Li Ta-chao at this point, we find that they were at one in their uncompromising hostility to traditional Chinese culture; that they both looked to the West for philosophic guidance and accepted this guidance uncritically. Yet, while Ch'en Tu-hsiu found in democracy and science specific solutions for China's problems — social, political, and cultural — Li Ta-chao's thought remained on the cosmic level, looking forward to some cosmic act of liberation. We are not surprised that he was the first to accept the messianic message of the October Revolution.

Such, in outline, are the major features of the thought of Ch'en Tu-hsiu and Li Ta-chao before 1919. If we are to understand the sweeping shifts in their thought during the 1918–1920 period, however, we must turn our attention to the depressing milieu in which they lived and to the impact of external events. For it must be emphasized that neither of these men was a leisurely thinker; neither had time or inclination to meditate deeply on ultimate problems. They were rather men deeply engaged in the situation of their native land who had cast aside traditional Chinese solutions and were anxiously looking westward for new solutions. It is, therefore, impossible to understand the development of their thought (even in its philosophic reaches) in isolation from the immediate political circumstances of the time.

By 1919 it had become glaringly apparent that the revolution of 1911 had failed. Sun Yat-sen's Kuomintang had disintegrated like the "sheet of loose sand" to which he was fond of comparing the Chinese nation. Republican, constitutional ideas had failed to rally his followers behind him, while no attempt had been made to propagate these ideas among the masses. In the vacuum of power left by the death of Yüan Shih-k'ai, power had gravitated into the hands of the generals who cynically manipulated the whole constitutional apparatus. As Ch'en dolefully wrote in 1919, "The false signboard 'Chinese Republic' has been hanging for eight years now but it is still the old medicine which is being sold." [23] The world powers were still continuing their inroads into China's politico-economic life, while Japan's Twenty-one Demands threw a glaring light on China's impotence. Meanwhile, as a result of exactions by rapacious warlords, landlords, and moneylenders, and of the decline of home industry, the peasantry was gradually sinking into hopeless penury.

For a moment Ch'en Tu-hsiu had hoped that China's participation in the first World War would shake off her age-old lethargy and set her on the road to democracy and science.[24] This hope too was soon dispelled.

It was in the midst of this most disheartening atmosphere that Lenin seized power in Russia and proclaimed his messianic message. While it would be grossly inaccurate to say that the distant events taking place in Petrograd created an instantaneous ferment in China's intellectual circles (particularly since Lenin's ultimate victory over the Whites was still in doubt) one man, Li Ta-chao, was immediately attuned to his message.

In Li's article entitled "The Victory of Bolshevism," [25] written in October 1918, we already find him seizing upon the October Revo-

lution as the very act of cosmic liberation which he had been awaiting. "The real victory," he explains, "is not the victory of the Allies
against the Germans, but the victory of the Bolsheviks . . . Henceforth all national boundaries, all differences of classes, all barriers to
freedom will be swept away." [26] The eternally youthful spirit of the
universe had shaken off by this one act the dusty accumulations of
the past. Using his favorite image of spring and autumn, he exclaims,
"The Russian Revolution has shaken off the last dismal autumn
leaves from the tree of the world . . . although the word Bolshevism
was created by the Russians, its spirit expresses the common sentiments of twentieth-century mankind. Thus, the victory of Bolshevism is the victory of the spirit of all mankind." [27]

It is interesting to note, however, that while Li Ta-chao had already accepted the messianic claims of the Russian revolution, he
was still not a Marxist in any strict sense of the word. This very
article entitled the "Victory of Bolshevism" states that "the history
of Mankind is a record of its common spiritual experience. A change
in the sentiments of the individual is a reflection in miniature of a
change in world sentiments." [28] In other words, he still conceived of
the historic process as a movement of the world spirit. He had still
not "turned Hegel right side up." In Marxist terms he was still an
"idealist." He hardly seemed to realize at this point that the acceptance of the Bolshevik message involved the acceptance of its dogmatic base.

Ch'en Tu-hsiu's responses were much slower. He was too firmly
committed to his program of democracy and science to be swept off
his feet by events occurring in Petrograd. Thus, the very issue of
Hsin Ch'ing-nien in which Li Ta-chao greeted the victory of Bolshevism also carried Ch'en's article on the "Von Ketteler Monument." [29] It seems that during the enthusiasms attendant upon the
1918 armistice, a Peking mob had seized the occasion to shatter the
monument to the German minister Von Ketteler, slain at the time
of the Boxer Rebellion. The presence of this monument had long
been regarded as an affront by patriotic Chinese. Ch'en Tu-hsiu took
the occasion to present his own views on the significance of the incident and of the Boxer Rebellion itself. The Von Ketteler monument,
he said, was indeed a disgrace to China, but a disgrace which the
Chinese had brought on themselves. The forces behind the Boxer

movement had been the superstitious notions of Taoism, the supernatural fantasies of Buddhism, and the authoritarian servility of Confucianism. Unfortunately these forces were still dominant in Chinese life and were still acting as a bar to progress. "There are now," he concluded, "two paths open to us, one, the enlightened path to republicanism, science, and atheism; the other the obscurantist path of despotism, superstition, and theocracy. If our people wish to prevent another Boxer incident, another shameful memory like the Von Ketteler Monument, which path should it choose?" [30] The viewpoint expressed here is, of course, much closer to Voltaire than to Karl Marx. There is no hint that foreign imperialism was responsible in any way — no attempt to make a "class analysis." Like Voltaire, he found his enemy in the gross defects of his country's traditional culture and like him he exclaimed "écrasez l'infâme!"

Nevertheless, interest in the Russian revolution gradually deepened throughout the Chinese intelligentsia. If Li Ta-chao was alone in his prompt acceptance of the message of the revolution he was not alone in his interest. The spectacle of a vast historic transformation carried out by a small group of men in a vast nation which had for long held a peculiar fascination for the Chinese intelligentsia [31] — the spectacle of an attack on the West from the West itself — could not fail to arouse the most widespread interest in the most varied circles. The attacks on capitalist western civilization which emanated from Moscow did not necessarily affect traditional-minded Chinese in the same manner in which they affected western conservatives. On the contrary, there is evidence that among many it caused a certain glow of satisfaction.[32] The pro-western intelligentsia (except for some of its more extreme representatives such as Ch'en Tu-hsiu) had been considerably embarrassed by the fact that the very West which had been the source of all enlightenment had also been the source of China's degradation. Now, however, there existed the possibility of judging and criticizing the capitalistic West from a western point of view. Finally, Sun Yat-sen, involved as he was in the actual struggle to achieve political power, could not help but be most interested in Lenin's achievement. There is some evidence that he appreciated Lenin's political philosophy before the actual founders of the Chinese Communist Party themselves.[33]

One of the first concrete manifestations of this widespread interest in the Russian revolution was the founding of the Society for the Study of Marxism (*Ma-k'o-ssŭ-chu-i Yen-chiu-hui*) at Peking University in the spring of 1918.[34] Li Ta-chao soon realized that one could not accept the messianic message of the Russian revolution and yet completely ignore the doctrinal presuppositions on which it was presumably based. The society itself was formed at his instance while Ch'en Tu-hsiu in his capacity as head of the Literature Department of Peking University lent his tacit support, although he seems to have taken no active part in its activities. Its members were made up primarily of students, many of whom, such as Chang Kuo-t'ao and Mao Tse-tung, the librarian's helper, were later destined to play leading roles in the Communist movement.

At its inception, however, the society seems to have been nothing more than its name implied, that is, a society for investigating the doctrine which the Russian revolution had brought into such prominence. This is amply shown by the fruits of its investigations which can be found in a special number of the *Hsin Ch'ing-nien* devoted to Marxism, which appeared in May 1919. We are surprised to find that the spirit which pervades this symposium is not one of violent partisanship, but rather one of critical and detached scholarship. Li Ta-chao's own contribution, entitled "My Views on Marxism," is written in a much cooler spirit than his "Victory of Bolshevism," and at the very outset he candidly reveals his own motives for investigating Marxism in the following terms: "I have not engaged in any extensive research in Marxist theory and if I nevertheless make so bold as to discuss it, it is only because the Russian Revolution has produced such wide repercussions. The Austrian, German and Hungarian social revolutions are all based on Marxism and due to these tremendous upheavals Marxism has naturally drawn to itself the attention of the world." [35] A close reading of the article reveals to our amazement that essentially it is a rejection of Marxism. Li was loath to renounce his view that the human spirit is a dominant creative force in human history. Had he not greeted the Russian revolution itself as a proof of the creative potentialities of the human spirit? He was willing to concede that the economic factor played an important role in human evolution, but unless changes in economic structure were accompanied *simultaneously* by a transformation of the human spirit, they would be fruitless. (He did not share the Marxist faith that a change in economic structure would itself engender a transformation of the human spirit.) Furthermore, Marxism itself was, in the final analysis, a product of its times. Before the nineteenth century, religion and politics had been dominant forces in European society. With the rise of industrialism, however, economic factors had come to play a dominant role, while religion and politics had been swept into the background. It was in this milieu that Marx's views on historic materialism had arisen and they must consequently be considered a product of their period. As history moved on into new periods these views would naturally be superseded. Such, in brief, were the views of Li Ta-chao on Marxism as late as May 1919.

The other articles in the issue are, for the most part, dispassionate expositions of Marxist doctrine, many of them highly critical in tone. One hardly derives the impression from these articles that the Society for the Study of Marxism was indeed the forerunner of the Chinese Communist Party.

In short then, at the outset of the May Fourth Movement we find that Li Ta-chao had accepted without reservation the messianic message of the Russian revolution, but had not yet accepted its doctrinal base although he felt in duty bound to investigate it, and that Ch'en Tu-hsiu had followed Russian events with great interest but still clung tenaciously to his faith in democracy and science. Yet, the latter months of 1920 would find them both solidly within the Marxist-Leninist camp and along with them a host of student-disciples, who had hitherto been pursuing every conceivable wisp of doctrine.

It would thus appear that 1919–1920, the period of the May Fourth Movement, was a most crucial period in their development. We know, of course, that this was the period in which the fires of nationalism smoldering among China's student elements finally burst into flame. The supine attitude of the Peking government toward Japanese pressure and the betrayal of Wilsonian idealism at Versailles were the sparks which finally called forth an active reaction in the form of boycotts and demonstrations. Although we have spoken of Li Ta-chao and Ch'en Tu-hsiu as the spiritual leaders of the student generation, and although they are often spoken of as leaders of the May Fourth Movement, it is only too evident that they played little part in creating the defiant nationalism of the student generation of 1919. As we have seen, while both of them were completely preoccupied with the problems of their native land, neither of them had looked to a nationalist solution. Both of then were to some extent the heirs of a tradition which thought always in terms of man in general and of the world in general (*T'ien hsia*, "Under Heaven"), an intellectual tradition which did not make for responsiveness to purely nationalistic passions. Foreign imperialism had always been a fixed feature of their environment and neither of them had tended to find in it the major cause of China's difficulties. Ch'en Tu-hsiu had implied in all his writings that if the West had been able to exploit China, China herself was to blame. The dynamism of the West was in itself an admirable quality worthy of emulation. Li Ta-chao, on the other hand, had always thought in cosmic terms and sought universal solutions. He had long felt that the rebirth of China must be part of the rebirth of the world. Indeed, in welcoming the Bolshevik revolution, he had explicitly expressed the conviction that it would dissolve national boundaries and create a united mankind.

It is, therefore, not to these men and their contemporaries that we should look as a source of inspiration for the nationalism of the student generation of 1919.[36] This generation was in the aggregate quite different in temper from the generation of Li and Ch'en. In general its education in classical Chinese culture had been much scantier and, superficially, it was much more at home in the framework of western ideas. It did not have to maintain the struggle with the emotional tug of a classical education which we constantly feel in the writings of Li and Ch'en. It was accordingly much more susceptible to the contagion of the nationalistic passion which had risen to fever pitch in Europe and particularly in Japan.

In his capacity as head of the Literature Department at Peking University, Ch'en Tu-hsiu was to become, it is true, deeply involved in the nationalistic activities of his students. With a moral courage which characterized him throughout his life, he consistently and loyally supported them in their clashes with the Peking government, and even suffered imprisonment on their behalf. It was because of this, as well as because of his leading role in the literary renaissance, that he was later to become known as a leader of the May Fourth

Movement. Actually, however, he was in no sense a leader of the movement in its nationalistic, political aspects. It would, perhaps, be more accurate to say that it was rather the activities of his students which eventually forced him to come face to face with the whole phenomenon of imperialism, finally leading him into the arms of Lenin.

However, while the influences which were to lead Ch'en to Lenin were already present in 1919, their effect was to be delayed by a strong counterinfluence — the social philosophy of John Dewey.

The lectures delivered at Peking University by Bertrand Russell and John Dewey in 1919 and 1920 were by no means the least important events in the intellectual ferment of those years. The appearance of both of these men in the flesh in the midst of the intellectual ferment of the May Fourth Movement produced effects which can hardly be conveyed by the term "visiting professor." While Russell's influence was to prove restricted and evanescent,[37] Professor Dewey [38] was to leave a lasting mark on Chinese thought in the sphere of the philosophy of science, if not in the sphere of social philosophy. Yet, it was precisely this social philosophy which Ch'en Tu-hsiu seized upon in order to bolster his much shaken faith in democracy. In his lecture on "Social Philosophy and Political Philosophy," Professor Dewey had outlined a conception of democracy which exceeded in breadth and depth anything that Ch'en Tu-hsiu had understood by that term. For a moment it occurred to him that perhaps the reason for the failure of democracy to take root in China had lain in China's miscomprehension of the whole concept — a miscomprehension which he himself had shared. And for a moment, in his article on "The Basis for the Realization of Democracy" (December 1919), he accepted wholeheartedly Professor Dewey's broader conception.

"I am not disheartened about the future of democracy," exclaims Ch'en.[39] If democracy had failed it was because Chinese had thought of democracy only in terms of constitutions imposed from above. Professor Dewey had amply shown that "facts have the power to create laws, but laws do not have the power to create facts." [40] Democracy must have a grass-roots social basis. It must be part of the fabric of the lives of the people and begin in every village and in every city block. Discussions concerning cabinet organization, parliamentary organization, even about centralism versus federalism, are unreal so long as the people as a whole are not thoroughly imbued with democratic attitudes and do not participate in processes of a democratic life. Nothing was to be expected from political parties which had not the slightest notion of the meaning of popular sovereignty or from generals who sold the old medicine of despotism behind the signboard of the republic.

In the past China had been ruled by a despotic bureaucracy which, had had little direct relationship with the people except in its capacity as a taxgatherer and law court. This tenuous hold of the government had had one positive effect in that it had allowed all sorts of local guild and village mutual benefit societies to spring up. While these organizations were far from modern ideals of popular sovereignty, they did provide some historic basis for grass-roots democracy in China.

The propensity we note here to find positive elements in traditional Chinese institutions is a rather unexpected note in Ch'en's thought and can itself be traced to the influence of Professor Dewey's more even-tempered evaluation of the role of tradition. It is a note which was to disappear entirely and forever with Ch'en's conversion to Marxism-Leninism.

Professor Dewey had turned Ch'en's attention to the question of economic democracy. Specifically, therefore, he recommends the establishment of nation-wide industrial organizations to be organized in every village. In these local organizations the people would finally find their voice and democracy would extend from them into the highest spheres of government. We are somewhat amazed to find that as late as December 1919 Ch'en still does not feel that separate organizations for workers and management are justified. "In the average Chinese artisan shop, after all, the position of managers and workers is more or less alike." [41] This man who by the end of 1920 was to see only proletariat and bourgeoisie, still thinks in December 1919 that modern capitalist industry is a negligible force in Chinese society. It is thus patent that the rise of the proletariat was not the factor which led Ch'en into the Communist movement.

Even while Ch'en was attempting to apply Dewey's formulas to Chinese realities, however, the counter pull of the Leninist world view was already beginning to exert itself.

Unlike the leaders of social democracy in the West, Lenin had begun to occupy himself with the problem of the "backward areas" at a relatively early date. As a man who thought, above all, in terms of political action it had occurred to him that the nascent nationalism of the world's "backward areas" could itself be utilized as a force in realizing the world revolution. Thus in February 1916 he writes in *Sozialdemokrat*: "Not only would we carry out our whole minimum program with decisive means, but we would at once systematically start to incite rebellion among the peoples now oppressed by the Great Russians — and all the colonies and dependent countries of Asia (India, China, Persia, etc.)." [42] This policy was, of course, to find its theoretical framework in the famous Leninist theory of imperialism. The Leninist theory of imperialism confronted the Chinese intelligentsia with a grandiose, starkly melodramatic image of the world. Within this theory almost the entire onus for the wretchedness of the backward areas is laid at the door of international finance capital. [43] In 1919, the picture in its crude outlines seemed simple enough. On the one side was the concert of capitalist-imperialist powers — on the other, the Soviet State of Workers and Peasants, which represented the interest of the toilers as well as of all the oppressed nations and colonies. In 1919 it was an image which seemed to reflect most accurately the events of the time. Had not the Allies acted in concert at Versailles in support of Japanese imperialism? Had not the Soviet Union placed itself squarely on the side of China in its Karakhan proposal? [44]

Li Ta-chao had been won by this melodramatic vision even before the events of 1919, conceiving of it in terms of the conflict between the dead spirit of the past and mankind's self-renewal. After the events of 1919, Ch'en also began to feel its magnetic pull.

In his lectures at Peking University, Professor Dewey had made clear his rejection of all-embracing solutions for mankind's political and economic difficulties. He had viewed human experience as a sea of separate problems and had specifically stated that the only scientific approach to human problems was "to search for concrete methods to meet concrete problems according to the exigencies of time and place." Yet, it was precisely such all-embracing solutions which Ch'en Tu-hsiu had sought in the West. He had hoped that "democracy and science" would have the potency of western technology, while the implementation of the democratic program he had himself outlined in his "Basis for Realization of Democracy" would, on the contrary, have demanded long years of prosaic and undramatic work. It would have required a "going to the people" on the part of the intelligentsia with the aim of carrying on the political education of the people and of helping them to organize themselves along democratic lines. This would, in turn, have required a spirit of utter self-effacement on the part of the intelligentsia, a willingness to play a modest role in the background with no hope of immediate spectacular results. It was a role which neither Ch'en nor his students were ready to play, and a role for which traditional Chinese civilization provided few precedents. Leninism, it is true, would also require a "going to the people" and would in the next few years lead many young students to sacrifice life and career. However, the role it offered to the intelligentsia was a spectacular role of leadership in an atmosphere supercharged with the promise of imminent redemption. It called upon the intelligentsia to agitate and to organize and then to lead the organizations thus formed. It was a type of "going to the people" which Sun Yat-sen was later to find compatible with his own elitist convictions. The fact that Ch'en clearly understood the implications of Leninism on this point is indicated by a statement made in December 1920 to the effect that "a political revolution must begin with those who have knowledge, with the urban intelligentsia, while the social revolution must begin from the organized producers — the laborers." [45] It need hardly be added that like Lenin, he felt that the social revolution must be led by the political revolution.

The very issue of the *Hsin Ch'ing-nien* which carried Ch'en's article on "The Basis for the Realization of Democracy" also carried the first symptoms of his transformation. In one of his miscellaneous notes on current events, Ch'en exclaims: "They accuse the Bolsheviks of disturbing the peace. Do not the Great Powers disturb the peace when they violate the sovereignty of small and weak countries? It is the anti-Bolshevik Omsk government which has bombarded our gunboats and protested against Mongolian autonomy in the name of the Sino-Russian Treaty. It is these gentlemen who are disturbing the peace!" [46] The emotional impact of the Leninist world image was soon to efface every trace of Dewey's influence.

By September 1920, Ch'en Tu-hsiu had accepted Marxism-Leninism *in toto*. None of the philosophic hesitations which mark Li Ta-chao's approach to Marxist doctrine stood in the way of his final leap. "Democracy and Science" had failed; Professor Dewey's program would require years of undramatic self-effacing work for its implementation, and even then offered no hopes of any overall redemption. Here, at last, was a view of life marked by drastic, melodramatic contrasts and hopes of total redemption. What was more, the drama it envisaged was a global drama which finally brought China onto the stage of world history.

The same events and the same atmosphere which carried Ch'en Tu-hsiu into the Marxist-Leninist fold also served to overcome the last scruples of Li Ta-chao on the matter of Marxism. In an article entitled "Material Change and Ethical Change" published in the *Hsin Ch'ao* review in December 1919,[47] we still find, however, evidence of mental conflict. In this article Li Ta-chao tries to reconcile his fervent faith in the power of the human conscience with Marxist doctrine. He reiterates his belief that "the existence of a moral sense is something we must all accept," and that "the call of duty exists in the human heart." [48] However, the source of this moral sense need not be traced to any supernatural source, but can be found in the social instinct which the human race has developed in the course of its struggle for social existence. He thus explains the origin of the moral sense by his own peculiar version of Social Darwinism (a version in violent conflict with Thomas Henry Huxley's, as well as with other versions of European Social Darwinism).

While the moral sense itself can be explained in terms of "Darwinism," however, the positive content of various ethical systems is to be explained only in terms of changes in the mode of production. Man may indeed act out of a sense of duty, but his concept of where his duty lies is determined by the economic system in which he lives.

It is in this manner that Li finally comes to terms with Marx. Strictly speaking, of course, Marxism does not deny the existence of a sense of morality. Like religion and art, morality is also part of the ideological superstructure of human society. To maintain, however, that the moral ideals preached in a given society are actually the springs of action in that society is to overlook a basic concept of Marxism, namely the concept of man's alienation from himself in presocialist society. The whole "ideological" life of man in pre-socialist society serves the function of concealing from his view the true nature of his existence. Thus, Confucian morality was not an effective source of action in "feudal" Chinese society, but rather an ideological reflection of that society which served to conceal its true nature.

Li sins against Marxism still further by seeking the foundation of his moral sense in the biological rather than the social sphere. In spite of the fact that Marx was fond of seeking parallels between his own concepts and those of Darwin, he did not accept the Darwinist propensity to explain social phenomena in biological terms. The Italian Marxian theorist Labriola has explicitly attacked Social Darwinism as an explanation of social phenomena (*Essays on the Materialist Conception of History*). The explanation of social facts must be sought in the social environment.

Having, to his own satisfaction, made the peace with Marxism required by acceptance of the messianic message of the Bolshevik revolution, Li was now free to proclaim himself a Marxist-Leninist without reservation. In his article entitled "The Value of Historical Materialism in Modern Historical Science" (*Hsin Ch'ing-nien*, December 1920) [49] he announces his complete conversion. In spite of its scholarly title, this article is permeated with an undertone of rage and defiance. While the "Victory of Bolshevism" had been his enthusiastic greeting to the forces of regeneration, this article represents his final repudiation of all the forces of evil. As in the case of Ch'en Tu-hsiu, the events of 1919 and 1920 (both internal and external) had aroused in him a bitterness sufficient to sweep away all reservations.

Li now bluntly informs us that all pre-Marxist theories of history are tools of the ruling class designed to stupefy the people, and that only the materialist concept of history provides us with the possibility of a new life in the future. Nowhere does he attempt to reconcile this new conception of ideology as a means of deception with his recently proclaimed belief in the autonomy of the human conscience. Nowhere does he attempt to answer the doubts regarding Marxism which he had expressed in 1918. Having aligned himself with the forces of regeneration he cannot help but accept the doctrine with which these forces are associated.

In discussing the evolution of Li Ta-chao and Ch'en Tu-hsiu toward Marxism-Leninism, I have so far failed to discuss the impact of the Chinese labor movement on their thought. To some this may seem a glaring omission. We know, of course, that the first World War had occasioned a spurt in Chinese industry and that this had had as its concomitant the rise of a visible proletariat. We also know that the May Fourth Movement was accompanied by a growing self-consciousness on the part of this Chinese proletariat. Having come into existence at a time when world trade unionism was a highly developed movement, when socialist and anarchistic philosophies exalting the proletariat were rife throughout the world, it was exposed to these influences almost from birth. We also know that in the early years of the Chinese Communist movement, Chinese labor did provide a substantial mass following for it. However, a close reading of the writings of Ch'en and Li does not suggest that the rise of a Chinese proletariat was itself an important factor in their conversion. It would be more correct to say that Leninism turned their attention to the proletariat rather than that the proletariat turned their attention to Leninism. Li Ta-chao had never mentioned this problem before his "Victory of Bolshevism," while Ch'en Tu-hsiu, as we have seen, had as late as December 1919 considered the industrialized proletariat a negligible factor in Chinese society. This should not be taken to imply that their concern for the deplorable living conditions of the Chinese industrial worker after 1920 was not genuine. It does, however, indicate that at its inception, it had extraneous ideological roots.[50]

In their movement into the Marxist-Leninist camp, Ch'en and Li carried with them a whole host of students who were, no doubt, influenced by the sheer weight of their intellectual authority. Among the men under their immediate influence were Chang Kuo-t'ao, Ch'ü Ch'iu-pai, Li Han-chün, Mao Tse-tung, and Chou Fu-hai, all of whom were to play prominent roles in the future. When we attempt to follow the intellectual development of some of these men during the ferment of the May Fourth Movement, we find them flirting with every conceivable variety of doctrine. We find Ch'ü Ch'iu-pai, a student of Russian literature, translating the works of Tolstoy.[51] Chou Fu-hai did indeed consider himself a socialist, but a guild socialist of the British type. State socialism, he said, would merely foist a new bureaucracy on the Chinese people which had suffered so long from bureaucratism. As for Marxism, it is one-sidedly materialistic and he cited with approval Bernstein's revisions of Marxist doctrine.[52] Mao Tse-tung, according to his own testimony, was for a time under the influence of anarchism, as were some of the Chinese intellectuals in France.[53] Chang Kuo-t'ao, one of the favorite students of Li Ta-chao, was an early collaborator in the Society for the Study of Marxism, and followed the evolution of his teacher into the Communist movement. Mao Tse-tung, who lived on the fringes of academic life as a ˙library employee of Li Ta-chao, was greatly influenced by his mentor, who undoubtedly provided the first impulse for his association with the Communist movement.[54]

Some of those brought into the movement by the authority of Li Ta-chao and Ch'en Tu-hsiu were soon to come in conflict with it. Others, such as Mao Tse-tung, soon proved themselves better able than either Li or Ch'en to understand the implications of Leninism as a program of action.[55] (The same may be said of Sun Yat-sen.) There can be no doubt, however, that these two were indeed the spiritual fathers of Marxism-Leninism in China, and the first founders of the Chinese Communist Party.

Reviewing, then, the intellectual evolution of Ch'en Tu-hsiu and Li Ta-chao, we find that both of them had set out from a consciously antitraditional predisposition, that both had sought light in the West. Both of them, in spite of the different bent of their intellects gravitated by predilection toward world views which offered sweeping all-embracing solutions. Li Ta-chao's vague but optimistic metaphysical views had prepared him to accept the messianic message of the Bolshevik revolution, while the events of the ensuing year solidified his faith to such an extent that he soon succeeded in brushing aside all philosophic reservations. Ch'en Tu-hsiu had committed all his hopes to a combination of liberal democracy and materialistic science. His ardent, impatient nature, however, was soon discouraged by the impotence of "atheistic republicanism" in China. For a moment his discouragement was stemmed by John Dewey's broader definition of the concept of democracy. However, Dewey's undramatic, gradualistic program was unable to withstand for long the brilliant glare of the melodramatic Leninist world image with its neat dualism and its promise of a spectacular role for the revolutionary intelligentsia.

It would thus not be incorrect to say that Marxism was carried into China in the wake of the messianic message and the concrete political program of Lenin.

II *THE FOUNDING OF THE PARTY*

While Ch'en Tu-hsiu had become totally committed to Marxism-Leninism, he hardly seemed aware of the perplexing problems involved in this commitment. The whole problem of the "inevitability of the capitalist stage" which had perplexed a whole generation of Russian Marxists, the problem of how to cope with the national factor which had so long preoccupied Lenin, did not seem to exist for him. It had, after all, been precisely the escape from complexity provided by the clear-cut antinomy between capitalism, as the source of all evil, and socialism, as the harbinger of all good, which had so strongly attracted him.

Thus in June 1920 we find him baldly stating that "I recognize the existence of only two 'nations,' the 'nation' of the capitalists and the 'nation' of the workers. At present the 'nation' of the workers exists only in the Soviet Union. Everywhere else we have the 'nation' of the capitalists." [1] In this statement Ch'en evinces no awareness of the strenuous efforts currently being made by Lenin to harness the nationalist passions of the "backward" areas to the services of the world revolution.

His position concerning the capitalist stage and the role of the bourgeoisie is equally uncomplicated.

During the latter part of 1920, Bertrand Russell and a young Chinese journalist, Chang Tung-sun, roused a violent controversy among Shanghai's young socialists by contending that the root of all China's misery lay in its poverty and low productivity, that this could be alleviated only through industrialization and not through "empty discussions regarding this or that ism," [2] and that however much one might object to capitalism on ethical grounds, it appeared that only capitalism could achieve such an industrialization.

These contentions infuriated Ch'en and his young disciples. In reply he exclaims: "We all agree that it is essential to develop education and industry. On this there is complete agreement. The question is, however, whether in developing industry and education we shall use the old methods of capitalism or the methods of socialism. My own view is that while capitalism may have been effective in advancing education and industry in Europe, America and Japan, it has, at the same time made European, American and Japanese society mean, fraudulent, close-fisted and conscienceless. The world war and the coming economic revolutions are all fruits of capitalism. Of this we are all aware. Fortunately, we, in China, are beginning our task of industrialization and education while capitalism is still undeveloped. We can thus use methods of socialism to develop our education and industrialization, thus avoiding the errors of Europe, America and Japan." [3] He refuses to draw a distinction between an exploiting foreign capitalism and a progressive native capitalism. "If capitalism is good," he states, "it should be welcome whether at home or abroad. If it is evil, it should be opposed whether at home or abroad. . . Only our workers can attain the goal of independence for China. So-called national capitalists are all directly or indirectly compradors of foreign capital. They merely help foreign capitalists to exploit China." [4]

Nevertheless, Ch'en is forced by his opponents to confront the problem of the "capitalist stage" in Marxism. His answer is very simple. "In the Soviet Union the republic overthrew the feudal system only to be replaced by socialism a half year later. This is clear proof that there need not be any long interim between feudalism and socialism." [5] His opponents also force him to admit grudgingly that "as long as there is a quarrel between the democratic and despotic factions of the bourgeoisie, we must support the former against the latter. As soon as they are victorious, however, they become our enemies. . . We can not follow the German social democrats in their practice of using the political instruments of the bourgeoisie in carrying on our activities." [6]

We thus find that the attitude of Ch'en Tu-hsiu during this brief period before he becomes subject to the discipline of the Comintern might best be designated as "proto-Trotskyist." He is, as it were, a Trotskyist by instinct before Trotskyism had emerged as a distinct phenomenon and without Trotsky's ingenious theoretical rationalizations. He has not committed himself to socialism only to contemplate a long dreary period of capitalism. He has not committed himself to a universal, messianic creed only to be forced to make annoying distinctions between foreign and national bourgeoisie.

It would probably not be wrong to say that *emotionally*, Ch'en's basic attitude was close to that of Lenin, who spent his life chafing against the strictures of his own Marxist orthodoxy. There is, however, little evidence to indicate that Lenin would have supported Ch'en's attempts to draw an easy parallel between Russia and China. In spite of his acute appreciation of the dynamic potentialities of the backward areas, Lenin nevertheless tended on the whole to draw a sharp distinction between Tsarist Russia — a world empire, where capitalism had already made some inroads, where a small but vigorous proletariat already existed — and the "colonial" and "semicolonial" areas which were victims of imperialism and where a modern industrial proletariat hardly existed, if at all. In 1912, Lenin had ridiculed the "petty bourgeois socialism" of Sun Yat-sen who had also entertained the notion of the possibility of by-passing capitalism in China.[7] After the October Revolution, however, when Lenin was anxiously scanning the horizon for signs of world revolution, his views tended to fluctuate. The profound influence of the October Revolution on young Asiatic intellectuals, and the first signs of industrialism in India and China were arousing hopes of other possibilities. Thus, while his "Thesis on the Colonial and National Questions" of June 1920 still admits the "necessity of the Communist parties coming to the aid of the movement for democratic bourgeois emancipation,"[8] one month later, after hearing an optimistic report by the young Indian Communist, Roy, Lenin expresses the hope that "if the triumphant revolutionary proletariat carries on a systematic propaganda among backward peoples, if the Soviet governments come to their aid, it would be erroneous to suppose that the capitalist phase of evolution is necessary."[9] It will be noted, however, that this possibility is predicated on the assumption that "Soviet governments" exist or in other words, that the world revolution will already have been successful in several metropolitan states. Barring this possibility, Lenin tends to revert to his thesis that, in semicolonial areas, "The Comintern must conclude temporary alliances with the democratic bourgeoisie . . . but never fuse with it and retain its independence, even if in embryonic form."[10] This seemingly clear statement was to become the subject of voluminous exegesis during the next few years revolving about the meaning of the words "temporary" and "independence." Whatever its ambiguities, however, it hardly justifies Ch'en's faith that China was simply free to choose whether it would travel the road of capitalism or that of socialism.

If Ch'en hardly seemed aware of the enormous difficulties which still obstructed the path to socialism, he was equally unaware of the role of the party in the Leninist scheme. In his writings of 1920 we find vigorous polemics against anarchists and liberals but little discussion of the organizational principles of the Communist Party. Neither Ch'en nor his disciples had, after all, lived the lives of professional revolutionaries in the Russian sense and it was to take some time for them to understand the role they were expected to play. It was only with the help of such Comintern agents as Voitinsky, Yurin, and Maring that they were to come to some appreciation of the Leninist concept of party organization.

When Ch'en left the hostile environment of Peking for the freer atmosphere of Shanghai in 1919, he had not yet achieved such an understanding. Here too, as in Peking, the May Fourth Movement had aroused a febrile activity among the intelligentsia and every conceivable type of "advanced" doctrine from the West had found its coterie of supporters among the Shanghai intellectuals. Ch'en's prestige, which had been enormously heightened by his heroic role in Peking, soon made him the center of intellectual life in the city. Anarchists such as Yuan Chen-ying, Chin Chia-feng, and Kuei Ken-chin, intellectual followers of Sun Yat-sen such as Tai Chi-t'ao, and "socialists" of every variety, soon surrounded him.[11] Ch'en carried on verbal polemics against them but seemed quite willing to work with them in practical affairs. It was clear in his view that the task which faced all "men of learning with a conscience" (*yu liang-hsin ti hsüeh-che*) [12] was the organization and education of the proletariat. He seemed willing to work with all those who shared this conviction. Thus, we find that the "Socialist Youth Corps" finally organized by Ch'en in August 1920 was made up of a loose array of Anarchists, Marxists, and even "anti-Confucianists." [13] In Peking, Li Ta-chao, who was probably even less conscious of the meaning of party organization than Ch'en, organized a labor group made up of six anarchists and two Communists.[14]

In June 1920, however, a new factor had appeared on the scene in the form of the Comintern agent Gregory Voitinsky. Sent to China by the Eastern Bureau of the Comintern, Voitinsky had met Li Ta-chao in Peking and had been referred by him to Ch'en Tu-hsiu in Shanghai. Voitinsky established his headquarters in Shanghai and proceeded forthwith with the task of forming a Communist Party. It may well be presumed that many of his meetings with Ch'en were devoted to the task of explaining to him that a Communist Party was something other than a loose grouping of "learned men of conscience" devoted to the common task of labor organization. Nevertheless, the Socialist Youth Corps which finally formed in August with the financial aid of Voitinsky [15] was, as we have indicated, a most nebulous grouping. This most un-Leninist toleration of heterodoxy may have reflected Voitinsky's feeling that many of these vague, young radicals could be transformed into Communists, or else it may merely have reflected the foreigner's inability to distinguish subtle differences in points of view among a group of young Chinese radicals.

We find, for instance, that one of these young men — Tai Chi-t'ao, a close collaborator of Sun Yat-sen — had come to Marxism in 1919 even before the conversion of Ch'en Tu-hsiu. Both he and Hu Han-min, another close collaborator of Sun, had in the latter months of 1919 begun publishing articles on Marxism-Leninism in the Kuomintang organ *Reconstruction (Chien-she)*.[16] They had, however, come to Marxism by an entirely different road. It was precisely the nationalist implications of the Leninist theory of imperialism, as it pertained to China, which attracted them to it. It was precisely the Leninist insistence on an authoritarian, highly disciplined elite group which attracted them by its crystallization of Sun's own elitist theories. "It is impossible," states Tai in February 1920, "to talk of revolutionary activities without, at the same time, aiming at making revolutionary groups really powerful. . . We must have a scientifically organized revolutionary army." [17] To Tai and Hu, the paramount problem was the attainment of a strong independent state. By underplaying the factor of class conflict, they actually felt that Marxism-Leninism could serve as an ideological base for their nationalistic program.[18]

Proceeding from this base, it was possible for Tai Chi-t'ao to collaborate in the activities of the Socialist Youth Corps, and even to coöperate with Ch'en in forming a "Marxist study group" within the youth group. It was, however, precisely at the point where the Comintern began to assert its position of authority that the abyss between Ch'en and Tai revealed itself. Tai, the staunch nationalist, could not for a moment tolerate the interference of a foreign power in the internal affairs of a Chinese party. Viewed in this light, Tai's transformation from "Communist" to extreme "anti-Communist" does not appear as sweeping as might appear on the surface. It is significant that some of Tai's later polemics against the Communists still employed the categories of Marxism-Leninism.

Under Voitinsky's guidance, however, Ch'en's education proceeded rapidly. In September 1920, a meeting was called to discuss the formation of a bona fide Communist Party, based on a clear-cut Communist ideology.[19] The task of weeding out dissenters had begun. Since the most recalcitrant among the dissenters were the anarchists, we find that much of Ch'en's writing during the latter months of 1920 and the early months of 1921 was directed against these young men who refused to believe that "coercion could be used for good in the proper hands." [20] By May 1921, his impatience with their annoying objectic s had increased to such an extent that he exclaimed: "The anarchism now so rampant among our youth is not completely a Western product. In the final analysis, it is nothing more than a revival of our own Taoism. It is a Chinese variety of anarchism." [21] Since there was nothing more repugnant to Ch'en than the Taoist laissez-faire tradition in Chinese life, this charge reflects the full measure of his animosity. It did not occur to him, however, that his own easy acceptance of the belief in a benevolent elite might itself reflect the influence of that very Confucian tradition which he had so emphatically repudiated. The fact that anarchism with its fear of state power, per se, was to remain an exotic growth in China, while Marxism-Leninism, with its confidence that state power "in the proper hands" could lead man to the good society, was to win wide and lasting acceptance, may perhaps itself reflect the abiding influence of Confucian habits of thought in Chinese life.

In the course of the heated controversies with followers of Bertrand Russell, anarchists, "social democrats," nationalists, and others, there finally emerged the hard nucleus of the future Communist Party. In the early months of 1921, Ch'en received an invitation from the warlord of Kwangtung, Ch'en Ch'iung-ming, to reorganize the education system in his province. Ch'en seized the opportunity to begin organizational activities in Canton and in a short time succeeded in forming a small group centered about Ch'en Kung-po and T'an P'ing-shan. In Peking Li Ta-chao had formed a similar group including such future notables as Chang Kuo-t'ao, Ho Meng-hsiung, Lo Chang-lung, and Teng Chung-hsia. In Hunan province, Mao Tse-tung, who had already won somewhat of a reputation as a result of his many organizational activities, had, according to his own testimony, begun to engage in labor organization activities under the influence of Marxist theories and the Russian revolution as early as the winter of 1920.[22]

By July 1921, a Communist Party ostensibly existed in Peking, Canton, Shanghai, and Hunan and the stage was set for the First Party Congress. This "Congress," attended by a handful of men, was held in secrecy in a girl's school in the French Concession of Shanghai. Its deliberations were, however, interrupted by the Concession police. The members fled to Shaohsing in Chekiang and concluded their remaining business in a boat on the waters of Niehpu lake. No records of the Congress have been preserved.[23]

When we examine the roster [24] of those in attendance, we are somewhat struck to find that even this nucleus of convinced Communists still included the names of Ch'en Kung-po and Chou Fu-hai, whose motives for embracing Marxism-Leninism later proved to have been much closer to those of Tai Chi-t'ao than to those of Ch'en Tu-hsiu.

We have, furthermore, one account of the deliberations of the First Congress, which, if reliable, would indicate that the Communism of this hard core was still most superficial. This account states that "there was no harmony of views at the Congress. Ch'en Tu-hsiu's proposed agenda which called for a people's government led by the Chinese Communist Party was considered by some too radical . . . Li Han-chün made the remarkable suggestion that delegates be sent to Germany and Russia to examine the relative merits of the German and Russian revolutions. In this he was supported by Ch'en Kung-po and others." [25] The question of joining the Communist International was not even raised.

It would thus appear that the commitment of many of these young men to Communism was still a most tentative and superficial affair. They were still the young men of the May Fourth period experimenting with various doctrines but profoundly committed to none. They had come to Communism in the same spirit in which they had previously accepted guild socialism, Tolstoyanism, or theories of free love. The Leninist theory of imperialism, the Karakhan proposals, and the messianic hopes aroused throughout the world by the October Revolution had simply created an emotional atmosphere favorable to the acceptance of Communist doctrine. It was only by hard experience that they were to learn the meaning of total commitment in thought and act and the meaning of iron discipline.

It is somewhat significant in the light of future events that Mao Tse-tung was probably one of the few among these early party members equipped by experience to appreciate Leninism as an organizational technique rather than as simply another doctrine. While his contacts with Li Ta-chao and Ch'en Tu-hsiu may have introduced him to Marxist doctrine, it was his experiences in organizational activities in Hunan which had made him realize that "only mass political power secured through mass action could guarantee the realization of dynamic reforms." This insight is, of course, one of the vital elements of the Leninist technique — not simply for realizing dynamic reforms — but for seizing power.

In spite of the vagaries of the party founders, however, the First Congress does mark an important step in their education. With the aid of the Russian advisers and under the leadership of Ch'en Tu-hsiu (who was not present at the Congress) the party now began to crystallize as a political entity. According to Hatano, the Congress devoted some time to the question of party organization and established a party constitution and a Central Committee which was constituted under the chairmanship of Ch'en Tu-hsiu.[26] The main task which the party set itself, however, was the organization of a labor federation. While we do find certain vague references to the necessity of forming a "people's government" led by the Chinese Communists, there can be little doubt that Ch'en Tu-hsiu regarded labor organization as the paramount task of the party. Since the Communist Party was the party of the proletariat, since the proletariat was the instrument for the realization of socialism, all else was secondary.

Teng Chung-hsia, in his *Short History of the Chinese Labor Movement*, states that immediately after the Congress, a "China Labor Union Secretariat" was established by the party with the aim of coördinating and uniting all the scattered, amorphous labor unions which had sprung up since the end of the First World War.[27]

The events of 1922 would indicate that, having found a program of action and a way of "going to the people," Ch'en Tu-hsiu, the erstwhile professor, and his student followers devoted themselves to this task with unstinting zeal. The rapid growth of Communist Party influence in the railroad workers union, the organization of a Communist-led union at the Hanyehp'ing foundry by the talented young organizer, Li Li-san, and the leading position won by the Labor Secretariat at the First All-China Labor Conference held in Canton in May, must have buoyed Ch'en Tu-hsiu's hopes beyond all expectations.

It is, of course, true that the success of the Communists was due in no small measure to the fact that industrial labor in China was already ripe for organization. It was also true, as future events would show, that neither the Labor Secretariat nor the General Labor Federation which succeeded it had won the firm hold on Chinese workers which its imposing façade suggested. Teng Chung-hsia complains that the direct influence of the party on the workers was minimal, and that the party made little effort to draw workers into it on the ground that they were not yet ready to become party members. It would thus appear that the "Secretariat" was an apparatus superimposed upon the workers — an apparatus which they welcomed as long as it was able to win positive gains, but one with which they had few intimate ties.[28]

In 1922, however, all signs pointed to a mighty proletarian surge under the leadership of the Communist Party, and Ch'en Tu-hsiu was able to indulge at will in his rosy dreams of an early achievement of socialism. It is entirely possible that, if left to his own devices, Ch'en would have continued to bend all his party's efforts to this single task.

PRELUDE TO COLLABORATION

In the Kremlin, considerations of grand policy were pointing in quite another direction. As we have seen, Lenin himself had hardly been sanguine about the immediate prospects of communist parties in backward areas, barring the eventuality of world revolution. Furthermore, to judge from the biting remarks of Radek at the Fourth Congress of the Comintern, the Chinese Communist Party did not enjoy a high reputation in Moscow. At this Congress, held in November 1922 and attended by Ch'en Tu-hsiu himself,[1] Lin Yen-chin (Liu Yen-ching?), a young Chinese delegate, had pleaded that the Hong Kong strike had shown that "the Communist Party can be successful in agitating among the masses. It shows that the Communist Party in China will progress favorably unlike previous years when it was merely a study circle, a sect." [2]

In his scathing retort, Radek exclaimed: "Comrades, do not indulge in too rosy expectations, do not overestimate your strength. When our Chinese comrade told us here, 'We have struck deep roots in China,' I must tell him, 'Esteemed Comrade, it is a good thing to feel confident of one's strength when one starts to work. Nevertheless, things have to be seen as they are.' The comrades working at Canton and Shanghai have failed to associate themselves with the working masses . . . Many of our comrades out there locked themselves up in their studies and studied Marx and Lenin as they had once studied Confucius . . . You must understand, comrades, that neither the question of socialism nor of the Soviet republic are now the order of the day . . . The immediate task is: (1) To organize the young working class. (2) To regulate its relations with the revolutionary bourgeoisie elements in order to organize the struggle against the European and Asiatic imperialism." [3]

The charge of Radek concerning the failure of the Communists to agitate among the masses is manifestly unfair for it was precisely during the year 1922 that the Chinese Communist Party had made considerable progress in this direction. However, his remark that neither socialism nor the Soviet Republic were the order of the day might well have been directed precisely at the type of view held by Ch'en during the whole 1920–1922 period. The Kremlin had no intention at this time of basing all its hopes in China on the young immature Chinese Communist Party. The Soviet Union needed allies in Asia — potent allies — not merely the students and professors of the Chinese Communist Party. Nor was it too delicate in its search for allies. As early as 1920 the Soviet government was looking hopefully in the direction of Wu P'ei-fu who, by that power of class imputation which is the Kremlin's prerogative, was converted from the status of a feudal warlord to that of a bourgeois nationalist.[4] Later, when Maring had become somewhat impressed with the potentialities of the Kuomintang after his interview with Sun Yat-sen, the Kremlin's interests shifted in that direction.[5]

In the theoretical sphere, this urgent need to find allies in Asia inevitably led to a new emphasis on "bourgeois nationalism," on the need for an alliance with the "bourgeoisie" and the necessity of a capitalist phase of development in colonial and semicolonial areas. In Russia, it was true, Lenin had thought as early as 1905 that it would be possible to by-pass the bourgeoisie and consummate the bourgeois revolution in alliance with the peasantry. However, in a country dominated by imperialism, it was necessary to unite as many strata of the population as possible against the common enemy.

This strategy and theoretical formulation must, of course, have proved a shock to those within the party — including Ch'en — who had definitely felt that "socialism was the order of the day." The extraordinary tone of irritation in Radek's speech lends color to an account we find in one source which claims that throughout the year 1922 there had been considerable resistance to this formulation in the Chinese Party.[6] This source states that the Peking group was split in two on this issue and that the Soviet embassy lent its active support to the more "moderate" faction led by Teng Chung-hsia and Li Ta-chao. The moderate faction was of course the faction which accepted the perspective of a "bourgeois, national revolution." The hostile faction included Chang Kuo-t'ao, Lo Chang-lung, and Ho Meng-hsiung, and was supported by Ch'en Tu-hsiu. According to this same account, it was only by the application of severe pressure on the part of the Comintern that he was finally induced to accept this formula. He had, after all, come into the Communist movement in a mood of apocalyptic expectation. The world revolution and the achievement of socialism in China had both seemed immediate possibilities. Now, however, he was told that socialism was not imminent and that he would again have to temporize with the forces of nationalism. It was a reorientation which required some adjustment.

Just as he had formerly been forced to renounce the easy hope that "democracy and science" would redeem China, he was now forced to renounce the apocalyptic vision of 1920 — the hope that socialism would sweep away all forces of evil before it became necessary to temporize with these evils. He could merely comfort himself with the thought that what he had lost in immediate hopes he had gained in doctrinal consistency. Henceforth, his doctrinal writings would fit neatly into a pre-Leninist-Marxist scheme.

It is vital, however, that we have a clear conception of what Ch'en had so reluctantly accepted. The new approach which was embodied in the "First Manifesto of the Chinese Communist Party on the Current Situation" of June 1922 and in the "Manifesto of the Second Congress" (held July 1922) consisted of a series of general propositions to the effect that China was still under the sway of imperialism and that "due to the inroads of imperialism, China was still dominated by a feudal system of militarists and bureaucrats"; [7] that the survival of "feudalism" was inhibiting the emergence of capitalism in China, and that "until such time as the Chinese proletariat is able to seize power in its own hands, in view of the present political and economic conditions of China, and in keeping with the present stage of its historic development, the most urgent task of the proletariat is to unite with democratic groups against feudal militarism." [8] The "First Manifesto" goes on to suggest that a conference be held with a view to forming a united front of all democratic groups.

Does all this imply that the Communist Party had already lent its assent to the Kuomintang-Communist alliance in the form in which it finally emerged? Do all these statements contradict Ch'en Tu-hsiu's own contention made many years later that he had vigorously opposed the Kuomintang-Communist alliance in the form in which it was presented by Maring in August 1922? Much here hinges on the meaning of the phrase "united front." There is no reason whatsoever for assuming that "united front" meant anything more to Ch'en than the coöperation of independent political parties in the pursuit of certain common ends. The "First Manifesto," in fact, enumerates a list of common goals on which it would be possible for the Communist Party to coöperate with the Kuomintang.

The same document, however, makes it amply clear that "the Chinese Communist Party is the vanguard of the proletariat struggling for working class liberation and the proletarian revolution." [9] The "Manifesto of the Second Congress" adds that "if the proletariat extends a hand to promote the democratic revolution, this does not mean that the proletariat should capitulate to the bourgeoisie . . . The Chinese Communist Party is the party of the proletariat and its aim is to organize the proletariat, to use the methods of class welfare, to set up a workers and peasants dictatorship, eliminate the system of private property and gradually attain a Communist society . . . *Within the democratic alliance, the workers must not become an appendage of the petty bourgeoisie but must continue to fight for their own interests*" [10] (italics mine).

The party had thus accepted at face value the Marxist-Leninist concept that given political parties represent given economic classes and that classes do not merge with each other. How then could Ch'en have anticipated the suggestion of Maring that "the Kuomintang was not a bourgeois political party but a coalition party of all classes"? [11] There is no reason whatsoever for thinking that the phrase "united front," as used at the Second Congress, was meant to imply anything more than a limited coöperation with the Kuomintang within some sort of general democratic framework.

It was at this time, however, that the Comintern representative, Dalin, was carrying on his discussions with Sun Yat-sen, looking toward a Kuomintang-Communist alliance. It would appear that, in spite of his new-found enthusiasm for the Soviet Union, Sun Yat-sen proved a most hard bargainer. According to Ch'en Tu-hsiu, "He would allow the Chinese Communist Party to enter the Kuomintang only on the condition that they would submit to the Kuomintang and recognize no party outside of it." [12] Yet, the pressure from Moscow for a coalition on some basis seems to have continued unabated.

It was against this background that Maring suddenly decided to call a Special Plenum of the Central Committee of the Chinese Communist Party at Hangchow in August 1922. According to all accounts, the meeting was much in the nature of a surprise. According to the account of Ch'en Tu-hsiu, Maring made a motion that the members of the Communist Party join the Kuomintang on the ground that the "Kuomintang was not a bourgeois party but a coalition party of all classes," and that the proletariat should therefore enter that party and transform it into a driving force of the revolution. Ch'en states that Li Ta-chao, Ts'ai Ho-shen, Kao Yü-han, and he all vigorously opposed Maring's suggestion on the ground that "our union with the Kuomintang would simply confuse our class structure and curb our independence." Maring thereupon invoked the authority of the Comintern and the Chinese Communist Party leaders were forced to submit to party discipline.[13] A Japanese account adds that Ch'en even dispatched a wire to Lenin in which he complained, "There is great confusion of thought in the Kuomintang and its principles are extremely unclear. It would be very distressing for a Communist Party member to enter the Kuomintang." [14]

It must be observed here that Ch'en's account of this meeting was written many years later at a time when he was most anxious to defend his reputation against the Li Li-san leadership. There is thus, perhaps, some room for suspecting that it may be tendentious. It is, furthermore, most difficult to find external evidence to corroborate or refute his account.[15] Most of the meager literature available was written by orthodox Stalinists at a time when it had become a fixed feature of orthodox history to treat Ch'en as an arch-collaborationist. There is, nevertheless, one account by the orthodox historian, Hua Kang, which states that "while the party central committee respected the motion of the Internationale, *most of the comrades* [emphasis my own] had only approved a democratic revolutionary united front and were quite doubtful about entering the Kuomintang." [16] Ch'en's name does not appear in this account, but the issue as stated here is substantially the same as that mentioned in his account.

This was the very crux of the matter. It was one thing to suggest an alliance with the "bourgeoisie" and even a united front with the Kuomintang, although we have reason for believing that Ch'en had reconciled himself most reluctantly even to this prospect. It was quite another thing to suggest that Communists actually join the Kuomintang. The "bourgeoisie" was, after all, a somewhat indeterminate and abstract entity, while the Kuomintang was a most concrete group of politicians with whom Ch'en and his supporters had had a long acquaintance. The relations between the Peking intelligentsia and Sun Yat-sen had never been close. Ch'en's attitude, in particular, had always been distant and cool. We know that even during his youth in Japan, he had been repelled by what he had regarded as the narrowly anti-Manchu program of the T'ung-Meng-hui.[17] In his later writings he tended to look with disdain on Chinese political parties in general. In 1918 he stated that "we must abandon the idea of unifying the nation through the strength of one party." [18] In December 1919, he states that "while the Chinputang [Progressive Party] and the Kuomintang both advocate a republic, neither understands the true nature of democracy." [19] Sun Yat-sen had, during these years, stressed nationalism above all else, while Ch'en had despised nationalism. Sun had attempted to find a basis for his program in Chinese tradition, while Ch'en had dedicated himself to the task of extirpating these traditions. Sun had temporized with militarists while Ch'en had regarded all militarists as one of China's three scourges.

In an article written some time after the formulation of the Kuomintang-Communist alliance, Ch'en flatly stated: "I had always felt that the Kuomintang had failed in the revolution of 1911. All it had accomplished was the cutting off of queues and the setting up of the meaningless signboard of 'republic.' " He then went on to list as the past defects of the Party: (1) the narrowness of its slogan, "overthrow the Manchus," (2) its exclusive reliance on military force, and (3) its compromising tendencies. "Even Sun," he said, "had been overly inclined to compromise." He ended the article by expressing the hope that these past errors would be overcome in the future.[20]

The "First Manifesto" of June 10, even while calling for a united front, was highly critical of the Kuomintang. "The democratic party which expressed the demands of the liberal social strata," it complained, "resorted to compromises with the counterrevolutionary classes of feudal lords . . . It possesses only a relative amount of democratic, revolutionary spirit." It added that "if the Kuomintang wishes to play a definite role in the revolutionary struggle for the consolidation of democracy in China, it must renounce once and for all every policy of vacillation compromise and endless zigzag." [21]

In the light of this attitude, it does not appear at all incredible that Ch'en and many other members of the Central Committee viewed Maring's proposal with utter consternation. Furthermore, quite apart from the question of their attitude toward Sun Yat-sen and the Kuomintang, Maring's proposal must have seemed most confusing to these men who had just begun to absorb the major tenets of Marxist-Leninist philosophy.[22] Within the Marxist-Leninist frame of reference, political parties are nothing more than political superstructures concentrating the political power of given economic classes. The Leninist concept of the "party" with its insistence on the organic relation between the Communist Party and the proletariat had, if anything, reinforced this aspect of Marxism. In 1920, it is true, Lenin had urged the British Communist Party to enter the British Labor Party. He had specifically denied, however, that this involved a confusion of classes on the ground that the British Labor Party was a genuine proletarian party which simply lacked the proper proletarian leadership.[23] In Russia, however, it had been taken for granted that the Cadets represented the bourgeoisie and later, when the Bolsheviks laid claim to a monopoly of the proletariat, it was assumed that the Mensheviks represented the petty bourgeoisie. With the emergence in China of the notion of a "coalition party of four classes," however, the whole concept of the organic relationship of party and class was placed in jeopardy. The Kuomintang, it now appears, was a political organization which was, somehow, assumed to lead an autonomous existence above and beyond the existence of the classes which it embraced. As Trotsky sarcastically remarked in May 1927, "The classes come and go but the continuity of the Kuomintang goes on forever." [24]

In his later debates with Stalin on this very problem, Trotsky constantly hammered at Stalin's "bureaucratic apparatus-like attitude," [25] at his tendency to see in the Kuomintang a force independent of the classes which presumably lie at its base. Here, as elsewhere, Trotsky was the more orthodox Marxist-Leninist, but a candid view would suggest that Stalin's political instincts were the more accurate. In the course of his climb to power in the Soviet

Union through the control of an effective political machine, Stalin had probably come to realize subconsciously, as it were, that political power is not merely an adjunct of economic power, and that a well-organized political machine is a social force to be contended with in its own right. In the Kuomintang, the Kremlin saw ready at hand an established political organization with roots within the country. From the distance of Moscow the Kuomintang's influence in China may, indeed, have loomed much larger than it actually was. In 1922, however, the prospect of a union with this political force must have seemed most attractive since it promised to provide a firm base for the spread of Soviet influence in China. Later, the influence of Borodin on Sun Yat-sen and the strategic positions won by the Communist Party within the Kuomintang must have heightened still further the hopes of direct control over the Kuomintang.

It was, I think, this type of strategic consideration which induced the Kremlin to compromise with Sun Yat-sen's severe conditions for the establishment of a united front and to devise the doubtful theory of the "bloc of four classes." [26] Stalin's error, we shall find, I think, lay not so much in the fact that he instinctively thought of the Kuomintang as an autonomous political machine [27] as in his easy assumption that he could gain control of a machine organized on Leninist lines and led by others as self-willed and determined as himself.

While these may have been the strategic considerations behind Maring's proposal, the theoretical framework in which they were embodied must have seemed most puzzling to the members of the Chinese party fresh from their Marxist-Leninist textbooks. It is precisely to this difficulty that Ch'en Tu-hsiu's objection pointed. How could two economic classes, each with its own historic destiny, be fused into the same political party?

Viewed in the light of these considerations, I think that we may conclude that Ch'en's later account has the ring of authenticity.

Whatever may have been its objections, however, the Central Committee was forced to accept Maring's proposal. Shortly after the Plenum, Li Ta-chao was invited by the Kuomintang stalwart Chang Chi to join the party. Li replied that he would join on the condition that he be allowed to maintain his membership in the Communist International. Sun Yat-sen, who was in a much more pliable mood since his loss of power in Canton, acceded to this condition.[28] Although the alliance between the two parties was not formalized until after the issuance of the Joint Sun-Joffe Declaration in 1923, the formula on which it was to be based had been found. Communists would enter the Kuomintang "as individuals" but the Communist Party would continue to maintain its separate existence.

IV COLLABORATION

The period of Kuomintang-Communist collaboration (1923–1927) is, without a doubt, one of the most confusing and complex periods in modern history. Almost all the sources, and the Communist sources in particular, are open to grave suspicion. Furthermore, there is some room for doubting whether in the turmoil and complex maze of events of these years any of the major actors pursued a clear-cut consistent policy. Nevertheless, I feel that it is possible to discern the outlines of certain major trends within the Chinese Communist movement. It goes without saying, of course, that this is a period in which Moscow played a most direct and detailed role in guiding the destinies of the Chinese Communist Party. During these years, China was inundated with hosts of Comintern agents, and both the leadership and the opposition in Moscow followed events in China with rapt attention. It shall, nevertheless, be our effort to concentrate our attention on trends within the Chinese Communist movement itself while bearing clearly in mind that most of these trends cannot be considered in isolation from developments in Moscow.

The So-Called "Right Wing"

In Communist literature of the Stalinist school after 1927, it is customary to refer to Ch'en Tu-hsiu and those closest to him in the party, during these years, as "right opportunists." He was, it is alleged, a supine capitulator to the Kuomintang who clung convulsively to a policy of appeasing the "bourgeoisie" long after the Kremlin had moved to a bolder and more radical position. Throughout the period, according to this version, he consciously misinterpreted the bold directives of the Kremlin in a conservative sense.

Is it true that this man who in the 1920–1922 period had clamored for the immediate realization of socialism, who had regarded with repugnance the policy of fusion with the Kuomintang, had suddenly become an ignominious capitulator?

In answering this question we are confronted with a peculiar difficulty. Ch'en was, after all, the chairman of the Chinese Communist Party during all these years and the executor of Comintern policy. How then can we extricate his own views from the views he was forced to express as party leader? In answering this question we have, of course, Ch'en's own testimony as given in the "Letter to Our Comrades." We have certain contemporary writings of Ch'en and of P'eng Shu-chih who was closely allied with him. Finally, we have the hostile testimony of Chinese and Russian critics — testimony which often reveals more than it intends. By comparing and sifting these sources, we can at least attempt to reconstruct an over-all view of Ch'en's own attitude during these stormy years.

There can be little doubt that in the period between the Hangchow Special Plenum of August 1922 and the Third Party Congress of June 1923 certain factors induced Ch'en and his colleagues to take a friendlier view of the Comintern's theory regarding the bourgeois-democratic nature of the Chinese revolution and even of the Kremlin's formula for Kuomintang-Communist alliance.

In the first place, we know that Ch'en Tu-hsiu was present in Moscow at the Fourth Congress of the Comintern (November 1922) where Radek administered his stinging rebuke to the Chinese Communist Party for its illusions regarding the achievement of socialism in China.[1] We cannot but think that much pressure was brought to bear behind the scenes to impress Ch'en with the Kremlin's point of view.

Of even greater significance, however, was the "February Seventh" incident. On February 7, 1923, the strike of the powerful Peking-Hankow Railway Workers Union was suppressed by Wu P'ei-fu in a gory blood bath. The effect of this incident was so demoralizing that it put a halt to the whole surge of the Chinese labor movement and led to the wholesale arrest of union organizers. In the words of Teng, "Most of the labor unions so carefully built up by the Communist Party during the previous two years — except for certain unions in Canton and Hunan — were crushed and the Chinese labor movement entered into a period of decline."[2] According to Ts'ai Ho-shen's hostile account, "If Ch'en Tu-hsiu exaggerated the power of the proletariat during the 1921–1922 period, after the failure of the Peking-Hankow railway strike, he swung over completely to a basically Menshevist position and lost all faith in the power of the proletariat." [3] The "Short History" adds that "the defeat in the Peking-Hankow strike spurred on the movement of collaboration." [4]

Allowing for hostile exaggeration in Ts'ai's statement, it is nevertheless true that if Ch'en's adherence to the "bourgeois perspective" of the revolution had been somewhat perfunctory before the strike, it became less so after the strike. The extravagant hopes roused by the surge in the labor movement had evaporated and Ch'en was able now to perceive all those defects in the young Chinese proletariat which had been somewhat obscured by the messianic visions of the previous years. "The Chinese proletariat," he now wrote, "is immature both quantitatively and qualitatively. Most of the workers are still imbued with patriarchal notions and their family ties and regional patriotism are extremely strong. These former handicraft workers carry over the habits of their previous existence even when they become industrial workers. They do not feel the need for political action and are still full of ancient superstitions." [5] He was now ready to face the prospect of a prolonged capitalist stage before the achievement of socialism and even went on to state in what might be called a pre-Leninist-Marxist vein (although a vein quite in harmony with the new Comintern line) that "the class consciousness of the workers depends on the development of class division as a result of the progress of industry. It cannot be fostered by the human will or negated by the human will." [6]

Ts'ai Ho-shen charges that at the Third Congress in June, Ch'en dwelt at length on the "patriarchal clannish ideas" of the proletariat but evaluated somewhat highly the role of the bourgeoisie. "While all classes of a semicolonial or colonial society are somewhat immature," Ch'en declared, "the strength of the bourgeoisie is, after all, more highly concentrated than that of the peasantry and more solid than that of the proletariat and it would be a grave error for the national movement to ignore the bourgeoisie . . . A semicolonial Chinese society must, without doubt, go through a bourgeois democratic revolution and if, in the course of the revolution, it loses the aid of the bourgeoisie, it loses its class significance and social basis." [7]

Not only did Ch'en revaluate the role of the "bourgeoisie," but at the Third Congress he is said to have spoken of the Kuomintang-Communist alliance in terms of unreserved approval. Since he had but recently returned from the didactic lectures of Radek in Moscow, this would hardly seem cause for surprise. Nevertheless, in proving that Ch'en had been an arch-collaborator of the Kuomintang, Ch'en Tu-hsiu's later detractors, such as Ts'ai Ho-shen and Li Li-san, lean heavily on the evidence of Ch'en's remarks at the Third Congress where he is alleged to have said that the Communist Party had been born too soon and that all activities should be carried on within the framework of the Kuomintang.[8]

Now Ch'en, himself, informs us that this period marks, as it were, a high point in his own acceptance of Comintern policy. He adds, however, that this was due to the fact that, at the time, "the Communist Party was still relatively free in respect to the Kuomintang. At the time, we could still severely criticize the compromising policies of the Kuomintang." [9]

In support of Ch'en's claim it must be remembered that this was the period *before* the Kuomintang had been reorganized into a tightly knit party of the Leninist type. It was thus the period before the Communist Party had become subordinated to the "democratic centralism" of the reorganized Kuomintang. It was the period before the rise of Chiang Kai-shek. It was quite possible at this time to hope that the Communist Party could still maintain a large degree of independence in shaping its own policies.

Furthermore, in spite of Ch'en's alleged "capitulationism," the Manifesto of the Third Congress, which could hardly have been drafted without Ch'en's approval, still sharply criticizes the Kuomintang for its past defects and calls upon the proletariat "to maintain its connections with the world proletariat." It adds that "since this is a struggle which must advance from the stage of a Chinese national revolution to the stage of a world social revolution, the proletariat must, by all means, maintain its class consciousness and unity and must be aware of its own inevitable goal. It is the duty of the Chinese Community Party and of the Comintern to bring about this awareness and unity." [10] It is thus made amply clear that whatever may be the Communist Party's relations to the Kuomintang, it still has its own separate goal which it must keep before it at all times.

It is precisely here, I submit, that we must seek the key to the real attitude of Ch'en and the so-called "right wing" during the whole 1923–1927 period. It is here, also, that we must seek the real source of any tension between the "right wing" and the leadership in the Kremlin during this period. Ch'en had sincerely accepted the theory that the revolution was a bourgeois democratic revolution and that the "bourgeoisie" was destined to play a large — even a dominant — role in the immediate future. As a Communist, however, he identified himself not with the "bourgeoisie" but with the proletariat. The proletariat was indeed young, immature, and not politically conscious. It might take some time to prepare the proletariat and the masses behind it for their historic role, but precisely this was to be the paramount task of the Communist Party. Since the Comintern had decreed that the Communist Party must carry on its activities within the framework of the Kuomintang-Communist alliance, he was willing to do so, *so long as this alliance did not hamper the Communist Party in the pursuit of what he considered its basic tasks.* On the other hand, to the leading group in the Kremlin, concerned as it was with global politics, the control of the Kuomintang as an effective political machine, either directly as at first or indirectly as later, by the achievement of "proletarian hegemony" (Communist Party control) within the Kuomintang was the paramount, overriding objective of all policy.

What is the evidence for this thesis?

We have already observed that the Third Congress of the Chinese Communist Party was held *before* the reorganization of the Kuomintang. We know that Ch'en Tu-hsiu, Li Ta-chao, and others held positions on the "Reorganization Committee" which brought about the reorganization of the Kuomintang on Leninist lines. Nevertheless, all sources agree that the chief actors in these deliberations were Borodin and Sun Yat-sen. The idea itself seems to have originated with Borodin. Sun Yat-sen later indignantly denied the charge of the Kuomintang right wing that "the political program of the Kuomintang was devised in toto by Ch'en Tu-hsiu's Communist Party." He states that "the draft was drawn up by Wang Ching-wei and myself. I doubt whether Ch'en even heard of it." [11] And Wang Ching-wei specifically states that "the reorganization of our party was carried out in January 1924 at the suggestion of Borodin." [12] The organization of the Whampoa academy was also carried out quite over the head of the Chinese Communist Party by Chiang Kai-shek, Galen, and Borodin.

Many Communists, it is true, won positions on the Kuomintang Executive Committee at the First National Congress of the Kuomintang in January 1924 and, under the leadership of Sun Yat-sen and Wang Ching-wei, the party was still able to carry on its activities in relative freedom within the framework of the Kuomintang itself. Nevertheless, by tightening what had been a comparatively loose organization and centralizing its leadership, the reorganization laid the foundation for all the troubles which were to emerge.

However, did the Communist Party completely forfeit its organizational independence as charged by Trotsky before the break with the Kuomintang and by Ch'en's enemies after the break with the Kuomintang? On the contrary, the evidence would indicate that under Ch'en's leadership the Communist Party did everything in its power to maintain its independence, to organize the masses albeit under a Kuomintang banner and to maintain control of these masses within the Kuomintang framework.

It was precisely on the issue of Communist Party independence that certain right-wing Kuomintang leaders began to attack the two-party alliance in 1924. In July 1924 the right-wing leaders Chang Chi, Hsieh Ch'ih, and Feng Tzu-yu, who had not previously opposed the alliance with the Communists,[13] issued "A Proposal for the Impeachment of the Communist Party" in which they openly charged that the Communists were not acting as "individuals" within the Kuomintang, but taking orders from the Central Committee of the Communist Party. They were quite easily able to prove their point. All they had to do was produce a Communist document entitled "Resolutions of the Socialist Youth Corps" (August 1923) in which the following statements appear: "When our party members enter the Kuomintang, they must adhere to the orders of the executive committee of this Corps . . . We must support all demands made by members of the Chinese Communist Party and be united with them in word and deed." [14] The proposal goes on to charge that Li Ta-chao's promise that the Communists would enter the Kuomintang as individuals had not been kept and that the Communist Party was, instead, acting as a party within a party.

In his marginal footnotes on these documents Sun Yat-sen attempted to comfort the right-wing leaders by the observation that the "experienced leaders of the Soviet Union are interested in working with *our* party and not with the inexperienced students of the Communist Party." He did not, however, deny the basic charge made in the document.

Actually, the notion of a Communist party member acting politically as an individual is a contradiction in terms. The corporate action of party members is part of the very essence of the Leninist conception of a Communist party and a principle which the leadership of the Chinese party had had ample time to absorb. There is no evidence that the party represented anything other than a unified, disciplined caucus within the Kuomintang during the whole period of Kuomintang-Communist collaboration in spite of the divergences which may have existed in its ranks. It would be difficult indeed to find instances in which Communist party members of the upper levels acted as "individuals" rather than as party members.

What is more, the Communist Party not only succeeded in winning a dominant position in the mass movement, but also bent every effort to maintain its separate control of that movement within the Kuomintang framework.

The tremendous surge of mass energies kindled by the May Thirtieth incident of 1925 was, it is true, somewhat in the nature of a spontaneous outburst. The hatred of the Japanese imperialists aroused by the strikes in the Japanese textile mills of Tsingtao and Shanghai called forth a wave of mass sentiment in large coastal cities which soon spread to the countryside and, to the surprise of all, even aroused the wretched peasantry of central and south China from its lethargy.[15] The Communist Party was, however, quick to take advantage of this popular surge and the young enthusiasts of the Communist Party soon stole a march on the non-Communist elements of the Kuomintang in the matter of mass organization, for in spite of Sun Yat-sen's lectures the non-Communist elements in the Kuomintang failed, even at this early date, to show a proper appreciation of the potentialities of mass power.

Even more significant, however, is the fact that, having won an initial advantage in mass activities, the Ch'en leadership made every effort to maintain control of the mass movement. In spite of the fact that it operated under the Kuomintang banner, it made every effort to maintain full Communist control of the "All-China Labor Federation" [16] as well as of the newly formed "Peasant Associations." A statement which appears in the "Resolution on the Peasant Question" of the Enlarged Executive Plenum held in July 1926 throws a clear light on the attitude of the party leaders during all these years. "The peasant associations," it states, "must be organizationally independent of the Kuomintang and must not become an appendage of the party." It adds, however, that "our party must make every effort to win a leading position in peasant movement activities. We must have branch organizations in the local units of all peasant associations to act as the backbone of all activities in these organizations." [17]

In 1928 Shih Ts'un-t'ung, by that time a renegade from the party, charged retroactively in a pamphlet entitled *Problems of the Chinese Revolution* that there had been a basic contradiction in the Chinese Communist Party's relations to the Kuomintang. Although the Communist Party had loudly proclaimed its belief that the Kuomintang should have a mass base, it had been unwilling to relinquish control of the masses to the Kuomintang. In his reply, Yün Tai-ying, at that time a voice of the official party line and no friend of Ch'en Tu-hsiu, did not deny Shih's allegation, but simply stated that "the reason why the party had refused to encourage the workers and peasants to enter the Kuomintang was because it feared that they might be influenced by the bourgeoisie." In 1927 the Comintern delegate, Mandalian, in his pamphlet, *Why Did the Communist Party Fail?* quotes Ch'en Tu-hsiu to the effect that he did not want the workers to enter the Kuomintang since they might become subject to right-wing influences.[18]

Even Trotsky and Isaacs in all their attacks against the Stalinist line tacitly assume that the Chinese Communist Party had achieved effective control of the mass movement. Indeed, Trotsky's call for the establishment of peasant and worker soviets after April 1927 [19] could hardly have been proposed had he not assumed that the Chinese Party possessed sufficient control of the masses to institute such a radical shift in policy.

It is thus clear that the Chinese Communist Party had not relinquished its organizational independence, had not shirked its organizational tasks among the masses and had, on the contrary, managed to win a dominant position in such activities before the non-Communist elements of the Kuomintang were able to show any effectiveness in this field. *In the area of policy*, however, it was tied hand and foot by its peculiar alliance with the Kuomintang. If any "opportunism" existed, this was its root. Hence, in judging the question of Ch'en Tu-hsiu's "opportunism," his attitude toward the Kuomintang-Communist alliance must serve as our major yardstick.

According to Ch'en's own account, his relatively friendly attitude toward the alliance began to change once more after the appearance of Tai Chi-t'ao's anti-Communist pamphlets in 1925.[20] He claims that, at the Enlarged Plenum of the Central Committee held in Peking in October 1925, he stated that "the pamphlets of Tai Chi-t'ao are no accidental, isolated phenomenon. It is evidence of a plot on the part of the bourgeoisie to consolidate its own class strength, to crush the proletariat and go over to the reactionary camp. We must prepare to withdraw from the Kuomintang and act independently. It is only by acting independently that we can maintain our political physiognomy, lead the masses and be freed from the restraints of Kuomintang policy." [21] Here again we find a striking corroboration of Ch'en's claim in Mandalian's pamphlet. "From the very moment that the Communist Party entered the Kuomintang," he says, "the right wing of the party was constantly thinking of withdrawing from the Kuomintang. Their pretext was that they did not wish to maintain an alliance with the bourgeoisie, on the ground that such an alliance was a disgrace to the proletariat." [22] Mandalian makes it quite clear elsewhere in this pamphlet that he regards Ch'en Tu-hsiu as the spearhead of the right wing.

Ch'en further states that after Chiang Kai-shek's *coup d'état* of March 20, 1926, in which the latter seized effective power, dissolved the Hong Kong strike committee, and removed many Communists from prominent positions, he (Ch'en) sent his young lieutenant P'eng Shu-chih to Canton to urge that at least some of the arms being brought in from the Soviet Union be given to the peasantry rather than to Chiang Kai-shek's forces. He alleges that Borodin replied that "armed peasants will not be able to crush Ch'en Ch'iung-ming or carry out the northern expedition. It will merely serve to arouse the suspicion of the Kuomintang and lead to resistance on the part of the peasantry against the Kuomintang." Ch'en adds that, after the events of March 20, in a report to the Comintern he expressed the private view that instead of carrying on collaboration within the Kuomintang, "we should carry on our alliance on an extra-party basis. Otherwise, we would not be able to carry on an independent policy and would lose the trust of the masses . . . After the Comintern saw my report, Bukharin published an article in Pravda severely criticizing the view that the Communist Party ought to withdraw from the Kuomintang." [23]

This account contrasts most sharply with the charge later made by Ts'ai Ho-shen that Ch'en had been an "unprincipled capitulator" [24] at the time of the March Twentieth incident. In Li Li-san's writings we find an interesting variation of this charge. It seems that by March 20, a conflict had already developed in the party between the Communist Party Central Committee in Shanghai and the Kwangtung Provincial Committee in Canton. At bottom, this conflict may well have been one of personalities rather than viewpoints. It undoubtedly reflected a long-standing tension between Ch'en Tu-hsiu and Borodin since the Canton Committee prided itself greatly on its closeness to the illustrious Comintern representative. According to Li Li-san, the view of the Kwangtung Committee was "that to step out of the Kuomintang would be to abandon the broad laboring masses. It would be tantamount to yielding the revolutionary banner of the Kuomintang to the bourgeoisie. This would be an irremediable loss. We must therefore adopt for a time a conciliatory policy, and at the same time positively prepare a new struggle for leadership." "On the other hand," Li adds, "certain comrades in Shanghai considered March 20th a disgrace to the proletariat and wished to withdraw from the Kuomintang, while Ch'en Tu-hsiu and the Central Committee were of the view that the party should capitulate." [25] In support of this account we do indeed have a letter from Ch'en Tu-hsiu to Chiang Kai-shek, printed in the party organ *Guide Weekly* on June 9, 1926, in which Ch'en indignantly denies Chiang's charges that the Communists had conspired against the Kuomintang, and humbly states that "Chiang Kai-shek is one of the pillars of the national revolution. Unless the Communist Party were the tool of the imperialists it would surely not adopt such a policy of disrupting the unity of the Chinese revolutionary forces." [26]

What conclusion, if any, can be drawn from this welter of conflicting evidence? While we are here on most uncertain ground, there are certain salient facts which must be borne in mind. In the first place, there is the fact that while Borodin had initially been highly disturbed by Chiang Kai-shek's coup, he had later come to an agreement with him and had even agreed to Chiang's demand that a northern expedition be launched as soon as possible. Secondly, that the leadership in the Kremlin had refused to be diverted, at any cost, from the policy of Kuomintang-Communist alliance. Its first reaction to the events in Canton was, in fact, to deny what had happened and dismiss it as an imperialist rumor.[27] Neither Stalin nor Borodin had abandoned the hope that the Kuomintang apparatus could still be controlled. In this hope they were further lulled by Chiang Kai-shek's complete willingness to use the language of world revolution and by his attack on the Kuomintang right wing.

It is thus obvious that, as the executor of Comintern policy, Ch'en Tu-hsiu had no alternative but to propitiate the actual leader of the Kuomintang since Chiang had been recognized as such by no less a person than Borodin himself. It is significant that Li Li-san is forced to admit that the "Kwangtung" faction had also opposed withdrawal from the Kuomintang. However, while referring to their view as "a conciliatory policy" he uses the word "capitulation" to describe the identical policy as applied by Ch'en Tu-hsiu. It is not unreasonable to suppose that Ch'en's "Letter to Chiang Kai-shek" was an expression of Ch'en the chairman of the Communist Party, rather than of his personal views. In view of his statement at the October 1925 Enlarged Plenum, it would appear most likely that his personal views were closest to those of the "Shanghai comrades" mentioned in Li Li-san's account.[28]

The fact that Ch'en did not actually regard Chiang Kai-shek as a "pillar of the national revolution" is amply proved by his attitude on the question of the northern expedition. Here we find ourselves once more on the solid ground of contemporary evidence. Ch'en had, after all, grown up in a land where anarchic military power had time and time again frustrated all attempts to establish a civilian order. All his pre-Communist writings were permeated with a hatred of the military, whom he regarded as one of the scourges of China. The criticisms of the Kuomintang in the precollaboration Communist Party pronouncements constantly criticize Sun Yat-sen for relying on the treacherous support of the militarists. It was a deep-rooted aversion which probably ran much deeper than his attachment to Marxist-Leninist categories. The fact that Chiang was a militarist loomed larger in Ch'en's mind than the fact that he was presumably a leader of the "national revolutionary classes," or the fact that he was quite willing to use the phraseology of revolution. "The northern expedition," Ch'en complained in the June 1926 issue of *Guide Weekly*, "is intended as a military action aimed at extending the southern revolutionary forces northward and at overthrowing the Peiyang militarists. It was thus intended to be part and parcel of the national revolution. Now the real aim of the national revolution is the overthrow of imperialism and militarism by the masses of all classes and the liberation of our whole people — particularly the workers and peasants. However, if the northern expedition is carried on by a motley crowd of military adventurers and politicians interested in achieving their own private ambitions, even if victory is achieved, it will only be a victory for the military adventurers and not for the revolution . . . In view of present conditions within the national government, of its actual strength, fighting power and revolutionary consciousness, a northern expedition would be premature at this time. Our slogan should be not 'the northern expedition' but 'defend the base of the revolution — Canton.' " [29] In August of the same year he went so far as to say that the "present national government is simply a special organ of military leaders." [30] Ch'en's fears are quite patent. The Kuomintang had been captured by what he rightly or wrongly regarded as "new warlords," whatever might be their Marxist class designation. Any northern expedition carried on by these wardlords before the Communist Party could reassert its power by its influence on the left wing of the Kuomintang would simply result in another militaristic regime.

The northern expedition was nevertheless launched with the final blessing of Borodin and the Comintern. Its results, however, did not wholly correspond to the expectations of either Ch'en Tu-hsiu or the Kremlin. It was no ordinary military adventure, for it opened an immense area of activity for the aggressive organizers of the Communist Party. On the other hand, it increased immensely the power and prestige of Chiang, making him much more independent of Borodin and the Kremlin. Anxious as Chiang was to receive material aid from the Soviet Union, he was henceforth more anxious to free himself from Kremlin control.

The new situation in China thus confronted the Moscow leadership with new pressures. The phenomenal spread of Communist influence among the masses, the growing prospects of defection on the part of Chiang Kai-shek, and the attacks of Trotsky on the Kuomintang Alliance were all factors which demanded a new statement of policy. This new statement finally found its expression in the "Theses on the Chinese Situation" of the Seventh Plenum of the Executive Committee of the Communist International held in December 1926.

Before discussing this statement and its effect on the Chinese Communist Party, we must point once more to a peculiar feature of the Communist party line as it applied to China. The term "party line" is used in this book to designate the theoretical framework devised to encompass a given strategic approach within a given period. Such a theoretical framework is, needless to say, essential within the Marxist-Leninist tradition since it is assumed that the political actions of the party leaders are derived from their theoretical insights into the course of history.

In general, when we examine a given party line we find that it is composed of certain constant elements. There is, first of all, a theory concerning the historic nature or the "content" of a given historic stage. Is it a bourgeois democratic stage or is it a socialist stage or a transition between the two? Secondly, we have a theory regarding the "class forces" of a given stage. Which are the classes destined by history to accomplish the tasks of a given stage? (It is an interesting feature of Leninism that the "class forces" can no longer be deduced from the mode of production as is the case in pre-Leninist-Marxism.) Thirdly, we have an estimate of the direction of the historic process of any given stage generally expressed in terms of upsurge and decline, or "rising waves" and "falling waves." In general, the question of the relations of political parties can be assumed to reflect the relations of class forces.

The concept of the Kuomintang, however, as a political apparatus existing above and beyond the classes which compose it introduces a new variable into the ordinary conception of a party line. It is no longer possible to deduce the "analysis of class forces" from the attitude toward the Kuomintang or to deduce the attitude toward the Kuomintang from the analysis of class forces. "The classes come and go but the continuity of the Kuomintang goes on forever."

Thus, the hard fact which lay at the core of the Seventh Plenum Theses was the determination to continue the alliance with the Kuomintang. There was some awareness in Moscow that Chiang Kai-shek was a doubtful ally, but this doubt was completely outweighed by the immense diplomatic advantages to be derived from the successful advance of the nationalist forces and by the belief that "the apparatus of the national revolutionary government can provide a very effective way to reach the peasantry." [31] At the same time, realizing that it would henceforth be impossible to control Chiang directly, the Comintern now called upon the Chinese Communists to make a direct bid for "proletarian hegemony" within the Kuomintang — that is, for a control of the Kuomintang by the Communist Party.

This hard fact was, however, effectively disguised behind a more "radical" theory of the relations of class forces. The revolution in China, declared the Theses, continues to be a bourgeois democratic revolution directed against foreign imperialism and "feudal remnants." There has, however, been a shift in class forces within the Kuomintang. "In this stage the driving force of the new movement will be a bloc of still more revolutionary nature of the proletariat, peasantry and certain strata of the big bourgeoisie which may for a certain period continue to march with the revolution." [32] The latter remark is obviously meant to legitimize the continued support of Chiang Kai-shek who had been categorized as a representative of the "big bourgeoisie." Finally, the Theses assert that "at this stage, the hegemony of the movement passes more and more into the hands of the proletariat." [33]

The Theses thus accomplish the task of reaffirming the Kuomintang alliance, of countering Trotsky's challenge by presenting a more "radical" analysis of the class situation and of burdening the Chinese Communist Party with the task of capturing the Kuomintang. The net result was to make the Ch'en leadership more vulnerable than ever. If it continued to oppose the alliance with the Kuomintang, it could be accused of abandoning the peasantry and the petty bourgeoisie. If it did not succeed in capturing the leadership of the Kuomintang, it could be accused of having sabotaged the truly radical program of the Comintern. We shall find that both these charges were made simultaneously.

Actually, the evidence would indicate that the "right-wing" leadership was privately more reluctant than ever to continue the alliance with the Kuomintang. Mandalian thus charges that in January 1927 Ch'en refused to allow the workers to enter the Kuomintang on the grounds that "they would become subject to right-wing influences," and adds that "it was only due to the pressure of the Third Internationale that the Chinese Communist Party grudgingly recognized the necessity of carrying on its activities within the Kuomintang." [34] Ch'en claims that although P'eng Shu-chih, Lo I-nung, and he were shocked by the Comintern's order of March 1927 that the Shanghai workers bury their arms in order to avoid a clash with Chiang Kai-shek's forces, he again submitted to Comintern discipline. He further claims that "the shameful" Joint Declaration which he drew up together with Wang Ching-wei on April 4, 1927,[35] was itself the result of Comintern pressure and contrary to his own inclinations.

After Chiang Kai-shek's April *coup d'état* in Shanghai, Ch'en claims to have been just as averse to the alliance with the "Left Kuomintang" as he had previously been to the alliance with Chiang Kai-shek. The politicians and generals of the Wuhan regime seemed to him not a whit more trustworthy than those of the right-wing Kuomintang. He claims that, at a Politburo meeting held in Hankow before the Fifth Party Congress, he asserted: "Our coöperation with the Kuomintang is becoming more precarious day by day. Superficially, we seem to be in conflict about various, separate problems but actually what they want is complete hegemony. There are now only two roads open to us — either we abandon the fight for hegemony or break with them!" [36] He further claims that after general Hsü K'e-hsiang carried out his military coup against the Communists in Ch'angsha on May 21, he twice suggested that the Communist Party withdraw from the Kuomintang.[37]

This account is substantially confirmed by Mandalian whose pamphlet was written before the final formal break with the Kuomintang. "Until today," he states, "Ch'en Tu-hsiu, the man who has been most clearly and decidedly the leader of opportunism in the Chinese Communist Party, is still calling for withdrawal from the Kuomintang." [38] He further charges that "the right wing opposed the policy of bringing Communist Party leaders into the national government structure because it wished to maintain its 'independence' and 'purity of principle.' "

A further confirmation of the "right wing's" attitude during these years is provided by the theoretical writings of P'eng Shu-chih. P'eng Shu-chih, like his rival Ch'ü Ch'iu-pai, had studied in Russia immediately after the outbreak of the revolutions and both were regarded as young men of promise within the party. According to Li Ang, a bitter rivalry had developed between them which may have begun by being personal, but had soon developed serious, ideological overtones. All sources tend to link the name of P'eng Shu-chih with Ch'en Tu-hsiu. Ch'en himself speaks of him as a faithful lieutenant, while the writings of Ts'ai Ho-shen,[39] Pavel Mif, and Mandalian all treat Ch'en and P'eng as fellow opportunists. A Japanese biography of Ch'ü Ch'iu-pai specifically states that "Ch'en adopted the views of the opportunist P'eng Shu-chih and wouldn't cast a glance at the theories of Ch'ii Ch'iu-pai." [40] In later years P'eng's name was to continue to be linked with Ch'en's and both were to suffer arrest together. There is, then, every reason to believe that P'eng's theoretical writings reflect the views of Ch'en himself. Since P'eng was not the direct executor of Comintern policy, there are indeed grounds for believing that his writings may reflect Ch'en's innermost misgivings more freely than Ch'en's own writings of the same period.

In an article entitled "Who Are the Leaders of the Chinese National Revolution?" written in the latter part of 1924, P'eng said that almost all segments of the Chinese "bourgeoisie" had already become antirevolutionary. The banking bourgeoisie was tied up with the militarists and imperialists. The commercial bourgeoisie had become a "compradore class" interested only in business relations with the imperialists. The "national industrial bourgeoisie" should objectively have been revolutionary, but due to its weakness and to the domination of most Chinese industry by the imperialists it was subjectively timid and tended to think only in terms of its own petty calculations. It thus could not play a separate political role of its own. As for the peasantry, it could participate in the national revolution but, as Marx had so often explained, it could not lead the revolution due to its backward nature. The bourgeoisie, completely involved with the landlord class, was incapable of leading the peasantry, which could therefore be led only by the proletariat. The proletariat, moreover, was much stronger than the industrial bourgeoisie since it was present in both nationally owned and foreign-owned industries. Hence, the "natural leader" of the revolution was not the bourgeoisie but the proletariat which should place itself at the forefront of the masses. However, if the proletariat was the natural leader of the revolution, why did it not convert the revolution into a socialist revolution? First, because the proletariat still had to contend with the forces of imperialism and militarism. It still had "bourgeois democratic" tasks to perform. Secondly, there were many elements of the petty bourgeoisie and peasantry who could be led by the proletariat only so long as the revolution did not take a socialist turn.[41]

The significance of this theory lies in its political implications. The only class really capable of revolutionary political initiative, according to P'eng, is the proletariat. Hence, why should it yoke itself in a political apparatus with classes he regards as downright reactionary or impotent? The Kuomintang, in his view, does not even represent the national bourgeoisie. It is rather a coalition of "bureaucratic, compradore" elements and "new warlords" while its troops are drawn from the ranks of the *lumpenproletariat*. As for the national bourgeoisie, "it is a cipher" and plays no political role whatsoever.[42]

We are thus not surprised to find that, like Ch'en, P'eng opposed the northern expedition on the grounds that "the military activities of the Kuomintang are not activities of the armed masses but of armed bandits and warlords." [43] Later, when the expedition had already swept northward, he is quoted to the effect that "if the revolutionary army is successful, the compradore class will inveigle itself into the government under a national bourgeoisie disguise. If it is defeated, it will cast off this disguise." Acocrding to Ch'ü Ch'iu-pai, when Chiang's troops drew close to Shanghai, P'eng Shu-chih became a strong advocate of an alliance with the Shanghai merchants on the grounds that while the merchants of Shanghai were weak (national bourgeoisie) and would have to depend on the proletariat, Chiang's army represented the formidable forces of the compradores and "new warlords." His program for the Communist Party was that it disassociate itself from Kuomintang military activities and devote itself to a "scientific, socialist" program of educating and organizing the masses against the day when they would be ready for uprisings leading to the proletarian revolution — all this to be done outside of the framework of the Kuomintang.[44]

We cannot be certain that P'eng's theoretical analysis was endorsed by Ch'en in all particulars. It is quite likely in the light of his reaction after the Peking-Hankow strike that Ch'en was by no means as sanguine about the prospects of a proletarian revolution in the near future as his younger colleague. Nevertheless, we have a passage written by him in June 1926 which is remarkably similar to P'eng's writings. "Our present revolution," he writes, "is still a bourgeois revolution since the bourgeois revolution begun in 1911 has not yet been completed. At the same time, because the world has already moved into the stage of the world revolution, and because the Chinese proletariat has already demonstrated that it has its own independent political power and *that it is actually the leader of the present revolution* [emphasis my own], our aims will not be the same as those of the French revolution. Our present aims are national independence and the overthrow of feudal society. At the same time, in conjunction with the tide of world revolution we shall combine our forces with the forces of world revolution. We shall wipe out all remnants of feudalism and capitalism to build a proletarian society." [45]

From all this, I think, we can attempt to reconstruct at least an overall view of the real inclinations of Ch'en and the so-called "right wing" in contrast to the policies which they were forced to implement by the Comintern. In the first place, the "right wing" seems to have accepted without hesitation the notion that "semicolonial China must go through a bourgeois phase." It did not, however, willingly accept the implication that the Chinese Communist Party must link its destinies to those of the Kuomintang in the peculiar form of the "coalition party of four classes." On the contrary, it profoundly distrusted the Kuomintang and was inclined to regard it as a collection of "new warlords" and "new bureaucrats." These new warlords and new bureaucrats may merely have represented the bourgeoisie as Ch'en maintained, or may have been a coalition of "compradore, bourgeoisie and feudal elements" as P'eng asserted, but they did not represent the "four revolutionary classes." Under such conditions, the task of the Communist Party was to preserve its independence and to educate the proletariat and the masses.[46] In other words, during the bourgeois period, the Communist Party should have acted as a "party in the field," supporting such measures of the national government as seemed to be beneficial, but working without pause to build up its base among the masses in preparation for the future revolution.

This does not mean that the "right wing" favored a bold, Trotskyist type of program or that it endorsed Trotsky's call of a separate Soviet regime. There is no evidence that it shared Trotsky's conviction that the time had come for the seizure of power by workers' and peasants' soviets. On the contrary, the "right wing" was obsessed with the fear of the military power concentrated in the hands of the "new warlords" and tended to think more in terms of preserving the gains which had already been made, of "protecting the proletariat," rather than in terms of seizing power. Ch'ü Ch'iupai charged in March 1927 that "actually our program has been one of self-preservation." [47] One aspect of this "protection" was Ch'en's determination to keep the urban proletariat completely under the control of the Communist Party. Hence, the charge of Mif that, at the Fifth Party Congress of April 17, Ch'en "never raised the question of the workers gaining control of the bloc of classes in the Kuomintang," [48] or Mandalian's charge that "all the actions of the Chinese Communist Party were calculated to isolate the proletariat and its party from all the other laboring masses." It need only be observed here that the Mandalian formula for drawing the party close to the masses was to integrate its activities into the Kuomintang. It would thus appear that the "right wing's" basic attitude was conservative in the etymological sense of the word. In the face of what was considered to be the formidable power of the enemy, it wished to conserve its strength for the future.

Whatever may have been the private inclinations of Ch'en and the "right wing," however, in the implementation of policy they bowed to the superior wisdom of the Kremlin. What grounds are there, then, for the later orthodox, Stalinist version of Ch'en's role after the Seventh Plenum of the ECCI as that of an arch-appeaser of the Kuomintang who wilfully sabotaged the Comintern's truly radical policies?

In the first place, it is interesting to note that the two attacks we have on the "right wing" written prior to the final break between the Comintern and the Kuomintang and before the orthodox version had as yet crystallized — that is, the pamphlet of Mandalian and the writings of Ch'ü Ch'iu-pai (see next section, below) — do not accuse Ch'en of appeasing the Kuomintang. On the contrary, they accuse him of attempting to withdraw from the Kuomintang. Finally, Bukharin himself states on July 14, 1927, that the opportunist leaders of the Party of the type of Ch'en Tu-hsiu advocated withdrawal from the Kuomintang.[49]

Aside from this solid fact, however, is it true that the Chinese Communist Party leadership sabotaged radical Comintern directives? Let us examine, for instance, the orthodox claim that while the Comintern was calling for a "deepening of the agrarian revolution,"[50] the Chinese Communist leadership was pursuing a compromising policy on the agrarian question.

It is quite easy for Ts'ai Ho-shen and other hostile writers to find passages in Ch'en's writings full of strictures regarding the peasantry. They are, however, the strictures which run through all Marxist-Leninist literature. "The peasantry's cultural level is low," he writes, "their forces are scattered and they incline toward conservatism . . . Being independent producers they are not easily socialized," etc.[51] All these statements are actually Marxist-Leninist platitudes even though they may have been reinforced by Ch'en's earlier attitudes on this subject. At the same time, however, he had learned from Lenin that the peasantry could serve as a revolutionary supporting force. "The peasantry," he states, "constitutes the overwhelming majority of the Chinese people and is, of course, a great force in the national revolution. If the Chinese revolution does not enlist the peasants, it will be most difficult for it to succeed as a great national revolution."[52] Far from "surrendering the peasant movement to the bourgeoisie" the Chinese Communist Party made strenuous efforts during these years to gain control of the peasant movement. The organizational activities of P'eng Pai[53] and Mao Tse-tung were, after all, carried on under Ch'en's leadership. He may have been surprised by the dynamism displayed by the peasantry in the May Thirtieth period, but so were others including Mao Tse-tung.[54]

The fact is that the agrarian program of the Communist Party was as radical as it could possibly be *within the framework of the Kuomintang alliance* since the leaders of the Kuomintang, both of the left and right, were not particularly interested in the supplementation of a radical agrarian program *particularly under Communist leadership.*[55] Actually, the program of the Comintern, drawn up at the Seventh Plenum of the ECCI, was not substantially more radical for precisely this reason. Thus, if we compare the concrete agrarian program drawn up by the Executive Committee of the Chinese Communist Party at its Enlarged Plenum of July 1926 with the agrarian resolutions of the Theses of the Seventh Plenum of the ECCI, we find that once the Comintern's statement is stripped of its radical phrases concerning the urgency of agrarian reform, not much new has been added. The July Plenum calls for "a united front of farm laborers, tenant farmers, independent cultivators and middle and small landlords, the neutralization of big landlords who are not positively evil and an attack on the most reactionary big landlords." [56] The Seventh Plenum "Theses," after expressing certain general sentiments concerning the urgency of thoroughgoing agrarian reform, recommends the "confiscation of monasterial and church lands and lands belonging to *reactionary* [emphasis my own] militarists, compradores and gentry." [57] The latter resolution does indeed use the word "confiscate" rather than "attack," but adds significantly that the agrarian movement must "march together with the Kuomintang to the very end."

The July meeting calls for an arming of the peasantry for self-defense and the Seventh Plenum also calls for arming "poor and middle peasants" *under the authority of the Kuomintang* and with the proviso that such arms be used for self-defense.[58]

Ch'en was later to be blamed for statements deploring "excesses" on the part of the landless peasantry (during the Wuhan period). According to Ch'en, all such statements were inspired by Moscow. It is significant that T'an P'ing-shan, the Communist Minister of Agriculture in the Wuhan government, who issued directives concerning the "curbing of excesses" had participated in the Seventh Plenum of the ECCI, and had but recently returned from Moscow, presumably with a firsthand knowledge of the Kremlin's point of view.[59]

Finally, Stalin's famous letter of June 1, 1927,[60] is often cited as proof that Stalin had called for bold action in China before the break with the Kuomintang. It is claimed that his orders had been frustrated by the Chinese Communist leaders. This letter does indeed call for "a confiscation of land from below," organization of an army of the twenty thousand members of the Communist Party, "elimination of unreliable generals," and replacement of reactionary elements in the government by progressive elements. At the same time, it still calls for a "curbing of excesses" through the peasant associations rather than by the use of Kuomintang troops. It still stipulates that the land of army officers not be confiscated. It suggests that reactionary generals be tried by the civilian authorities of the Kuomintang. It *fails* to enlighten the Chinese leadership, however, on what methods it is to use to control the troops of the Kuomintang generals, how it is to restrain the peasantry from seizing the land of army officers, where it is to obtain the weapons with which to arm the Communists, how it is to dislodge the "reactionary" leaders of the Wuhan government, or how it is to prevail on them to try the reactionary generals.

In short, the crux of the dilemma is pithily expressed in a statement of Ch'en Tu-hsiu: "The Internationale asks us to implement our own policies. On the other hand, it will not allow us to withdraw from the Kuomintang. There is thus no way out."[61] In order to implement a radical agrarian program, the Chinese Communist Party would either have had to act independently or gain control of the Kuomintang. How was it to gain such control? The Kuomintang may not have been merely the political party of the bourgeoisie as Trotsky contended, but neither was it an abstraction which existed apart from those who controlled it. During the Wuhan period, it was controlled by an uneasy coalition of politicians and generals who were, however, determined to maintain their own power, who were quite well aware of the Comintern's plans for establishing "proletarian hegemony" and quite determined to prevent this from happening. It is one thing for a Communist party to gain control of a loosely organized, democratic organization which is not aware of what is happening. It is quite a different matter for it to gain control of a centralized machine organized along Leninist lines which is quite aware of what is happening and determined to prevent it.[62]

In sum, then, there was during these years little discrepancy between the *specific directives* of the Comintern and the official policies of the Communist Party leaders. Where such discrepancies did exist, where the Comintern did recommend a more "radical" course than the Chinese leadership was pursuing, it was impossible for this leadership to implement such recommendations since the stipulation was constantly added that they be implemented through a political apparatus which the Communist Party did not control.

The Ch'ü Ch'iu-pai Faction

Sources on the collaboration period point to Ch'ü Ch'iu-pai as the focal point of opposition within the Communist Party during the early months of 1927. It is impossible, of course, to reconstruct all the complex crosscurrents of factionalism and personal antagonisms which existed in the ranks of the Communist movement in China during the 1923–1927 period. Most of the later sources merely hint at these crosscurrents without giving any conclusive information regarding them. We have already noted Li Li-san's reference to a Kwangtung faction which "correctly" interpreted the intentions of the Comintern as opposed to the Shanghai faction and the Central Committee faction.

We do, however, have more definite information concerning the emergence of an "opposition" faction after the Seventh Plenum of the ECCI. Pavel Mif, in his account of the Fifth Party Congress of April 1927, states that the Ch'en Tu-hsiu, P'eng Shu-chih leadership had plotted to postpone the summoning of that Congress "because they were aware of the growth of opposition within the local organizations and among some important Central Committee leaders (united under the leadership of Ch'ü Ch'iu-pai and Chang Kuo-t'ao)." [63] Mandalian often quotes Ch'ü Ch'iu-pai with approval in his attacks on Ch'en Tu-hsiu. Finally, we have the significant fact that the Emergency Conference of August 7, 1927, which marks the deposition of Ch'en Tu-hsiu from the position of leadership also marks the rise of Ch'ü Ch'iu-pai. The conflict between the two factions became focalized in the personal conflict between P'eng Shu-chih and Ch'ü Ch'iu-pai to which we have already referred.[64]

It is thus legitimate to assume that Ch'ü Ch'iu-pai's pamphlet of March 1927, *Controversial Questions of the Chinese Revolution*,[65] written in reply to P'eng Shu-chih's *Basic Problems of the Chinese*

Revolution,[66] accurately reflects the attitudes of the "opposition" insofar as this attitude was "ideological" at all.

Basically, the whole approach of Ch'ü Ch'iu-pai is a reflection of Bukharin's views as expressed at the Seventh Plenum of the ECCI. The phenomenal surge of the peasantry in China after May 30 had, strangely enough, served to provide Stalin and Bukharin with a weapon against Trotsky's demand for independent action on the part of the Communist Party. The dynamism of the peasantry, they asserted, proved that the revolution in China was closer in form to what Lenin had described as a "democratic dictatorship of the peasants and workers." The only factor which differentiated the Chinese revolution from the Russian revolution of 1905, however, was the fact that the Chinese revolution was still a semicolonial revolution directed against imperialism. In such a revolution the "national and petty bourgeoisie" could for a time still play a positive role. Since, by Stalin's definition, the Kuomintang was a coalition party of peasantry, petty bourgeoisie, and national bourgeoisie, any abandonment of the Kuomintang by the Communist Party would be tantamount to an abandonment of the rising peasantry to the bourgeoisie within the Kuomintang. Thus, instead of abandoning the masses, the proletariat should strive to gain "proletarian hegemony," that is, Communist control within the Kuomintang. Once such a hegemony was achieved, it was not impossible that the revolution might undergo a "non-capitalist development." [67]

This formula offered the Stalinist leadership two advantages. It allowed it to maintain the Kuomintang Communist alliance in the face of Trotskyist opposition and at the same time to present itself in a leftist role while casting Trotsky into a "rightist position." Trotsky, it now appears, wished to abandon the masses to the bourgeoisie while Stalin wished to gain proletarian hegemony over the masses — all within the framework of the Kuomintang.

It is substantially this formula which Ch'ü employed against P'eng. P'eng, as we have seen, had considered the "national bourgeoisie" a cipher and had regarded the Kuomintang as a coalition of "bureaucratic compradores and feudal militarists." This Ch'ü vehemently denied. The national bourgeoisie, he maintained, was still a strong force and still "capable of participating in the national revolution." [68] While it would, in the course of time, betray the revolution, its political power as represented by the "new right wing" (Chiang Kai-shek) of the Kuomintang was still very great. By underestimating the power of the national bourgeoisie, by stating that the proletariat is the "national leader of the revolution," P'eng was, in effect, making it possible for the national bourgeoisie to capture control of the revolution.[69]

What is more, Ch'ü continues, P'eng fails to appreciate the revolutionary role of the peasantry in the bourgeois democratic revolution. Both P'eng Shu-chih and Ch'en Tu-hsiu ignore the fact that the peasantry is becoming ever more revolutionary, and that the bourgeois revolution in China is tending more and more to take on the character of a peasant revolution. P'eng is thus abandoning the control of the peasantry to the bourgeoisie.[70] P'eng's failure to understand the important political role of the national bourgeoisie and peasantry has resulted in his false analysis of the class composition of the Kuomintang. How can a Marxist treat "militarists" as a separate social category? "What class do the militarists in question represent?" he asks. "Unless we can clarify this point, so long as we treat the military as a sort of armed force independent of all classes, we may commit grave errors of policy." [71] By placing the northern warlords and the leaders of the northern expeditionary force under the identical category of "militarists," P'eng is ignoring the immense difference between militarists who represent the feudal classes and militarists who represent the forces of the national revolution. "This is sheer Trotskyism!" he shouts.[72] Finally, P'eng Shu-chih bares his Trotskyist inclinations by dividing the revolution in China into two sharply divided stages: the bourgeois democratic stage in which the proletariat cannot play any substantial role and the proletarian revolution. This, according to Ch'ü, is a reflection of Trotsky's hated theory of "the permanent revolution." [73] The Comintern had indicated, on the contrary, that the bourgeois democratic revolution and the socialist revolution can proceed simultaneously provided that the proletariat captures "hegemony" within the revolutionary united front.[74]

What is the concrete political meaning hidden behind the radical phraseology of this analysis? In simple terms, it means that Ch'ü Ch'iu-pai, acting as the faithful voice of the Comintern, was firmly opposed to any inclination to withdraw from the Kuomintang. Since the Kuomintang was the party of the peasantry, petty bourgeoisie, proletariat, and national bourgeoisie, and since these classes all still had a role to play in the revolution, an abandonment of the Kuomintang by the Communist Party should be considered a reactionary move. In general, one is tempted to suspect that the theory concerning the "class compositions" of the Kuomintang was deduced from the strategic desirability of coöperating with the Kuomintang rather than vice versa.

Like the Comintern, of course, Ch'ü calls upon the party leadership to capture the hegemony of the Kuomintang. Nowhere, however, does he suggest precisely how the party leadership is to proceed to gain hegemony over Chiang Kai-shek. (Ch'ü's pamphlet was written before the April *coup d'état*.) His constant exhortations that the Communist Party gain control of the masses within the Kuomintang framework ignore the fact, already pointed out, that the Communist Party had already accomplished much along this line. They ignore the fact that one does not capture an organization organized along lines of "democratic centralism" and resting on military power simply by influencing the masses.

It is precisely this glaring omission which lends color to Li Ang's charge that Ch'ü's writings are motivated, to an unusually large extent, by personal ambitions [75] and by jealousy of the favor enjoyed by P'eng Shu-chih. It is possible that Bukharin and even Stalin in far-off Moscow really believed that the Communist Party could achieve "hegemony" within the Kuomintang — that they seriously underestimated the shrewdness of the Kuomintang leadership. Ch'ü Ch'iu-pai, however, was on the scene and presumably was thoroughly familiar with the difficulties of the situation. Since he was not in a position of primary responsibility, however, he was able to exploit to the full the embarrassing position of the party leadership. He could simultaneously present himself as the faithful interpreter of Comintern policy and attack the party leadership for becoming caught on the horns of the dilemma implicit in that policy.

This impression of ulterior motivation is further heightened by Ch'ü's studied effort to identify P'eng — and Ch'en behind him — with the Trotskyist opposition in Moscow. There could, of course, be no more effective way of discrediting the Chinese party leadership in the eyes of Stalin.

On what does Ch'ü rest his attack? He rests it on the grounds of presumed resemblance between P'eng Shu-chih's theory and the Trotsky theory of "permanent revolution."

What exactly is the theory of the "permanent revolution"? Since we shall meet this term constantly in our further investigation, it is appropriate that we attempt to define it here. The phrase itself is taken from Marx, but the theory, devised at the time of the 1905 revolution in Russia, was the joint creation of Parvus and Trotsky.[76]

Trotsky contended that, while the Russian proletariat was still small, it had come into being in an era in which world capitalism had already reached a high degree of maturity. In such a period, the Russian revolution could hardly be expected to follow the old paths of bourgeois revolution in the West. For, in spite of its small size, the Russian proletariat had the immense advantage of having access to the socialist experience of the proletariat in the West, while the Russian bourgeoisie on the other hand had been kept weak by the power of autocracy. It was thus to be expected that when the bourgeois democratic revolution broke out, the proletariat would easily be able to capture the leadership of the revolution and of the nonproletarian masses. "Once the revolution is victorious, political power necessarily passes over into the hands of the working class which has played the leading role in the struggle." [77] The working class, moreover, was the class destined by history to achieve socialism. "The political supremacy of the proletariat is incompatible with its economic slavery." [78] Hence, the victorious proletariat would of necessity have to break out of the groove of bourgeois democracy and carry the revolution forward to socialism. Meanwhile, the spark of the successful revolution in Russia might finally ignite the long overdue socialist revolution in the West, thus fusing the socialist revolution in Russia with the world-wide socialist revolution.

It has often been pointed out that Lenin's theoretical rationalizations of his seizure of power in October 1917 were essentially much closer to this theory than to this own previous theory of the "democratic dictatorship of the proletariat and peasantry." By 1927, however, the use of the phrase "permanent revolution" had become anathema.

Is there then any reality to Ch'ü's charge that P'eng's theory resembles Trotsky's because of his division of the revolution into two sharply divided stages? On the contrary, as we have observed, the very essence of Trotsky's theory is the denial of any such sharp division. The whole theory stresses the continuous flowing over of the bourgeois democratic revolution into the socialist revolution. P'eng's theory does resemble Trotsky's only in his insistence that the proletariat will be the natural leader of the revolution when its time comes, and that no other class of Chinese society is capable of real revolutionary initiative. On the other hand, Bukharin's suggestion, echoed by Ch'ü — that if the proletariat is able to win the hegemony of the revolution (within the Kuomintang), the bourgeois revolution may gradually "pass over" into the socialist revolution — comes perilously close to Trotsky's formulation. It is closer to Trotsky's formula than to Lenin's theory of "democratic dictatorship of the workers and peasants," which had on the contrary drawn a sharp distinction between the two stages of the revolution. P'eng is esssentially no closer to Trotsky than Bukharin himself. From all this confusing hairsplitting, we can see how tenuous are Ch'ü's efforts to couple the name of P'eng with that of Trotsky. His motives for doing so, however, are amply clear.

Ch'ü and his group were, of course, to reap the benefits of their appearance of superior loyalty to the Kremlin. After the catastrophic defeat of April 12, 1927, there appeared some tendency in Moscow to shift the blame on to the shoulders of the Ch'en leadership. This tendency in turn considerably strengthened the hand of the Ch'ü group at the Fifth Party Congress of April 27. At this congress, Ch'en was forced to make a confession of past errors and Ch'ü Ch'iu-pai, Chang Kuo-t'ao, Li Li-san, and Li Wei-han all won positions on the Politburo.[79] However, the full fruits of Ch'ü's zeal on behalf of the Comintern were finally reaped in August after the final rupture in the Kuomintang-Communist alliance.

Mao Tse-tung — a Side Current

The "Report on an Investigation of the Agrarian Movement in Hunan" by Mao Tse-tung, published by the *Guide Weekly* of March 20, 1927,[80] is a document so unique in content that it justifies us in treating its author even at this time as the representative of a unique trend within the Chinese Communist movement.

It would be an error to assume that Mao Tse-tung's insight into the potentialities of the peasantry was simply the fruit of his own peasant background. We know that immediately after his adhesion to the Communist Party he had followed the obvious course of devoting all his energies to labor-union activities. Since the future lay with the proletariat, it seemed clear that it was the bounden duty of every Communist to turn his attention in this direction. Mao himself admits that he did not realize the degree of class struggle among the peasants until the outbreak of the May Thirtieth incident.[81] There can be little doubt, however, that once the peasantry had begun to display its unexpected revolutionary dynamism, there were few in the Communist movement better equipped than he to appreciate its significance or better able to understand the psychology of the Hunanese peasant. Having once decided to devote his energies to peasant organization, moreover, he plunged into this activity with singular devotion. The "Report" is essentially a reflection of his experiences during 1926 — a year in which the peasant associations had achieved spectacular success. It is the work of a young man, deeply immersed in an undertaking which he regards of transcendent importance, and impatient of any external consideration which interferes with that undertaking.

The "Report" is almost completely bare of Marxist trappings. It may be that the other contemporary writings of Mao mentioned in his interview with Edgar Snow — the "Analysis of the Different Classes of Chinese Society" and the "Tasks Before Us" [82] — do attempt to fit his experiences into a quasi-Marxist framework. The "Report," however, is simply a blunt and passionate plea that the peasant associations be given complete freedom of action, that the revolutionary surge in the villages be allowed to develop without hindrance. "The force of the peasantry," he cries, "is like that of the raging winds and driving rain. It is rapidly increasing in violence. No force can stand in its way. The peasantry will tear apart all nets which bind it and hasten along the road to liberation. They will bury beneath them all forces of imperialism, militarism, corrupt officialdom, village bosses and evil gentry. Every revolutionary party, every revolutionary comrade will be subjected to their scrutiny and be accepted or rejected by them. Shall we stand in the vanguard and lead them or stand behind them and oppose them? Every Chinese is free to pick his answer. However, destiny will force us to pick an answer soon . . . The broad masses of the peasantry have arisen to fulfill their historic destiny. The democratic forces in the village have arisen to overthrow the feudal forces in the village. The overthrow of feudal forces is, after all, the aim of the national revolution." [83]

The remarkable feature of this passionate utterance is the fact that it looks to the peasantry itself to accomplish the tasks of "burying imperialism and militarism"; that it looks to the village as the key center of revolutionary action; that it judges the worth of any revolutionary party by its willingness to place itself at the head of the peasantry. The most remarkable statement in the whole "Report," from a Marxist-Leninist point of view, is the statement in which Mao compares the relative importance of the city and the countryside in the revolutionary process: "If we were to compute the relative accomplishments of various elements in the democratic revolution on a percentage basis, the urban dwellers and military would not rate more than thirty percent, while the remaining seventy percent would have to be alloted to the accomplishments of the peasants in the countryside." [84]

The "Report" is permeated with a Jacobin hatred of the ruling classes. Only the poor peasants can act as the revolutionary vanguard in the village. Mao vigorously repudiates the objections raised in certain quarters to the presence of "vagabond and bandit" elements in the peasant associations. "They are not vagabonds and bandits," he insists, "but aggressive leaders of the peasant associations . . . Even if some of them have been vagabonds, most of them have taken a turn for the better since their assumption of leadership." [85]

As for the so-called "excesses" of the peasantry, most of them are entirely justified. There is, after all, nobody better qualified to distinguish between "bad gentry" and "good gentry" than the peasant himself. "The revolution is, after all, no banquet. It's not quite as dainty an occupation as writing books or painting flowers . . . A revolution is a violent action on the part of one class to overthrow the political power of another. The agrarian revolution is a revolt of the peasantry against the political power of the feudal landlord class . . . We must build up the vast power of the peasantry. We must not allow anyone to criticize the peasant associations. We must wipe out the political power of the gentry, throw them to the ground and even trample them underfoot. All the excesses of the peasantry in this second period have a revolutionary significance." [86]

All this is, of course, extremely radical and full of elemental revolutionary spirit. On the whole, however, it might just as well have been written by a Russian *narodnik* as by a Marxist-Leninist. Nowhere here do we find those strictures on the independent revolutionary role of the peasantry which run through all Marxist-Leninist literature. On the contrary, there is here the constant implication that the peasantry itself will be the main force of the Chinese revolution. It is our intention to discuss the question in some detail in a later chapter. It might be interesting, however, by way of contrast to cite here one of Lenin's numerous reflections on the question of the relations of city to countryside. "The city," he tells us, "inevitably leads the village. The village inevitably follows the city. The only question is, which of the urban classes will the village follow?" [87]

The influence of Lenin's tactical lessons is, to be sure, present in Mao's insistence that the poor peasants be made the "vanguard of the revolution." Nowhere, however, does he add the vital condition, "under the hegemony of the proletariat." The article, written under the obvious stress of high emotion, simply ignores all such ideological considerations. It is interested in only one fact: the peasantry has proved itself, in the author's view, to be the major force of the revolution and any revolutionary party must base itself on this force if it is to win a leading position in the revolution.

There can be little doubt that Mao thought of himself at this time as a thoroughgoing Marxist-Leninist — that he entirely appreciated the Leninist formula of a professional revolutionary elite basing itself on the motive power of the masses. On the other hand, his own peasant background and experience in the peasant movement had already convinced him that the peasantry could furnish all the motive power necessary, at least for the completion of the "democratic revolution." We find no echo of the Leninist insistence on the necessity of an industrial proletarian base. The "Report" is even bare of the type of rationalization which was to be devised during the Soviet period to disguise the movement's lack of such a base. Even at this time, Mao demonstrated his readiness to turn his back on the industrial proletariat in the face of all theoretical considerations in order to take full advantage of the elemental forces which he found in the village.

It would nevertheless be an exaggeration to claim that Mao had already found his complete "formula for success." Nowhere in this "Report" do we find any discussion of the question of military power. In his enthusiasm, Mao seems to feel that "the raging wind and driving rain" will somehow sweep away everything in its path. Awareness of the question of coördinating mass support with military power and of the importance of a territorial base is not yet to be found here.

In his interview with Edgar Snow, Mao Tse-tung stressed Ch'en Tu-hsiu's "right opportunist policy" and declared that Ch'en "did not understand the role of the peasantry in the revolution and greatly underestimated its possibilities at this time." [88] This is, of course, an orthodox interpretation which does, nevertheless, contain a large element of truth. It must be pointed out, however, that anyone honestly committed to Marxism-Leninism would have had to object to the general tone of the "Report" — a tone evidently also reflected in Mao's other writings of this time. How could a consistent Marxist-Leninist accept the proposition that the peasantry could be the principal creative force of the revolution? All the objections which Ch'en raises in his writings against primary reliance on the peasantry may reflect his own deep prejudices, but they are also commonplaces of Marxist-Leninist literature.

Quite aside from doctrinal considerations, however, Mao completely ignores the fact that Ch'en Tu-hsiu was operating within the constraints imposed by Comintern policy. It has already been indicated that it was the Comintern which insisted that the Chinese Communist Party operate only through the organs of the Kuomintang. It has also been indicated that aside from their general phraseology, the specific directives of Moscow were hardly more vigorous or radical than the program which the Chinese leadership was attempting to implement, and that Stalin's famous letter of June 1, 1927, still spoke in terms of "curbing excesses." Finally, we also note that while Mao openly demands that local national government officials not be allowed to interfere with the peasant associations,[89] Stalin's letter still insists that all reforms be carried out through the officialdom. Mao's "Report," honestly considered, is not merely a protest against Ch'en's "opportunism," but is an implicit attack on the whole Comintern line.

Superficially, it might appear that in view of the tendencies represented in the "Report," Mao should be bracketed with the Ch'ü Ch'iu-pai faction within the party. Did Ch'ü not follow Bukharin's lead in stressing the importance of the peasantry, in insisting that the agrarian revolution was the main content of the bourgeois democratic revolution? We know, furthermore, that Mao Tse-tung joined forces with Ch'ü in August 1927 to discredit the Ch'en leadership.

It has been pointed out, however, that to Bukharin and Ch'ü the stress on the peasantry was intimately tied in with the proposition that the Kuomintang was the party of the peasantry and that all activities were to be carried on through the apparatus of the Kuomintang. We shall also attempt to demonstrate in a later chapter that there is a huge abyss between the proposition that the agrarian revolution is *the main content* of the revolution and Mao's proposition that the peasantry is the *main force* of the revolution. Finally, we shall find that the alliance between Ch'ü and Mao was to prove mainly an alliance of convenience which would very soon crumble.

It must further be pointed out that Ch'ü Ch'iu-pai, Chang Kuo-t'ao, Li Li-san, and the other leaders of the "opposition" were thoroughly urbanized intellectuals who were just as strongly committed to the doctrine of urban proletarian hegemony as Ch'en Tu-hsiu. In his pamphlet, Ch'ü Ch'iu-pai accepts without a moment's hesitation Marx's statement that the peasantry as a class cannot represent itself.[90] It would, indeed, be ridiculous to suppose that men like Ch'ü Ch'iu-pai and Li Li-san, who were to cling desperately to the dogma of the urban proletarian base in the bleak days of the 1928–1931 period, were not faithful to it in 1927 when the movement among city workers showed every promise of success.

There is thus every reason to believe that even at this time Mao Tse-tung represented a marginal exotic trend within the Chinese Communist movement.

We have here by no means attempted to give a full account of the complex crosscurrents and clique relationships within the Communist movement during the collaboration period, but we have tried to trace the main outlines of some of its most significant trends.

V
AN APPRAISAL OF KEY TRENDS

When we attempt to appraise the trends described above, as well as the major strategic tendencies in Moscow, in terms of their ultimate prospects of success (that is, historic not moral success), it is difficult to avoid the strange conclusion that they were all equally doomed to failure.

The official Stalinist line was based throughout on the fixed aim of controlling directly — or, later, of capturing — the Kuomintang. The "class analyses" of the Kuomintang, first as a bloc of four classes and after the April *coup d'état* as a bloc of three classes, reflect this basic political aim. Stalin was probably correct in assuming that if one could exercise a decisive influence over the Kuomintang, an organization with indigenous roots, with its own illustrious founding father, its own symbolism, and led by experienced politicians and military leaders, a long step would have been taken toward controlling the destiny of China. As late as April 5, 1927, we find Stalin asserting, "at present, we need the Right. It has capable people who still direct the army and lead it against imperialism." [1]

It is quite apparent that to Stalin, who had already begun to think in terms of "socialism in one country," that is, in terms of the Soviet Union as a Power among Powers, the prospect of a strong China peculiarly pliant to Moscow's will was a most attractive prospect. The fact that Sun Yat-sen eagerly complied with Borodin's advice, the fact that men such as Chiang Kai-shek and Hu Han-min did not hesitate to use Communist phrases and speak in terms of world revolution, must have vastly encouraged Moscow's hopes.

When hopes of controlling the Kuomintang leadership directly faded after the incident of March 20, the Stalinist leadership still seemed fully confident of its ability to capture the party organization by achieving "proletarian hegemony" within it. Had not the Chinese Communist Party made deep inroads into the lower echelon of the Kuomintang? Did it not control its mass organizations?

Stalin seems to have forgotten, however, that Borodin had reorganized the Kuomintang along the lines of "democratic centralism" and that one does not control an organization of this type simply by influencing its lower echelons or its mass basis. He had further overlooked the fact that at the center of this organization there was a group of political and military leaders who were quite determined to maintain their own independent power and were acutely aware of the Kremlin's plans to achieve "proletarian hegemony" within the Kuomintang. Stalin could hardly speak in terms of squeezing out the "Right" like lemons [2] and then expect the "Right" in the person of Chiang Kai-shek to act out the role assigned to him. Instead, of course, Chiang, who was at the peak of his political acumen, squeezed out the Comintern and the Chinese Communist Party like lemons and ruthlessly thrust them aside.

Above all, the Stalinist leadership overlooked the fact that it did not at any time control the military power of the Kuomintang. For this, too, the Ch'en Tu-hsiu leadership was later blamed. Actually, the Kremlin itself had not encouraged Communist activities in the army. As late as February 1927, the Comintern had asserted that "the Chinese Communist Party and class-conscious Chinese workers must not, under any circumstances, pursue a tactic which would disorganize the revolutionary armies just because the influence of the bourgeoisie is, to a certain degree, strong there." [3] Since the Kremlin had endorsed the northern expedition, it could not carry on vigorous Communist propaganda programs among the rank and file of the soldiery, since this might immediately alienate its officers and disrupt the whole campaign. It is axiomatic that when one is interested in the victory of an armed force, one does not proceed to disrupt it. This same axiom held true during the Wuhan period when the Kremlin was concerned, above all, to keep intact the forces of the Wuhan generals. (The spread of Communist influence among certain elements of Chang Fa-k'uei's troops was not the result of any plans framed in Moscow.) Since China was still a land in which military power controlled civilian power, this oversight proved catastrophic.

In brief, then, Stalin's error lay in his overweening confidence that from a distance of several thousand miles he could control and manipulate a centralized political machine whose leaders were quite as shrewd and strong-willed as he.

To some extent, the policies of the Stalin leadership (as well as of the Trotskyist opposition) were based on sheer ignorance of the local situation. Thus, Stalin's letter of June 1 calling for a trial of "reactionary generals" by the Wuhan government betrays a downright ignorance of the actual relationship of political and military power in the Wuhan government. The Comintern, it is true, had hosts of emissaries in China — men such as Borodin, Mif, Mandalian, Doriot, Browder, Roy, etc. All these men were obliged, however, to correct their observations to fit the prevailing official line. While a party line may originally be based on empirical observations, once it is established it becomes a priori truth as far as the lower echelons are concerned until such time as the leadership is again obliged by objective events to shift its grounds.

What of the Trotskyist line on China? Actually it was not until the conflict between Trotsky and Stalin had begun to assume an acute form that Trotsky began to develop his own clear-cut views on China. In the strategic sphere, Trotsky called for "an independent proletarian party which fights under its own banner and never permits its policies and organizations to be dissolved in the policies and organizations of other classes." [4] Thus far, his strategic line did indeed resemble the inclinations of Ch'en Tu-hsiu and P'eng Shu-chih as charged by Ch'ü Ch'iu-pai. After Chiang Kai-shek's April *coup d'état*, however, Trotsky issued a call for soviets of workers, peasants, and soldiers. He also frankly called for the subversion of the rank and file of the Kuomintang armies, since he clearly realized that it would be impossible to establish armed peasants' and workers' soviets until soldiers' soviets under Communist control were set up within the national armies. In other words, he frankly called for a "dual power" of the 1917 type in Russia. If the Wuhan national government should oppose the soviets, all well and good — real power would lie with the soviets.[5] At this point, of course, there is not the slightest resemblance between the bold course recommended by Trotsky and the cautious "self-protectionism" of Ch'en Tu-hsiu.

The theoretical aspect of the Trotsky line is marked by its insistence that the interests of the bourgeoisie of backward areas are not diametrically opposed to those of the imperialist bourgeoisie. On the contrary, its interests are already closely tied in with those of world imperialism. Imperialism has, indeed, already made "capitalist relations" the dominant economic relations in Chinese society even in the countryside.[6] The Kuomintang in Trotsky's view is thus primarily the party of the Chinese bourgeoisie. Hence, the proletariat must be allowed to lead the masses unencumbered by ties to this treacherous partner. The proletariat will still have certain "bourgeois" tasks to perform but it should do so with its own state power.

In general, then, Trotsky applies to China the basic features of his own theory of the "permanent revolution" which, he felt, had been so magnificently vindicated by the October Revolution in Russia. Trotsky cannot forget the events of October 1917. With all the differences in sophistication and brilliance, his image of the world remains very similar to that of Ch'en Tu-hsiu in the 1920 period. He is loath to renounce his image of the world as involved in a single melodrama to be resolved by a single apocalypse. With Stalin, on the other hand, the ardor to realize the world revolution has already receded before the power interests of the Soviet state. Thus, while Trotsky tends to draw the "backward areas" into what he regards as a unitary historic process, while he tends to exaggerate the extent to which the backward areas are already dominated by "capitalist relations," Stalin, the "empiric," is quite willing to perceive that the world process has not yet merged into a single drama. However clumsy his "theoretical" formulas, they are nevertheless designed to take account of differences which Trotsky finds it difficult to accept.

Stalin is thus not entirely wrong in stating that Trotsky's whole strategy in China is based on an unfounded analogy with Russia of 1917 [7] (although some of his own analogies are hardly more apt). In Russia, the soviets had existed as a ready-made instrument of power *before* Lenin had seized control of them. In China, the Communist Party would have had to take the initiative in creating this new state power. What would have happened if the Chinese Communist Party had begun to form "soldiers' soviets" in May 1927? Would not the generals, who crushed the Communist movement two months later, simply have crushed the attempt at the outset? Would the party have been able to win away the national army rank and file from their generals (a rank and file who had been led to believe that they were fighting for their own interests within the Kuomintang) before these generals were able to crush this movement?

Furthermore, even if the area under Wuhan control had been

sovietized, would the "revolutionary wave" necessarily have engulfed the whole of China? In Russia, the revolution had not broken the ingrained habits created by centuries of centralized government. Thus, seizing the heights of power in Petrograd and Moscow, Lenin had taken a long step toward establishing his regime as the government of Russia. In a fragmentized China which had long lost the habits of centralized government, the establishment of soviets in areas under the jurisdiction of the Wuhan government would not necessarily have produced sweeping effects in the areas under the control of Feng Yü-hsiang or Chang Tso-lin. The future history of the Chinese Communist movement was to illustrate this fact most vividly.

In evaluating trends within the Chinese Communist movement itself, we need not consider at length the views of the Ch'ü Ch'iu-pai faction since Ch'ü's main efforts were devoted to proving his unswerving loyalty to the Stalinist line of the post-Seventh-Plenum period. Like the Kremlin, he called at once for more "radical" policies and for the implementation of these polices through the organs of the Kuomintang. Like the Kremlin, he failed to indicate how these two aims were to be pursued simultaneously.

As for the tendencies represented by Ch'en Tu-hsiu and P'eng Shu-chih, they could succeed only within a framework of political democracy. Ch'en, it will be recalled, wanted the Communist Party to act as an independent party, to expend its energies in the area of mass "education" and mass organization until the time came for the seizure of power by the "proletariat." Such a program could be carried forward only in a state where a multiparty system was sanctioned by law and where civil rights were firmly established. Actually, Sun Yat-sen's theory of tutelage, reinforced as it had been by Borodin's reorganization of the Kuomintang, had made that party quite immune to notions of political democracy or to the notion of a multiparty system. The fact that the power within this party had gravitated into the hands of military men entirely unencumbered by notions of legality simply reinforced its undemocratic nature. After March 20, it is true, Chiang Kai-shek had himself suggested that the Communist Party carry on, on a separate basis.[8] There is, however, ample room for doubt whether he ever intended to allow the Communist Party to grow into a strong independent force.

In brief, then, the Ch'en program could be carried forward only within the framework of political democracy — even though its ultimate aim was to subvert such political democracy.

The tendency represented by Mao Tse-tung in his "Report" was, as we have indicated, a marginal tendency within the Communist movement. It is doubtful whether there were any others in the Chinese Communist Party or in Moscow prepared to stake the entire future of the Communist movement on the peasantry to the exclusion of all other considerations. Basic Marxist-Leninist dogma stood in the way of such an approach and was to continue to stand in its way as we shall later find. Furthermore, as has already been pointed out, Mao's "Report" still shows no appreciation of the importance of the role of military power in the Chinese scene. This was a lesson yet to be learned.

It is possible to speculate on what might have been the fate of the Chinese Communist Party if it had been allowed to go its own way from the very outset. We shall not indulge in such speculation here. We would suggest, however, that given the nature of the Kuomintang-Communist alliance as it developed during 1925 and 1926, with its peculiar relations of political and military power, almost any strategic approach adopted by the Communist Party would probably have suffered shipwreck.

It remains to inquire, however, whether the 1920–1927 period created any of those factors which were to account for the final victory of the Chinese Communist movement in the late forties. Superficially, there would appear to be little resemblance between the Communist Party of the early years and the Communist Party which finally won national hegemony under the leadership of Mao Tse-tung. It is possible, nevertheless, to find lines of continuity which underly all differences.

In the first place, as a result of its intimate contacts with Moscow, the Chinese Communist Party had had ample opportunity to become fully acquainted with the Leninist concept of party organization, as well as with the Stalinist practice of that theory during the period in which that practice was in the process of crystallization. While Ch'en Tu-hsiu's practice of Communist leadership may have been more in the tradition of Lenin, we shall find the future leaders of the party — Ch'ü Ch'iu-pai, Li Li-san, and even Mao Tse-tung

— thoroughly acquainted with the techniques developed by the Stalin leadership.

In the second place, the Chinese Communist Party had during these years acquired considerable experience in mass leadership. While its leadership of the labor movement was to prove abortive, its activities in the countryside were to have permanent results. It was during these years that Mao Tse-tung first learned to apply the Leninist formula of a revolutionary elite allied to the motive power of mass discontent. While the Kuomintang had already failed to appreciate the potentialities of mass power, the Communist Party was equipped by its *Weltanschauung* to take full advantage of this force. There was much yet to be learned at the cost of considerable ideological purity, but this formula was to remain as a potential source of power.

Finally, it was during these years that Marxism-Leninism began to exert its amazing influence on China's total intellectual life, in circles often far removed from the Communist movement. The groundwork for the later facile acceptance of Marxist-Leninist premises among the Chinese intelligentsia was laid during these years.

VI THE NEW LINE

The strategy adopted by the Stalinist leadership after the collapse of the Kuomintang-Communist alliance in July 1927 is a striking example of that technique of maintaining the appearance of infallibility in the midst of failure which has by now become a fixed feature of Communist technique.

In reading Lenin's writings, one is struck by the candor with which he often admits past errors without in the least diminishing the appearance of infallibility which hedges him about. His strategy on such occasions is never to engage in a defense of past actions but rather to turn on those who still cling to his own past views. His "charismatic" personality assures the success of this strategy. Stalin, however, whose leadership is of quite another order, has had to resort to other methods of maintaining the appearance of infallibility. In the face of Trotsky's constant attacks he felt obliged to assert not only the correctness of his present policies, but of his past policies as well. Whatever errors might have been committed must have stemmed not from the Comintern leadership, but from some other source.

Thus, immediately after the debacle of Wuhan, Stalin informs us that his policy throughout the 1923–1927 period had been entirely correct and that "only people who have no understanding of Marxism can demand that a correct policy must always lead to immediate victory over an opponent. The attainment of an immediate victory over opponents depends not only upon correct policy, but above all, on the relative strength of the class forces involved." [1]

It is immediately obvious, however, that Marxism-Leninism is supposed to furnish information concerning the relative strength of class forces. If a party line cannot furnish information regarding the relative strength of various classes, it means that there are important quantitative unknowns in political situations which are beyond the scope of the party line; hence, that the party line cannot serve as a guide for political action. As a matter of fact, both the Seventh and Eighth Plenums of the ECCI had devoted long analyses to a discussion of the relative strength of class forces in China. Furthermore, Stalin fails to mention the fact that what he was confronting in China was not merely the absence of an immediate victory but a defeat of major proportions — and major defeats have always been criteria of the failure of a line within the Leninist tradition.

We are not surprised to find that Stalin does not rest very long with this awkward makeshift. Instead, we find him turning more and more to another expedient, that of shifting responsibility for these failures onto the shoulders of the Chinese leaders. The Comintern line had been entirely correct. It had simply been misinterpreted and misapplied by the Chinese leadership. This approach is already foreshadowed in a statement of Bukharin of July 6 to the effect that "the Chinese Communist Party leadership has in recent times sabotaged the decisions of the Comintern." [2] Henceforth, the Comintern line was to consist of two propositions: (1) that the stage through which they had just passed had been a necessary historic stage and the party would now move on to a new "higher" stage; (2) that whatever gross failures had occurred during this stage had been due to the errors of the Chinese leaders.

This interpretation is supported by quoting general "radical" phrases from the past resolutions of the Comintern — phrases about the inevitable defection of the bourgeoisie [3] and the "deepening" of the agrarian crisis, etc., while scrupulously avoiding mention of concrete Comintern directives on specific issues. Certain speeches of Stalin and Bukharin are studiously ignored.

The Stalin leadership could not confine its attention, however, to a justification of past policy. The disastrous situation in China demanded a new positive program precisely at a time when the struggle for leadership in Moscow was at a most critical stage. The new line on China which was evolved during July and August was thus a response to various urgencies: the need to do something positive to salvage the situation, the need to demonstrate that Stalin had been correct in the past, and the need to prove that Trotsky had been incorrect. Both the strategic and theoretical elements of the new line can be understood, I think, only as a response to these needs.

In the theoretical sphere, the Kremlin insisted that the revolution was still a bourgeois, democratic revolution. The bourgeois tasks of completing the agrarian revolution, of wiping out the remnants of feudalism, and of overcoming imperialism had hardly begun. Stalin was determined to defend this theoretical bastion against Trotsky's claim that the defeats in China represented a consummation of the bourgeois revolution. The victory of the Kuomintang was, in Trotsky's view, a victory of the bourgeoisie, a victory which need not have taken place had it not been for the gross errors of the Stalinist leadership.

How could the revolution still be considered a bourgeois, democratic revolution when both the "grande" bourgeoisie (one of the bloc of four classes before the April coup) and most of the petty bourgeoisie (one of the bloc of three classes in the Wuhan government) had gone over to the feudal classes? Fortunately, Lenin had provided for this difficulty by making a sharp distinction between the content of a revolution and its class forces. The tasks of the revolution were indeed bourgeois tasks, but they would henceforth be met by what Lenin had called a "democratic dictatorship of peasants and workers."

Since the formula of the "democratic dictatorship of peasants and workers" was to remain a basic dogma of the Chinese Communist movement until the rise of the "New Democracy," it is perhaps appropriate that we consider its meaning at some length.

Like Trotsky's theory of the "permanent revolution," Lenin's theory of the "democratic dictatorship" was framed in response to the problems raised by the 1905 revolution in Russia. As against Trotsky, Lenin insists that "Marxists are absolutely convinced of the bourgeois character of the Russian revolution." [4] Russia must pass through her bourgeois stage. The consummation of this revolution cannot, however, be entrusted to the hated bourgeoisie itself since that class will simply seek an opportunity to make a deal with the autocracy. Only the proletariat in alliance with the peasant masses can effect a genuine bourgeois democratic revolution. The peasant parties themselves constitute, as it were, the bourgeois base of the revolution since the aims of the bulk of the peasantry are bourgeois in nature. Although there is a constant implication that the proletariat will inevitably be the senior partner in the alliance, this theory does represent a modification, to some extent, of the previous Marxist notion (one often echoed by Lenin himself both before and after 1905) that the peasantry can exercise no historic initiative whatsoever.

The dictatorship will be "democratic" because it will be based not simply on the proletariat, but on a coalition of classes which represent the overwhelming majority of the Russian people.[5] It is important to note here that Lenin takes it for granted that the collaboration of proletariat and peasantry will necessarily involve the collaboration of proletarian and peasant political parties. "The proletariat," he states, "constitutes a minority. It can only command a mighty overwhelming majority if it unites with the mass of semiproletarians, the semi-property-owners. Such a composition will naturally reflect itself in the composition of the revolutionary government." In other places he assumes that the dictatorship will involve an alliance with the Narodniks whom he regards as the legitimate representatives of peasant interests and peasant mentality. He vehemently rejects any notion that the Social Democratic Party should itself organize the peasantry as a whole. "In our opinion, there should be no Social Democratic Peasant Committees. If they are Social Democratic, that means that they are not purely peasant committees; if they are peasant committees that means that they are not purely proletarian, nor Social Democratic committees." [6] "The alliance between proletariat and peasantry must, in no case, be interpreted to mean a fusion of the different classes or parties of the proletariat and peasantry." [7] Once the democratic bourgeois objectives have been achieved, once the peasantry has been divided into various segments on the basis of property, the proletariat must break its alliance with the propertied peasants and pursue its own goal — the socialist revolution. Such, in outline, is the theory of the "democratic dictatorship of workers and peasants." We shall have ample opportunity to see to what extent this theory corresponded to practice in China.

After July 1927, however, this theory offered the Stalinist leadership certain solid advantages. It made it possible for Stalin to present the history of the 1926–1927 period as a sort of smooth continuous development. At the Seventh and Eighth Plenum of the ECCI, the Kremlin leadership had toyed with the idea that the Kuomintang alliance might almost be called a peasants' and workers' dictatorship. At the Eighth Plenum in May 1927, Stalin had asked: "Is the present Hankow government an organ of the revolutionary dictatorship of the proletariat and peasantry? No, so far it is not nor will it be very soon, but it has all the chances of developing into such an organ in the further development of the revolution." [8] Now, he could claim that this prognosis had been fulfilled. In the course of its development, the revolution had sloughed off the bourgeoisie and finally "advanced" to a stage where the peasantry and proletariat alone could carry forward the revolution. The defection of the Wuhan government had, as it were, cleared the ideological atmosphere and the revolution would now simply pass into "a newer higher phase." [9] The catastrophic events of July, the complete break between the Communist Party and the urban proletariat, were thus effectively hidden behind an appearance of smooth historic evolution.

Another advantage was the fact that the theory of "democratic dictatorship" had been Lenin's creation and had been partly directed against Trotsky. Thus, even though Lenin himself had treated it most cavalierly in 1917, the Kremlin leadership, by stressing this theory, was able to give the impression of solidarity with the dead spirit of Lenin against Trotsky.

The impression of a continuity of policy is further heightened by Stalin's insistence that the alliance with the Kuomintang as a party be maintained. On July 10 Stalin states in *Pravda*: "Does the departure from the nationalist government imply a break with the Kuomintang? In my view it does not." [10] The very Comintern instructions which call for a "demonstrative withdrawal" from the Wuhan government add that "the Chinese Communist Party should not withdraw from the Kuomintang in spite of the campaign of its leaders for the expulsion of the Communists." [11] The Nanchang uprising of August 1 was carried on under a Kuomintang banner and listed the names of Teng Yen-ta and Chang Fa-k'uei on its "Revolutionary Committee." It was not until the Politburo meeting of September 19 [12] that the Kuomintang banner was finally furled — and it was finally decreed that the Kuomintang would no longer serve as the vehicle for the "democratic dictatorship of workers and peasants."

It is, of course, possible to explain this insistence "theoretically." As has been pointed out, the democratic dictatorship presupposes an alliance of parties representing the proletariat and parties representing the peasantry (although *not* an alliance of the Kuomintang-Communist type). The Kuomintang could thus be considered as a party representing the peasantry and certain elements of the *petty* bourgeoisie. We shall later find, however, that this theoretical factor does not prevent the Comintern from dropping its affiliations with all other parties.

Actually, it seems to me that here, also, the political relationship between Trotsky and Stalin is a much more vital factor. Trotsky had in the past made the alliance with the Kuomintang the center of all his attacks. Hence, any abrupt break with the Kuomintang would simply have lent color to Trotsky's views. With the departure of the Wuhan government leaders, all that remained of the Kuomintang to appropriate were a few Left Kuomintang leaders and the hold of Kuomintang symbols on certain elements of the population. The real sources of power in the Kuomintang, however, now lay well outside of Stalin's control. In fact, Stalin had already begun to think in terms of Trotsky's previous slogan of "Soviets." On July 26 he already declares: "The Communists must immediately begin to propagandize the idea of Soviets so that in case they fail in their fight for the Kuomintang, they may lead the masses to the formation of Soviets. In case of success in our struggle for the Kuomintang, the perspectives of a growing over of the Kuomintang into Soviets should not be excluded." [13] If such a shift were to be made, however, the Stalin leadership was determined to avoid the impression that the disasters in China had confirmed the rightness of Trotsky's policies. A shift to soviets must be made to appear as a smooth historic shift from one stage to another. It must not appear that Stalin had taken a leaf from Trotsky's book.

In estimating the future direction of the revolution in China, Stalin adopts a prognosis diametrically opposed to Trotsky's. Trotsky's view was that the disasters of July had completely shattered the previous rising revolutionary wave. Stalin, on the contrary, maintained that Trotsky had been premature in postulating a rising wave in May. Actually, the revolutionary wave was just now climbing toward its crest.

It might be well to pause here for a moment to consider the imagery of the rising and falling wave (often expressed by other terms such as "rising tide" or "falling tide," or simply "rise" and "fall") in the Communist party line. In general, the party's knowledge of the future upward or downward trend of history is ostensibly not simply based on a "mechanical" analysis of empirical data. Throughout the course of human history, great statesmen have often succeeded in gauging future political trends from the general political situation in which they operated. The Communist postulation of rising and falling waves, however, is often applied to far-off places with which the Kremlin is unfamiliar or even to the whole globe. It is thus presumably based on some superior insight into the inner flow of the historic process vouchsafed only to the leaders of the Communist Party by virtue of their status as vanguards of the proletariat. One suspects, however, that the postulation of rising or falling waves is often as likely to be determined by some present political consideration as by any dialectic insight into the future flow of history.

Stalin's postulation of a "new rise" in China after July 1927 may have been partially based on the genuine belief that the workers and peasants in China were ripe for revolution. It may have been influenced by Trotsky's previous confidence that the masses in China were ready to sweep all before them. It is difficult to avoid the conclusion, however, that it was mainly motivated by political considerations. In the dramatic words of Trotsky, "In trying to insure themselves against the sins of the past, the leaders criminally forced the trend of events." [14] Stalin needed victories in China.

The most solid accomplishment of the new line lay not in the theoretical but in the strategic sphere. Since it was no longer possible to capture the real centers of power in the Kuomintang, the Comintern was now ready to sanction the establishment of a separate military force under Communist control. We have already pointed out that in spite of the Comintern's former policy, Communist influence had strongly infected many sections of the Kuomintang forces. It is not likely that the emergence of "Red Armies" under the leadership of Ho Lung, Yeh T'ing, Chu Teh, and others was a direct result of the Comintern shift, but the new Comintern line did provide them with official sanction.

The Nanchang uprising of August 1 was the first large-scale attempt to implement the new line. Thus the attempt to capture

Nanchang was predicated on the assumption that a new revolutionary rise was imminent, hence, that any bold act might kindle the flames of revolution anywhere. In keeping with the party line the "Revolutionary Committee" set up at Nanchang operated under the banner of the Kuomintang and included the names of such Kuomintang leaders as Teng Yen-ta, Soong Ch'ing-ling (Madame Sun Yat-sen), and Chang Fa-k'uei (who later crushed the uprising). The avowed aim of the Committee was to establish a "workers' and peasants' republic." [15] The failure of Nanchang did not immediately draw the censure of Moscow. We shall find, however, that when the Comintern line was again modified after the Canton Commune, the leaders of the Nanchang uprising were duly criticized for implementing the Comintern's previous line.

The real significance of the Nanchang uprising is the fact that it marks the emergence of military power as a factor within the Chinese Communist movement.

The August Seventh Emergency Conference

We are not surprised to find that the most vigorous protagonists of the new Comintern line are such men as Ch'ü Ch'iu-pai, Li Li-san, Chang Kuo-t'ao, and the extremely flexible Chou En-lai — in other words, the leaders of the "opposition" faction who were now in a position to reap the fruits of their superior loyalty. According to Li Ang,[16] the Emergency Conference of August 7, called to reconsider the policies of the Ch'en Tu-hsiu leadership, was planned and executed by Ch'ü himself. Other sources claim that the conference was called at the instance of the new Comintern delegate, Lominadze.[17] Whatever may be the case, the August Seventh Conference does mark the removal of Ch'en Tu-hsiu from his position of leadership and the rise of Ch'ü Ch'iu-pai to party leadership.

The main accomplishments of the conference, which is often referred to as a "turning point" in the history of the Chinese Communist movement, were its confirmations of the new Comintern line. The *Manifesto of the August Seventh Conference* presents an elaborate account of the new orthodox version of Ch'en Tu-hsiu's errors. The Comintern and the party rank and file, it appears, had always pursued a correct policy. This correct policy had, however, been sabotaged by the leaders of the party whose opportunism was a "reflection of the influence of the bourgeoisie on certain Communist Party members." [18]

This device of referring wrong policies to the tainted class connection of the executors of policies is, of course, well within the Leninist tradition. The party qua party can commit no historic error. It is, however, rather ironic to observe that the same August Seventh Conference which has suddenly discovered that "the leadership of the party is generally composed of intelligentsia and bourgeoisie" is itself made up primarily of intelligentsia and bourgeosie, many of whom will themselves be subject to similar accusations in the future.

The program of the conference adhered in all respects to the new Comintern line. The new historic stage of the revolution was still a bourgeois democratic stage. Its political expression was the "democratic dictatorship of workers and peasants" and the Kuomintang still remained the political vehicle of this dictatorship. It still asserted that "under present conditions, unless the party wins hegemony within the Kuomintang, it cannot win the hegemony over the Chinese proletariat itself. We must reorganize the Kuomintang into a genuine organization of the working masses of town and country." [19] It was stressed, however, that henceforth the Kuomintang apparatus was to serve as nothing more than a front for the Communist Party which would maintain its full independence. The door was also left open for a possible shift to the slogan of soviets. "The organization of the revolutionary Kuomintang developing to a higher stage will enable our political power to advance to the stage of workers', peasants' and soldiers' Soviets in such a manner that the transformation can be carried out easily and painlessly." [20]

A peculiar feature of the *Manifesto* is the fact that it still leaves a door open for the "bourgeoisie." Since the Comintern still insisted on clinging to the Kuomintang, since the Kuomintang had but recently been a three-class bloc, it was not unreasonable to assume that the Comintern had not yet completely lost hope of recapturing segments of the "bourgeoisie." "The wavering elements of the bourgeoisie should be won over by the resolute, revolutionary action of the proletariat." [21] The bourgeoisie might still play an anti-imperialist role.

The unique accomplishment of the August Seventh Conference, according to later orthodox versions of Chinese Communist history, was its emphasis on the agrarian question. This emphasis was, of course, a logical consequence of the theory of "democratic dictatorship of workers and peasants." "The agrarian revolution" states the *Manifesto*, "is the crux of the bourgeois democratic revolution." [22] Great attention was devoted to this problem, particularly to an indictment of the failures of the Ch'en Tu-hsiu leadership. The question of the relationship of the Communist Party to the peasantry will be discussed in some detail in a later chapter. It should be pointed out here, however, that this greater emphasis on the peasantry was by no means meant to imply the abandonment of the party's tasks among the urban proletariat. On the contrary, while the agrarian problem might be the crux of the bourgeois revolution, "the basic task of the Chinese Communist Party is to organize the working class and lead their struggle." [23] The party must strive "to obtain a hegemony of the working class in order to realize a workers' and peasants' dictatorship." [24]

The conference also dealt in some detail with organizational matters. After violently upbraiding the Ch'en Tu-hsiu leadership for its dictatorial control of the party, it proceeded to suggest modifications in party structure which would tend to make the party less democratic than ever. Since the party now had to operate within hostile surroundings, the factor of secrecy had to be stressed. This provided the justification for an even greater tightening of party structure. "Our most important duty in the organizational sphere is to make our party a strong, secret combative organization." Within the Central Committee a seven-man "Emergency Politburo" was to be established to act as the kernel of the party. This bureau was to have its counterpart in each party headquarters and its own secret communications system.[25] The main motive for the reorganization was probably the need to separate the reliable from the unreliable elements within the party, for in spite of all his "opportunist errors," Ch'en Tu-hsiu's prestige in party ranks still ran high. It is not surprising that the party reorganization was soon followed by a wholesale series of expulsions.

The most important decisions of the party, however, lay in the tactical sphere. The Comintern, as we have seen, had postulated a new rising wave in the Chinese revolution. A rising historic wave, however, by its very nature, demands bold action on the part of the party. If the objective situation is ripe, then any "subjective" failure on the part of the party to take advantage of such a situation is criminal. We are thus not surprised to find that the August Seventh Conference calls for armed uprisings on every hand. "We must provide for the arming of the workers and must train them for uprisings and street fighting in order to coördinate these uprisings with agrarian uprisings in the village and thus directly prepare the overthrow of the antirevolutionary government." [26]

VII

THE CH'U CH'IU-PAI
LEADERSHIP

The New Line in Practice

Armed with this new line, the new leadership faced the actualities of the Chinese situation in the latter months of 1927. If the Comintern line of the previous period had not led to success and had considerably hampered the movements of the Chinese party, it had nevertheless allowed the party to increase its hold on the urban proletariat. The new line, however, ran directly counter to a harsh, intractable reality. There now began that long series of attempts on the part of the party to beat down the iron wall of proletarian indifference which were finally to end in complete failure.

After July, the Wuhan and Nanking governments had both turned their fury on the Communist Party and actually succeeded in breaking its control of labor unions. What is even more important, however, in the cities, the industrial proletariat was itself turning its face irrevocably against the Communist leadership. At the time, it was perhaps not clear how deep an abyss had been created. We now know that it was not to be bridged until Chinese Communist troops were to enter the cities as conquerors in the late forties. At the time of the August Seventh Conference, the process of alienation had not yet reached that degree of finality which it was to assume in the early thirties, but it had already begun.

Since this is not a history of the Chinese labor movement, it would perhaps be inappropriate to consider all of the reasons for this alienation. Certain factors, I think, should, however, be mentioned.

The first and most obvious factor was, of course, the "white terror," the factor of sheer repression. The "white terror" initiated by the Kuomintang in 1927 was a movement of awesome proportions.[1] The government did not stay its hand from eliminating all those who were Communists or even suspected of being Communists within the labor movement.

At the same time, however, it is to be noted that Communist literature of the 1927–1931 period does not consider the "white terror" sufficient to account for its inability to recapture its control of the workers. This literature pays much unconscious tribute to the effectiveness of the "reformist" policies which the Kuomintang was carrying on through the medium of the "Yellow Unions." Why then did the Chinese industrial proletariat prove so amenable to "reformism," so deaf to Communist blandishments?

The "Short History" [2] informs us that in 1920 when the Communists had first begun to court the labor movement, the workers had regarded the radical young students and intellectuals with no little suspicion. With the passage of time, however, as organized labor began to achieve unanticipated successes under its Communist leadership, it is evident that the workers began to take more seriously the slogans and pronouncements of their leaders regarding the messianic mission of the industrial proletariat. In the feverish, apocalyptic atmosphere of the 1925–1927 period, everything seemed possible. Their faith was, however, based on a belief in the infallibility of the Comintern and of the Chinese Communist leadership. They had come to the Communist movement easily and without struggle. Where Communism had won a hold in the labor movements of Europe, it had done so only after desperate struggles with social-democratic and other tendencies. By that very token, however, where it did win a hold, this hold was much more solid. The young Chinese labor movement, however, had come to accept the slogans of the Kremlin solely as a result of the extravagant hopes roused by the events of these years. The repeated disasters of the early months of 1927 were thus sufficient to shatter these hopes. Once again that strain of political cynicism which seems to be such a deep-rooted Chinese tendency reasserted itself. The Chinese workers again became immersed in their own private trials and tribulations. They were now interested only in improving their own economic position, precisely in that type of "reformism" and "economism" which the Comintern now refused to consider.

The August Seventh Conference did, it is true, pay lip service to the "daily economic struggles" of the masses, to the need for raising living standards, etc.[3] It was made amply clear, however, that all slogans of a purely economic nature, such as those concerning the eight-hour day, wage increases, etc., were merely meant to serve as stimulants to arouse the workers to political insurrection. In a period of "revolutionary upsurge," one does not confine one's attention to economic demands.

We are thus not surprised to find that the latter months of 1927 are marked by sporadic attempts to force insurrectionary strikes in Shanghai and elsewhere. While this period is generally known in the history of Chinese Communism as the period of the "autumn harvest uprisings," it would be an error to assume that the Ch'ü Ch'iu-pai leadership was inclined to ignore its tasks in the city. Hua Kang informs us that the Kiangsu provincial committee, at this time, armed red terrorists and attempted to manufacture a general strike by intimidating the workers in various Shanghai factories.[4] Similar abortive strikes took place in Changsha and elsewhere.

However, while the urban proletariat was turning its face against the party, the countryside was still ripe for insurrection. The peasantry of central China, which had been roused to action during the 1925-1927 period, was still ready for action against landlords, militarists, and officials, whether this action was led by the "Red Spears," the "Great Knives," or the Communist Party. For the first time, the Communist Party was confronted by the embarrassment of the "uneven development of proletarian and peasant struggles."

How are we to account for this difference? Here again, the first and most obvious fact was, of course, that the government's control of the vast and swamplike countryside was by no means as firm as its control of the large urban centers. Furthermore, in spite of the ostensible centralization of power achieved by the Kuomintang, the hinterlands were still largely controlled by semi-independent local warlords.

What is more, it would appear unlikely that the peasants had been greatly affected by the extravagant hopes of the 1925-1927 period. The small Chinese proletariat had been subject to a concentrated propaganda concerning its transcendental missions, while the appeal to the peasantry had been on the basis of elemental demands. It is precisely because the peasantry was not aware of its transcendental mission, precisely because its demands remained what they had been — "economic" demands for less taxation and for land —

that sweeping political reverses did not affect its desperate readiness to rise against its miserable conditions under any leadership.

While the Ch'ü Ch'iu-pai leadership did not intend to abandon its task of winning back its proletarian base, it was nevertheless forced to seek evidences of a rising revolutionary upsurge where it could find them. It was thus entirely prepared to take full advantage of the continuous restiveness in the countryside which it later hoped to coördinate with successful strikes in the city.

It was under these conditions that the "autumn harvest uprisings" took place. The leadership plausibly assumed that the peasantry would be particularly prone to insurrection during the harvest period when landlords and tax collectors make their burdensome levies.

According to the account of Mao Tse-tung, he himself was mainly responsible for the general developments of the uprisings. The Ch'ü Ch'iu-pai leadership had indeed sent him to Hunan with the general aim of fomenting peasant disturbances, but according to Mao's testimony it did not support him in all his activities.[5]

In late August and early September, Mao managed to assemble a patchwork army consisting mainly of peasants, some Hanyang miners, and deserters from the Kuomintang forces. This "First Division of the First Peasants and Workers Army" was the nucleus of what was later to become the famous First Army.[6] The sporadic uprisings fomented and led by this force over a large area all ended, of course, in failure and were to win Mao a dismissal from the Politburo. According to one source, after these events he was even placed on probation as a member of the Party.

Why did Mao fling himself into these activities with such ardor, and why was he "repudiated" by the Central Committee?[7] We have already seen how deep had been his faith in the revolutionary potentialities of the peasantry, how impatient he had been of all attempts to limit the "excesses" of the peasant movement prior to the break with the national government. It is thus not unlikely that after the break with Wuhan, he finally felt that the time had come for the "raging torrents and driving rain" to sweep all before it. He had, furthermore, during this period come to realize the importance of the factor of military organization. Since it was now legitimate in terms of the new Comintern line to engage in military activities, he probably felt that a judicious coördination of military organization with local peasant uprisings would provide the formula for a country-wide agrarian insurrection. His actions were predicated on the assumption that isolated uprisings fomented here and there would provide the sparks for a flame which would engulf the whole Chinese peasantry. The flame, however, did not spread. The fragmentized nature of the Chinese countryside did not make for the spread of political contagion beyond the area immediately affected. Mao had realized at an early date, in the face of Marxist dogma, that the peasantry could independently provide the mass base for a revolution. During 1927, he had come to realize that in a country where power tended to gravitate into the hands of the military, mass power must be coördinated with military power. He had not yet discovered that in a land as politically and economically fragmentized as China, the revolution would have to operate from a fixed territorial base.

The "autumn harvest" uprisings were, of course, a failure and it is probably in this fact that we must seek the main reason for Mao's fall into disfavor. Such failures, for which the Central Committee had to bear responsibility, did not increase its stature in the eyes of Moscow. According to Mao, however, the Central Committee had opposed his program even before the failure had become manifest.[8]

One obvious source of friction was Mao's cavalier adoption of the slogan of "organizing soviets." [9] The new Comintern line, as we have seen, had not yet authorized this slogan, and Mao's adoption of it at this time was a rather surprising breach of discipline which the Central Committee could not allow to pass unnoticed. This is the single occasion in Mao's autobiography in which he blandly admits that he had deliberately adopted a policy which was "opposed by the Comintern." [10]

Mao also implies, however, that the Central Committee objected to the whole procedure of organizing a military force. The memory of the Nanching uprising and of the failure at Swatow (Yeh T'ing and Ho Lung had occupied the city for a week only to be expelled) was still too fresh for the Central Committee to regard with enthusiasm further activities of a directly military nature.[11] Hua Kang, in his discussion of the failure of the autumn harvest uprisings, mentions as one of the main defects of the whole undertaking its "reliance on military force." [12]

Most important of all, however, the autumn uprisings were carried out with little regard for developments in the cities. To the minds of the party leadership, thoroughly wedded to the dogma of proletarian hegemony, any activity carried on in isolation from the city proletariat was bound to fail. Mao, himself, states that one of the main reasons for his disgrace had been the fact that "from the angle of the cities the movement appeared doomed to failure." [13] Hua Kang complains that the "rising peasants did not obtain any aid from the urban proletariat . . . At the time of the Hunan harvest uprising, Changsha simply had no workers movement whatsoever!" [14]

In spite of harrowing adventures Mao managed to keep a small force intact and finally took refuge in the winter of 1927 in the remote recesses of the Chingkanshan mountains lying athwart the border area between Hunan and Kiangsi.[15] This concentration of a small military force on a remote hinterland base may, at the time, have been nothing more than an expedient of despair. It was, however, to become the point of departure of a strategy which was to lead the Chinese Communist movement to ultimate success. It is thus most interesting to note that this whole development was inaugurated under a cloud of official disfavor, without the blessing of the party leadership, and most likely without the knowledge of Moscow.

It would, of course, be an error to suppose that Mao was the only one within the party at this time groping for a formula of agrarian revolution. It has already been pointed out that P'eng Pai had realized the potentialities of peasant organization at a much earlier date than Mao. His organizational accomplishments among the Haifeng peasantry during the early twenties had far outshone the accomplishments of Mao.[16]

After the break with Wuhan, P'eng Pai had served on the "Revolutionary Committee" at Nanchang and had later retreated with the armies of Yeh T'ing and Ho Lung to the Haifeng and Lufeng area where he had formerly carried on his work among the peasantry. Here, in November 1927, he organized a peasant militia and established the first Chinese Soviet government.[17] (The Comintern had authorized the shift to soviets on September 19.) During the Soviet period when orthodox histories of Chinese Communism revolved about the axis of the soviet, the Hailufeng venture was always cited as the first attempt to establish a Soviet government in China. Actually, it was a pioneering effort in a much more fundamental sense. It established an organized political power on a given territorial base. It won the support of the local peasantry by a policy of land division and burning of land deeds. Finally, it organized a peasant militia. In many respects, it thus provided an earlier prototype of the strategy later developed by Chu Teh and Mao Tse-tung at Chingkanshan. It is significant to note, however, that the Hailufeng experiment differs most from the strategy developed by Mao Tse-tung and Chu Teh in its underestimation of the military factor. The careful choice of a favorable terrain and the development of a rationalized technique of partisan warfare seem to have been truly original contributions of the Chu-Mao partnership.

The November Plenum

When the Central Committee of the Chinese Communist Party finally met in Enlarged Session on November 9 to reassess its accomplishments since the August Conference, the view was indeed bleak. It could contemplate in retrospect only a series of bloody failures in town and country. The Comintern, however, had not shifted its line an iota. On the contrary, its endorsement of the Soviet formula in September was interpreted by Ch'ü Ch'iu-pai as a call for even bolder action. The Stalin-Bukharin leadership in Moscow could hardly retract its postulation of a rising revolutionary wave so shortly after announcing it, particularly in the face of Trotsky's view that the revolutionary wave had decisively receded.

In fact, Ch'ü Ch'iu-pai and the Comintern delegate, Lominadze, had staked their future on their reputation for boldness and "true Bolshevik spirit." It would have been most difficult for them to reverse their strategy at a time when Ch'en Tu-hsiu, who still enjoyed a dangerous prestige in the party ranks, was openly calling for a policy of retreat.

Thus we find that the Enlarged Plenum stubbornly reiterates the claim that China is in the midst of a "rising revolutionary wave." [18] In support of its case, it points primarily to "objective factors" — that is, to the supposed weakness of the enemy and the desperate condition of the peasants and workers. A great deal of evidence is offered to prove that there can be no reconciliation of the "contradictions" between the bourgeois and feudal elements within the Kuomintang or among its various military cliques. "Stabilization" of the reactionary forces is thus out of the question.[19] How then are we to account for the failures of the July–November period? In the Plenum's view they can be traced, in most cases, to the "subjective" inadequacies of those involved. T'an P'ing-shan is charged with responsibility for the failure of Nanchang while Mao Tse-tung is made to bear the brunt of the failure of the autumn harvest uprising.[20]

The Plenum does, it is true, indulge in a certain amount of orthodox "self-criticism." While emphasizing that "in spite of new partial failures the whole experience of the last three months proves that our tactics, as a whole, have been completely correct," [21] it admits that the Central Committee may itself bear some responsibility for certain strategic errors. The main error mentioned, significantly enough, is the lack of coördination between the party in the cities and the party in the country. "In some localities one could have called the party a 'labor union party' or 'soldiers party' while in others one could have called it a 'peasants party.' " [22] "The coordination of worker uprisings and peasant uprisings is the most important problem facing the party . . . A purely peasant uprising without the leadership and help of the working class cannot achieve conclusive victories." [23]

The latter statement, later confirmed, by the Ninth Plenum of ECCI, throws an abundantly clear light on the reasons for the "repudiation" of Mao Tse-tung.

In general, the Report of the Plenum adhered scrupulously to the Comintern line. It did, however, contain one fatal statement which would provide Bukharin with an excellent handle for attack when the time came for Ch'ü's fall from power. "The Chinese Revolution," states the Report, "is protracted in nature and yet it is uninterrupted. It thus bears the nature of what Marx called a permanent revolution." [24]

Now there is an excellent reason why Ch'ü Ch'iu-pai dares to use the expression "permanent revolution" at this point. As has already been pointed out, in September the Comintern had sanctioned a complete break with the Kuomintang and had called for the establishment of a Soviet regime. In his earlier debates with Trotsky on the nature of the soviets, however, Stalin had argued that "the history of the workers' soviets in Russia shows that such soviets can exist and develop further only if favorable premises are given for a direct transition from the bourgeois democratic revolution to the proletarian revolution." [25] In other words, soviets appear only when the prospects of proletarian dictatorship are imminent. To Stalin, at the time (May 1927), this had served as an argument against the establishment of soviets in China. Now, however, that the Comintern had authorized the establishment of soviets in China, was it not legitimate to assume that the period of transition from the bourgeois democratic revolution to the period of proletarian revolution had arrived? Was it not now legitimate to speak in terms of "a permanent revolution" provided that one made it clear that one was referring to Marx's permanent revolution and not to Trotsky's? It would have indeed been a glorious destiny for the Ch'ü Ch'iu-pai leadership, if the proletarian revolution could be ushered in under its aegis.

After the failure of the Canton Commune, however, we shall find that Ch'ü Ch'iu-pai was made to pay the penalty for this logical indiscretion.

The Canton Commune

In general, the November Plenum laid the "theoretical" groundwork for the Canton Commune. It had reaffirmed the Comintern's postulation of a rising wave in China. It had stressed the fact that insufficient attention had been paid to urban centers. It had stressed the weakness of the enemy and called upon the party to take advantage of the conflicts among military leaders.

However, while the stage for urban insurrections may have been set by Ch'ü Ch'iu-pai and Lominadze at the Enlarged Plenum, there is much evidence that the events of Canton were inspired directly from Moscow. We know, of course, that the German Communist leader, Heinz Neumann, was to play a leading role in planning and executing the Canton uprising. Victor Serge and Souvarine have charged that the uprising was ordered directly from the Kremlin by Stalin who urgently needed a victory in China to vindicate his theory of the rising revolutionary wave in China at the Fifteenth Congress of the Communist Party of the Soviet Union.[26] Further strength is added to this claim by Li Ang, who claims to have been the corresponding secretary of the party at this time. "The Comintern," he says, "sent telegrams daily urging the Chinese Communist Party to bring about uprisings in Canton and other large cities. These telegrams were all extremely emphatic in tone and allowed no room for argument."[27] Li adds that Chang T'ai-lei, the secretary of the Kwangtung Party branch, vigorously protested that Canton was not ready for insurrection.[28]

Whatever may have been the source of the decision, however, Canton was probably chosen because: (1) it was the scene of a conflict between the contending forces of Chang Fa-k'uei and Li Chi-shen, thus providing the necessary "lack of stabilization in the reactionary camp"; (2) the existence of the Hailufeng Soviet government in the vicinity of Canton promised to provide the necessary "coördination of uprisings in the countryside, and uprisings in the city"; (3) Canton had been an important revolutionary center, and presumably its population was merely awaiting the signal to rise.

Actually, none of these considerations bore any relation to political reality. Since the defeats of Ho Lung and Yeh T'ing at Swatow the military potential of the Communists had become negligible. The "direct revolutionary situation" postulated by official policy was nonexistent and the inner contradictions between Li Chi-shen and Chang Fa-k'uei did not prevent them from uniting to crush the insurrection.

During the few days in which the Communists controlled the city (December 11–14), they did, of course, accomplish astounding military feats which belied their meager resources. They were not, however, supported by the urban masses or by any reserve forces of their own and were inevitably crushed.

During the few days of its existence, the Commune had an opportunity to establish a "soviet" of handpicked members which issued proclamations of an extremely radical nature. Trotsky has aptly pointed out that these slogans were actually much more in harmony with his own theory of the permanent revolution than with the official theory of the democratic dictatorship of peasants and workers. Its slogans called for workers' control of production, nationalization of large industries, etc., all under the sole leadership of the Communist party, that is, the party of the proletariat. "If these are the methods of the bourgeois revolution," he asks, "what will the proletarian revolution be like?"[29]

The failure of the Canton Commune was an event of such magnitude that it forced the Comintern to reconsider its party line in

China. It was now utterly impossible to speak in bland terms about a "revolutionary upsurge" in China. The new situation imperatively demanded a shift in line — a troublesome shift which was finally accomplished at the Ninth Plenum of the ECCI in February 1928.

The End of the Ch'ü Ch'iu-pai Leadership

While Ch'ü may not have been the major architect of the uprising at Canton, he was bound to suffer its consequences. He had, after all, never enjoyed the "patriarchal" prestige formerly enjoyed by Ch'en Tu-hsiu and others in the party. Li Li-san, Chang Kuo-t'ao, Hsiang Chung-fa, and Chou En-lai felt themselves his peers in every way. Li Li-san had, after all, been the "hero" of the May Thirtieth uprisings, while Chou En-lai had already won a reputation as an authority on military affairs. Hsiang Chung-fa was a man of genuine proletarian origins.

Ch'ü, who was basically a literary man — a "bookish student," in his own words [30] — had not been a particularly successful politician and had failed to build himself a personal machine within the party.

In addition to his political weakness and to the necessity of bearing the brunt of the failures of the past few months, the Ch'ü leadership was faced with serious problems of disorganization in the party. The long series of failures which the party had suffered since the beginning of the year were giving rise to all sorts of doubts within the party ranks concerning the very principle of "democratic centralism." While Ch'ü resorted to the now well-established practice of blaming failures on the "subjective mistakes" of local leaders, the local leaders were showing an increasing tendency to blame the center.

Ch'ü himself informs us in his *Chinese Revolution* that in Chihli (Hopei) a tendency had developed "to oppose the principle of centralism entirely, to advocate a sort of federal autonomy within the party and simply to follow at the heels of the masses." [31] The Chihli committee advocated a revision of the party constitution whereby the workers and peasants would be represented in the party according to a ratio of one representative for fifty workers and one representative for one hundred peasants.[32] This was nothing less than a call for political democracy! Worker members were quoted as saying that "the party doesn't seem to care that it has made us lose our jobs by its strikes or that it has gotten us thrown into prison. The party just brings the workers trouble." [33] There were further demands for rigid economic equality in party ranks and attacks on the "anti-democratic" decrees of the center.[34] After the Canton uprising the new Kwangtung Provincial Committee "placed the responsibility for the failure squarely on the shoulders of the central organs and said that they were responsible for the slaughter of several thousand people." [35]

These facts, cited by Ch'ü himself, point to a spirit of disaffection throughout the party rank and file and to the threat of all sorts of heresies within the movement.

Thus, the cumulative failures of the new line designed by the Comintern but implemented by the Ch'ü leadership, the growing signs of disintegration within the party, Ch'ü's own political ineptness, and the ambitions of other party leaders were all factors conspiring to undermine Ch'ü's leadership. Just as Ch'ü Ch'iu-pai had received the mandate of leadership after the failures of the early months of 1927, so now, Li Li-san, Hsiang Chung-fa, and Chou En-lai were easily able to unseat Ch'ü.

After the Ninth Plenum of the ECCI at which Ch'ü Ch'iu-pai was duly rebuked for his past errors, he remained in Moscow as Chinese Communist delegate to the Comintern. While this position was to win for him a reputation in the international Communist movement, it effectively removed him from any position of real power in China.[36]

In assessing the accomplishments of this period in terms of the subsequent history of Chinese Communism, we can point, I think, to only two factors: the emergence of the Red Army as a distinct military force and the discovery of a new strategy of revolution on Chingkanshan. The first step had indeed won the endorsement of the Kremlin; yet every attempt which had been made so far to apply independent military power had failed dismally.

As for the experiment on Chingkanshan, it would appear to have been the result of Mao Tse-tung's own desperate experiences, rather than of anything planned in either Shanghai or Moscow. It was born under a cloud of orthodox disapproval and, at the time, seemed to hold little hope of further development.

A NEW SHIFT IN LINE

A New Estimate of the Revolutionary Situation

The situation in China after the Canton Commune confronted the Kremlin with problems of a most embarrassing nature. After the failure in Canton — an event which had received world-wide publicity — it was no longer possible to continue the previous line intact. At the same time, Moscow could not radically modify its line without giving comfort to the forces of the opposition. Furthermore, this period marks the beginning of total reorientation in Kremlin global policy, a reorientation which was substantially in the spirit of the leftward course adopted in China.[1] The stabilization of world capitalism, it was contended, was now drawing to an end and history was now entering into a new "third period," when capitalism would begin to disintegrate, when a revolutionary wave would engulf the capitalist world. During this period, the proletariat would become "radicalized" and the Communist Party would succeed in wresting the leadership of the proletariat from the Social Democrats. During this revolutionary period, the Comintern would break all alliances with other political groups since it henceforth would be able to rely exclusively on its own mass support. All other political groups were to be considered simply as manifestations of the growing force of fascism. Thus, the Social Democrats would henceforth simply be called Social Fascists.

Now while Kremlin global policies are presumably designed to take into account the peculiarities of local conditions and the differences between countries of advanced capitalism and the backward areas, this consideration is counterbalanced by the desire to maintain a certain uniformity, a certain *gleichschaltung* in the tone of world-wide Communist propaganda. The Kremlin is thus not inclined to take a leftward course in its overall policies and a rightward course in China, or to speak of a rising revolutionary wave in Europe and a declining wave in China.

Considerations of this sort were, I think, what lay behind the new line on China as formulated at the Ninth Plenum of the ECCI, the Sixth Comintern Congress, and the Sixth Congress of the Chinese Communist Party.

In the strategic sphere, the new situation in China obviously demanded a new approach. It was no longer possible to maintain that "a direct revolutionary situation" existed, or that all the abortive uprisings since the August Seventh Conference had been successes. On the other hand, any admission that the revolutionary wave had definitely receded would set policy in China completely out of harmony with the general leftward course of Comintern policy and would further lend comfort to the Trotskyist opposition, which had announced immediately after the break with Wuhan that "we are in a period of ebb-tide in China." [2]

To meet this difficulty, Bukharin advanced an ingenious formula based again upon the imagery of waves. "The first wave of the broad revolutionary movement of workers and peasants," he declared, "which developed mainly under the mot d'ordre and, to a considerable degree under the direction of the Communist Party has already passed." [3] This bland assertion is somewhat astonishing when we consider the fact that every Comintern pronouncement until the very eve of the Canton insurrection speaks in terms of a revolutionary upsurge. We are now finally told that "this wave has ended in heavy defeats for the workers and peasants in several revolutionary centers." [4]

Having admitted a recession in the first revolutionary wave, however, Bukharin hastens to add that "numerous symptoms indicate that the workers' and peasants' revolution is approaching a new surge." [5] In support of this assertion he points to continued restiveness among the peasantry, soldiers' revolts, etc.

The image is thus that of two revolutionary waves divided by a momentary trough. For the moment — and only for the moment — "a certain consolidation of the forces of reaction has taken place." [6] The new wave is, however, imminent. This is in clear contrast to the views of Trotsky, who is inclined at this time to foresee not simply a trough but a long stretch of calm water, as it were. "There is not at the present time a revolutionary situation in China," he asserts. "It is rather a counter-revolutionary situation transforming itself into an inter-revolutionary period of indefinite duration." [7]

One result of the new formulation is that it enables the Comintern to censure the Ch'ü Ch'iu-pai leadership for its "putschist" tendencies, for its inclination to "play with uprisings." [8] A *Putsch*, of course, is an uprising carried on at a time when objective circumstances are unfavorable to its success. Since the Comintern had belatedly discovered that the latter months of 1927 had been a period of ebb tide, it was now obvious that the uprisings launched by the Ch'ü leadership had all been "putschist" in nature. (It is nowhere made clear why the Comintern had not previously informed the Chinese party that the ebb tide had set in, or why it had continued to speak in terms of an upsurge.)

An exception is made, however, for the Canton insurrection, thus lending color to the view that Moscow was directly involved in that event. In spite of the errors committed by its leaders, we are told that the Canton uprising was "a heroic attempt on the part of the proletariat to organize Soviet power in China." According to the formula later adopted at the Sixth Congress of the Chinese Communist Party, the Canton Commune was a "heroic rearguard action," rather than a *Putsch*.[9] It was a rearguard action in that it brought to a close a declining revolutionary wave. It was, however, a beginning in that it was the first large-scale attempt to establish a soviet as "the organ of the revolutionary democratic dictatorship of the workers and peasants." [10]

On the other hand, while postulating a new revolutionary surge, Bukharin nevertheless hedges his posulation about with cautious reservations. To prepare itself, as it were, against the consequences of future unsuccessful uprisings, the Comintern now warns that in the future, uprisings must be carefully prepared in advance. "The Communist Party will certainly be beaten," state the Resolutions of the Ninth Plenum, "if it fails to understand the necessity of winning over the masses and organizing them. If it does not fight against all attempts to distract its attention from the preparation of the masses for a new and broad revolutionary surge, preparation is the central task of the present period." [11]

Another reservation is based on a newly won insight into Chinese conditions. It was now realized that, under Chinese conditions, a revolutionary situation in a given area does not automatically engulf the whole nation. "The revolutionary situation is developing unequally in the different provinces of China." [12] This observation was to become the basis for the new formula of an "initial victory in one or several provinces." [13]

While these reservations served to protect the Comintern against future contingencies, they merely confronted the new Chinese leadership with new dilemmas. In a period of revolutionary upsurge it should, after all, be relatively easy to prepare the desperate masses for uprisings. If overmuch time is spent preparing and organizing the masses, might not the opportunity for revolutionary insurrection be missed? Might the party not then expose itself to charges of "opportunist passivity"? On the other hand, if the party should foment uprisings which ended in failure might it not be accused of having ignored the Comintern's warnings concerning the necessity of adequate preparations?

The formula of the "initial victory in one or several provinces," we shall find, involved similar difficulties.

Having made this revision in its "estimate of the revolutionary situation," however, the Comintern was now able to maintain intact the theoretical aspects of the old line in the face of Trotskyist attack. While Trotsky continued to maintain that the bourgeois revolution had already been consummated, that capitalist relations were already the dominant relations of the Chinese economy, that the next revolution — the third revolution — could only be a proletarian revolution, the Ninth Plenum of the ECCI stubbornly reiterated that "the present period of the Chinese revolution is a period of the bourgeois democratic revolution which has not been completed either from an economic point of view (the agrarian revolution and the abolition of feudal relations) or from the viewpoint of the national struggle for independence against imperialism (the unification of China and the establishment of a revolutionary government) or from the point of view of the class nature of the government (the dictatorship of the proletariat and peasantry)." [14]

As before, the Comintern accused Trotsky of failing to note the peculiarity which differentiated China from the Russia of 1917 — namely, the factor of imperialism — but while this argument had been used in the past to justify the alliance with the "national bourgeoisie" it was now used to justify the continued use of the formula of "democratic dictatorship of workers and peasants." The peasantry, it was asserted, was itself the victim of imperialism.

One of the more immediate by-products of this reassertion of the formula of "democratic dictatorship" was that it allowed the Comintern to censure Lominadze and Ch'ü Ch'iu-pai for having dared to use the expression "permanent revolution" at the November Plenum of the Chinese Communist Party. "It would be erroneous," declared the Resolutions of the Ninth Plenum, "to characterize the revolution as a 'permanent revolution' (the position of the representative of the ECCI).[15] The tendency to skip over the bourgeois democratic phase of the revolution is a mistake similar to that which Trotsky made in 1905."[16] The November Plenum in China had drawn a faultless syllogism based on Stalin's own theory of the nature of soviets, but this bit of independent deductive reasoning merely served to call down the wrath of the Comintern.

The Ninth Plenum nevertheless confirmed the directive of September 19. Henceforth, the soviet would be the political organ of the democratic dictatorship. Sufficient time had now elapsed to eradicate the impression that the Stalin leadership was borrowing a leaf from Trotsky's book in appropriating the notion of soviets for China. On the other hand, the fact remained that Stalin had proclaimed that soviets could be organized only during the transition toward the proletarian revolution. To meet this difficulty, the Resolutions state that "the transition to the proletarian dictatorship is possible in China only after a series of preparatory stages; only as a result of a whole period of the growing over of the bourgeois democratic revolution into the socialist revolution."[17] The notion of "transition" was thus combined with the notion of "stages" in a neat scholastic formula designed to eradicate any suspicious resemblance to Trotsky's theory of the permanent revolution.

The Resolutions of the Sixth Comintern Congress add another highly significant amendment to the formula of the "democratic dictatorship of workers and peasants." "The victory by the masses," it proclaims, "can be won *only under the hegemony of the proletariat*" (italics mine).[18] The phrase "hegemony of the proletariat" also appears throughout the "Resolution of the Sixth Congress of the Chinese Communist Party." In concrete political terms, this phrase means that only the proletariat is to be allowed a separate political voice within the alliance of peasantry and proletariat; that is, that the Communist Party alone is to monopolize the heights of political power. No political groups claiming to represent the peasantry are to be allowed any voice in the new Soviet government.

When we examine these amendments to the theory of "democratic dictatorship" as well as Trotsky's reservations on his own theory of "permanent revolution," it becomes apparent how tenuous and verbalistic the *theoretical* distinctions have become. Trotsky clings fetishistically to the image of the October Revolution. Stalin clings fetishistically to the phrase "democratic dictatorship of the workers and peasants." Yet, on the one hand, Trotsky admits that the proletariat still has a long uphill fight in China, that the proletarian revolution is "laid over into an indefinite future." [19] In spite of the dominance of capitalist relations, he admits that the proletariat will still have to "sweep from its road to socialism all feudal barbarism and every other type of barbarism." [20] While insisting that only the proletariat can exercise political initiative, he nevertheless admits that "it will have to conduct an intransigent struggle to win influence over the peasants, to guide the peasants directly — from a political point of view." [21]

On the other hand, the Stalin leadership, even while clinging to Lenin's phrase "democratic dictatorship of workers and peasants," simply annuls the basic features of that formula as originally conceived. How can one speak of a *democratic* dictatorship of proletariat *and peasantry* when the peasantry is not to be allowed any separate political voice of its own? The formula was, after all, originally designed to meet a situation in which a weak proletariat (the Social Democratic Party) would have to collaborate for a time with other political parties representing the peasantry.

Furthermore, while Lenin's original formula makes a sharp division between the bourgeois democratic stage and the socialist stage, Bukharin is forced to speak in terms of a "growing over" into socialism — a phrase which comes perilously close to the notion of permanent revolution.

Is there then any real difference between the "growing over" of the bourgeois democratic revolution into a socialist revolution under the "hegemony of the proletariat" in alliance with the peasantry (an alliance in which the peasantry was to have no separate political voice of its own) and a proletarian revolution protracted over a long period of time, still faced with the necessity of accomplishing certain bourgeois democratic tasks and "drawing the peasantry behind it"? The differences which developed between the Trotskyists and the Stalinists on the question of peasantry and proletariat were real enough, but were not implicit in the scholastic distinctions of their theoretical lines.

And yet, these shadowy theoretical differences were combined with diametrically opposed conceptions of political strategy, which would suggest that theory and practice are not always bound together by inner logical necessity. The combination of a given theory with a given strategy may often be due to political factors which have little to do with logic (either formal or dialectic) — a fact which we shall have to bear in mind in considering the rise of Maoism.

On the one hand, the Comintern leadership called for the overthrow of the existing regime in China, for the establishment of a new Soviet regime under the exclusive control of the Chinese Communist Party. It called for armed uprisings — or preparation for armed uprisings — both in town and country. Trotsky, on the other hand, maintained that the party would require some time to heal its wounds and win back its proletarian base. During this period of convalescence, it should advance democratic slogans calling for the convocation of a National Assembly, for drastic agrarian reform, workers' rights, and national independence.[22] This sudden turn to "formal democracy" — Trotsky took pains to emphasize — was simply a stratagem. These democratic slogans would rally the nonproletarian masses behind the proletariat. The "Assembly will provide the Communist Party with a tribunal from which to preach violent revolution and give the party time to regain its proletarian base." As in Russia, the party might then be able "to switch the revolution onto the rails of Soviet democracy"[23]

The Sixth Congress of the Chinese Communist Party

The Sixth Congress of the Chinese Communist Party, held in Moscow in July 1928[24] under the close supervision of the Kremlin, closely reflects the new shift in line. Its resolutions simply add concrete detail to the new formulations.

The fact that this Congress was held in Moscow under the very eye of the Kremlin has peculiar significance in the history of Chinese

Communism. The decision to hold the Congress in Moscow must again be understood, I think, in terms of Stalin's conflict with the opposition. In the Soviet Union itself, Stalin's victory over Trotsky was now fairly well consolidated. It now remained to eradicate heretical elements within the communist parties abroad. The Chinese party in particular, as we have seen, had shown peculiar tendencies toward heresies of various types. While China no longer loomed on the forefront of the Kremlin's horizon, the necessity of maintaining Stalinist control of the party nevertheless remained.

Li Ang, in his *Red Stage*, has presented a vivid account of the manner in which the Congress was used as a sieve to eliminate unreliable elements. He himself had been appointed delegate to the Congress from Hopei. On the way across Siberia, however, he and the members of his party had been abruptly detrained at Irkutsk and sent back to China.[25] "We later found out," he says, "that the reason why we could not attend the Congress in Moscow was because some of us (including myself) were under suspicion of belonging to the opposition."[26]

For this very reason, however, this Congress enjoys a peculiar odor of sanctity in the orthodox histories of Chinese Communism. The Japanese Stalinist, Nakanishi, attempts to prove in his numerous writings on the Chinese party that the whole Maoist development of Chinese Communism was outlined at this Congress under the unerring guidance of Stalin. "The mistaken policies of Ch'ü Ch'iu-pai and Li Li-san," he states, "continued until the Sixth Party Congress of 1928 when Mao's course was approved as the correct course."[27] Mao Tse-tung himself takes pains to point out in his autobiography that "with the new line adopted at that Congress, Chu Teh and I were in complete agreement."[28]

If, by this statement, Mao means that the Sixth Congress was willing, up to a point, to endorse the type of activity being carried on by himself and Chu Teh in the hinterlands as *one legitimate form of activity*, he is substantially correct. If he means, however, that the Sixth Congress meant to endorse the whole ulterior development of Chinese Communism under his leadership — the total isolation of the movement from its urban bases — then we have here, I think, a case of orthodox falsification.

It must be pointed out that whatever the nature of his acts, Mao

Tse-tung is a man committed to the Marxist-Leninist-Stalinist tradition. However anxious he has been in the last few years to prove that he is a theoretical innovator within that tradition, he is equally eager to prove that his power is legitimately based in terms of that tradition, that he is, as it were, in line of apostolic succession. If he can claim that the course pursued by the movement under his leadership is legitimately based on the Resolutions of the Sixth Congress, his leadership receives a historical legitimization which it might not otherwise possess.

The question remains, however, was the whole Maoist development of Chinese Communism contemplated and planned at this Sixth Party Congress? To answer this question, we must consider the whole question of the Communist attitude toward the peasantry, in general, and at this Congress in particular.

Proletariat, Peasantry, and the Communist Party

It is, of course, common knowledge that Marxism in its pre-Leninist form did not regard the peasantry as an independent, creative force in human history. Whether this attitude was purely the result of intellectual analysis or whether the intellectual analysis itself reflected certain set attitudes, we shall not here inquire. There can be little doubt, however, that while the peasantry is portrayed as a victim of feudal society, it is not the real agent of the overthrow of feudalism. This role is assigned to the urban bourgeoisie which is destined by the processes of production to play the truly creative role in smashing feudal relations. In the period of capitalism, the countryside gradually comes under the control of capitalist relations, but rural society as a whole remains subordinate to urban society and in the transition from capitalist society to socialist society the creative role falls to the urban proletariat.[29]

With Lenin, however, the question of the role of the peasantry becomes somewhat more problematic. A study of his life reveals that he first came to Marxism in recoil from the Narodniks who tended to regard the peasantry as a harbinger of human redemption, as a force which promised to lead Russia to an idyllic rural socialism, by-passing the horrors of western capitalism. Lenin, who loathed the "backwardness" of the Russian countryside, may well have been attracted to Marxism precisely because of its negation of any separate creative role for the peasantry. His first great work, *The Development of Capitalism in Russia*, greatly magnifies the extent to which the Russian countryside has already been invaded by capitalist relations.[30]

On the other hand, when peasant uprisings swept across Russia in the 1905 period, this man, so quick to apprehend political realities, immediately became intent on harnessing that force to the revolutionary wagon. The result was the theory of the "democratic dictatorship of proletariat and peasantry" already discussed. The peasantry, according to this theory, is capable of a certain limited historic creativity in Russia. It can help to consummate the bourgeois revolution, for the Russian bourgeoisie itself is incapable of realizing its own destiny. Lenin's views on the creativity of the peasantry continue to fluctuate, however, depending on the political situation. At the time of the seizure of power in 1917, when the Communist Party was able to establish its own dictatorship, he again tended to minimize its historic role.[31]

In contrast to his fluctuating views on the historic role of the peasantry, however, Lenin's views on the class nature of the Social Democratic Party (later the Communist Party) never waver. Here we find an iron consistency running through all his works. The Social Democratic, or Communist, Party is nothing more or less than the political organ of the industrial proletariat. It is only because of its organic relation to the proletariat that the Communist Party can act as the oracle of history. It is true that Lenin often speaks of the "rural proletariat" as an ally of the urban proletariat in the village and is even willing to absorb loyal elements of the rural poor into the party. There is, after all, a common denominator uniting the two groups: the fact that they have nothing to lose but their chains. At the same time, he makes it amply clear that the party can afford to absorb these elements only to the extent that it has its basis in the city proletariat. "There can be no doubt," he states, "that all elements of the party must strive toward the cities and industrial centers for only the industrial proletariat is capable of a resolute mass fight against absolutism." [32] The industrial proletariat shares its poverty with other downtrodden classes. Its uniqueness derives from the fact that modern industry has socialized it and given it a sense of historic direction. With Lenin, these unique virtues become incarnate in the proletariat's political organ, the party. The rural proletariat can be weaned from its petty bourgeois mentality only when led by the urban proletariat. In 1909, he attacks the Social Revolutionary Party on the grounds that "the fundamental idea of their program was not at all that of an 'alliance of forces' of the proletariat and peasantry is necessary, but that there is no clear abyss between the former and the latter, and that there is no need to draw a line of class demarcation between them; that the social democratic idea of the petty bourgeois nature of the peasantry — that distinguishes it from the proletariat — is false." [33] Lenin, on the other hand, insists on clearly drawn demarcations. Only when the class bases of the party are secure, can the party proceed to maneuver with other social classes.

To those who stand outside of the tradition, the organic connection between a Communist Party as conceived by Lenin and the proletariat may hardly seem obvious. Since all final authority is concentrated in the hands of a few men, as often as not of nonproletarian origin, who do not feel obliged to consult the actual proletarians (as opposed to the proletariat) in making important decisions, the connection may indeed seem most tenuous. To those within the tradition, however, the a priori belief in the organic connection between the Communist Party and the proletariat lies at the very heart of the faith. The faith does, however, require certain visible signs. However little the party may heed the will of the actual proletarians, the existence of an industrial proletariat, however small, and the existence of some actual relationship between the proletariat, or part of the proletariat, and the party are considered essential to the party's continued existence. The Communist Party can no more survive its proletarian base than the head can survive the body. Where the party's relations with the proletariat are weak, it is the party's first and paramount duty to strengthen these relations.

To those who stand outside of the tradition, it may also seem obvious that insofar as the October Revolution was the work of the masses at all, the peasantry played quite as important a role as the industrial proletariat. The point is, however, that factory workers *did play* a visible role, and this fact makes all the difference in the world since it satisfied the demands of doctrine.

Thus, we find that the dogma of the proletarian base is no adventitious element within the Marxist-Leninist tradition which can change with every change in party line. It is rather part of the vital core of faith which cannot be violated without casting doubt on the party's very bases of authority. The question of the legitimization of authority is one which no political system can ignore, nor is it a point on which Trotsky can adopt one point of view and Stalin another.

During the 1920–1927 period, the question of the proletarian base in China did not assume an acute form. A Chinese proletariat, small as it was, did exist and, for the most part, prove amenable to Communist leadership. On the other hand, when the peasant movement began to develop with unexpected *élan* after 1925, the Kremlin was prepared by its Leninist background to take advantage of it. Having a firm basis in the urban proletariat, the party could exert itself in the countryside within the framework of the Kuomintang. Such was the background of the famous statement in the Resolutions of the Seventh Plenum of the ECCI of November 1926, to the effect that the agrarian problem constituted the central content of the bourgeois democratic revolution.[34] Similar statements were to appear in the Resolutions of the Eighth Plenum of the ECCI, of the August Seventh Emergency Conference, and of the Sixth Congress of the Chinese Communist Party. It is this type of statement which is adduced as prime proof that the whole Maoist development of Chinese Communism was planned in advance by Moscow.

This interpretation rests on a complete confusion of two elements which are kept clearly distinct in any Communist party line; namely, the "content" or "central problem" of a given revolutionary stage and the class forces of the revolution. The content of a revolution, as already pointed out, designates the tasks to be accomplished by a given revolution. The "class forces" designate the classes which are destined to accomplish these tasks. It is thus false to leap to the conclusion that simply because the agrarian revolution is the central problem of the revolution, the peasantry can be the central revolutionary class or — what is even more incredible — that the Communist Party can base itself squarely on the peasantry. Actually, the statement that "the agrarian question is the basis of the bourgeois democratic revolution" was first used by Lenin himself, at the time of the 1905 revolution.[35] Even though he conceded to the peasantry a certain creative function at the time, he never for a moment meant to imply that the peasantry would play a central role. On the contrary, it was only by allying itself with the proletariat that the peasantry could hope to realize the agrarian revolution. Otherwise, it would fall victim to the Russian bourgeoisie which was not at all interested in bringing about agrarian revolution. To Lenin, the fact that the agrarian problem was the central problem of the revolution by no means signified that the peasantry was the central class of the revolution.

In 1926, when the Seventh Plenum of the ECCI speaks of the agrarian problem as the central problem of the revolution, it is still committed to the view that this problem is to be met through the vehicle of the Kuomintang, a coalition of four classes. All these classes together would presumably coöperate to liquidate feudalism in the countryside. Again, in May 1927, Stalin states at the Eighth Plenum of the ECCI that "the agrarian revolution constitutes the foundation and content of the bourgeois democratic revolution." He adds, however, "that the Kuomintang in Hankow and the Hankow government are the center of the bourgeois revolution." [36] The presumption is that the agrarian revolution will be carried forward by the three classes which presumably form the base of the Kuomintang.

After the break with the Wuhan government, the Emergency Conference of August 7 again declares the agrarian problem to be the crux of the bourgeois revolution.[37] Now, however, the necessity of the hegemony of the proletariat is unequivocally stated. The peasantry and the petty bourgeoisie are in theory still conceded some limited political role under the banner of the Kuomintang but it is made quite clear that the ruling role will be played by the proletariat itself. After the final abandonment of the Kuomintang banner, in September 1927, it was assumed, as has been pointed out, that the proletariat would alone guide and direct the agrarian revolution in spite of the fact that the new line envisaged a "democratic dictatorship of the workers and peasants." The peasants would, to be sure, be allowed a voice in the soviets, but basic policies were to be made by the Communist Party, the organ of the proletariat, and not by the soviets. The peasantry could furnish revolutionary motive power, but the direction of this motive power would lie with the proletariat. The peasantry would have no separate political voice of its own.

The Resolutions of the Ninth Plenum of the ECCI, the Sixth Comintern Congress, and the Sixth Congress of the Chinese Communist Party all devote a great deal of space to a consideration of the agrarian problem. They all repeat the assertion that the agrarian problem is the main content of the revolution — and all insist on the hegemony of the proletariat. Thus, the Resolutions of the Sixth Comintern Congress state that "the problem of the agrarian revolution constitutes the axis of the bourgeois democratic revolution in China." [38] At the same time, it insists that "the peasants can achieve their emancipation only under the direction of the proletariat just as the proletariat can lead the bourgeois democratic revolution to victory only in alliance with the peasantry." [39] Lest we suspect that the word "proletariat" is simply used as a synonym for the Communist Party, the "Resolutions" proceed to insist that "communist parties in colonial and semicolonial countries must become truly communist in their social composition . . . The party must improve its social composition by concentrating particular attention on the creation of party cells in the main branches of production, the main factories and railroad shops." [40]

The Resolution on the Land Problem and the Resolution on the Peasant Problem of the Sixth Congress of the Chinese Communist Party have, however, become the main source of evidence that the whole Maoist development of Chinese Communism was planned in advance in Moscow. These Resolutions are, it is true, much more detailed than any previous discussion of the Chinese agrarian problem. They echo within their pages a weighty discussion which had arisen among Soviet theoreticians concerning the nature of Chinese rural society and they endorse the final Stalinist solution of this theoretical controversy. Ostensibly, they establish a detailed policy to guide the party in its dealings with various strata of peasant society. Actually, their directives on this subject are much more ambiguous than might appear at first glance, and the degree to which they became guides to action is highly questionable.

In the theoretical sphere, the Resolutions, on the one hand, reject the Trotskyist claim that capitalist relations have already extended into the village economy.[41] On the other hand, they reject *in toto* the claim of Madyar, Wittfogel, and others that Chinese society is an example of what Marx referred to as an Asiatic society (a society in which property is "weak" and in which the bureaucracy is itself the ruling class).[42] Instead, it insists that "Chinese peasants suffer a combined feudal and capitalist mode of exploitation."[43] This analysis was, of course, a corollary of the new line which proclaimed that the feudal classes and the bourgeoisie were now in alliance with each other. The dominant force in the rural areas was, however, the feudal element. The word "feudal" is nowhere defined and its use was to give rise within the next few years to volumes of theoretical controversy. For various reasons, however, the Stalinist leadership clung to this term almost convulsively and in China it was used to refer to all those economic and social phenomena which cannot be understood in terms of a Western system of private property. The phrase "semifeudal" is used to indicate the fact that private property relations exist side by side with "feudal relations."

Feudalism is maintained in China by foreign imperialism which inhibits the emergence of a capitalist type of industrialization in China. "Imperialism has used these feudal remnants as instruments for carrying on exploitation . . . This system of exploitation manifests itself in the form of a close alliance between foreign finance capital and Chinese usurious commercial capital."[44]

In the strategic sphere, the Resolutions call for a total expropriation of all landlords as representatives of feudal land relations. The rich peasantry are the representatives of capitalism in the village, but also tend to engage in feudal modes of exploitation. Where they have maintained the revolutionary potentialities, they may become allies of the revolution. Where they "waver between revolution and counterrevolution," they should be "neutralized." An alliance should be maintained with the middle peasants while the poor peasants and hired hands should form the "main force" of the revolution in the village as prescribed by Lenin.[45] Much of this, it can be seen, is taken directly from the writings of Lenin on the agrarian problem.

The strongest arguments in favor of the contention that the Sixth Congress contemplated the Maoist development of Chinese Communism is its position on guerrilla warfare in the countryside. For the first time, this Congress lent its limited approval to the type of guerrilla warfare being carried on by Mao Tse-tung on Chingkanshan,[46] although it added that such warfare must "begin with the spontaneous demand of the masses and must be carried on simultaneously with propaganda and agitation." One need not seek far to find the reason for this kindlier attitude toward such activities. The situation in China at the time of the Sixth Congress was extremely bleak and the precarious pockets of resistance created by Mao Tse-tung, Ho Lung, Hsü Hai-tung, and others constituted the only positive development within the movement. The party was not so rich in successes at the time that it could afford to repudiate any encouraging signs in any quarter.

We must again ask, however, does the Sixth Congress's approval of this type of activity as *one* legitimate form of activity imply the prior endorsement of the whole Maoist development of Chinese Communism? We must reply, I think, in the negative. The Sixth Congress prescribed proletarian hegemony within the agrarian movement in no uncertain terms and made it amply clear that proletarian hegemony could be achieved only by recapturing the party's proletarian bases. The very passage of the Resolution on the Peasant Question which endorses guerrilla activities adds the significant reservation that "the spontaneous guerrilla warfare of the peasants in various provinces and districts can be a starting point in the national victories mass revolt *only on the condition that it is carried out in alliance with a new revolutionary wave among the proletariat in the cities*" [47] (emphasis my own). "The consolidation of working class leadership among the peasantry," it adds, "is a prerequisite to the success of the agrarian revolution." [48]

When we turn to the Political Resolution of the Sixth Congress the evidence becomes overwhelming. In seeking reasons for the "trough" in the development of the revolution, the Resolution points to the fact that "the number of those participating in the revolution is still insufficient and the urban proletariat has not yet been able to overcome the obstacles to its own victory." [49] The fact that, in general, the congress took a most conservative view of the possibilities of peasant guerrilla activities when considered in the total revolutionary picture is amply proved by the sober phraseology in which it described those activities. "The small worker and peasant armies which *are still in existence* promise to become an important factor in the new revolutionary rise." [50] What is more, the Resolution specifically censures tendencies which had appeared in the agrarian struggle to underestimate the importance of proletarian leadership: "In certain sectors of the agrarian struggle an inclination has arisen to treat lightly the leadership of the urban proletariat. All such deviations within the party must be strictly opposed." [51]

In outlining the future tasks of the party, the Political Resolution lays great stress on the importance of "proletarianizing the party." "We must restore," it proclaims, "party branches which have been destroyed and pay particular attention to the formation and development of branches in large-scale industrial centers, for it is here that the masses of the proletariat are concentrated. We must energetically seek members among the workers and continue to draw the most active elements among our worker comrades into the leadership cadres of the party in order to proletarianize these cadres." [52] "It is the party's major task to win over the majority of the proletariat, to win their support of the class vanguard, the Chinese Communist Party, to have them trust *the* party and accept *its* directives. We must pay more attention to the labor union movement, particularly among the industrial proletariat, *for it is only thus that we can strengthen the hegemony of the proletariat over the peasantry*" [53] (emphasis my own). This is still far from the time when the mere presence of avowed Communist leaders in rural areas is considered an adequate guarantee of proletarian hegemony.

In discussing the "Major Tasks of the Party in the Peasant Movement," the Political Resolution repeats the admonition of the Ninth Plenum of the ECCI that "the peasant movement in the village be coördinated with the revolutionary labor movement in the cities." [54] It adds the comment that "a peasant revolt unaccompanied by a proletarian revolutionary movement is bound to fail . . . The party must particularly emphasize activities among peasants in areas close to commercial and industrial centers (Shanghai, Wuhan, Canton, etc.)." [55]

Lest we think that the word "proletariat" (literally, "property-less class" in Chinese) is used here in a loose etymological sense simply to imply poor people or "toilers," the "Resolution on the Labor Movement" warns that "particular attention must be paid to textile workers, railroad workers, miners, tobacco plant workers, metallurgical workers, municipal workers, postal workers, etc. Recently a tendency has arisen among revolutionary workers to believe in the maxim 'the poorer, the easier,' to follow the path of least resistance and concentrate on artisans, store clerks and other types of non-industrial workers. The revolutionary unions must concentrate their activities among whatever Chinese proletariat we have. To concentrate our activities on workers in small establishments merely serves the purposes of the reactionary unions." [56]

The same Resolution makes it absolutely clear that the relations between the Communist Party and the urban proletariat are organic and indivisible. "We must correct," it insists, "all false ideas concerning the relations of party and class; all ideas which tend to regard the party as if it were a special force standing ahead of the class and capable of helping and directing the class. Such ideas completely ignore the fact that the party is simply the most conscious and advanced element of the proletariat itself." [57]

Finally, the fact that the Sixth Congress confirmed Li Li-san and Hsiang Chung-fa in the position of leadership is itself conclusive proof that neither the party nor the Kremlin leadership had any intention at this time of abandoning the task of recapturing the proletariat. Both of these men had been exclusively associated with the labor movement in the past, and there was every reason to assume that they would take their proletarian tasks most literally in the future. Li Li-san had first won fame as a labor leader at the time of the May Thirtieth incident, while Hsiang Chung-fa — one of the party's few genuine proletarians — had risen through the ranks of the All-China Labor Federation.[58] In spite of all the phrases concerning the importance of the agrarian problem, we find no inclinations in Moscow to cast the mantle of leadership over the obscure shoulders of Mao Tse-tung, Chu Teh, Ho Lung, Hsü Hai-tung, or other peasant leaders carrying on their precarious experiments in the hinterlands. The content of the bourgeois revolution was agrarian. It would, however, be led by the proletariat.

IX THE LI LI-SAN LEADERSHIP

What then were the mandates with which Li Li-san returned to China in the latter months of 1928? He had, first of all, received a mandate to complete the bourgeois democratic revolution — which, it had been agreed, was basically an agrarian revolution. At the same time, it had been made clear that the agrarian revolution could be completed only under "proletarian hegemony" and that such "proletarian hegemony" could be attained only when the Communist Party recaptured its bases among the urban proletariat. Hence, in a very real sense, the recapture of the urban proletariat was the first task of the party. The Comintern's optimistic forecast of a new revolutionary tide seemed to guarantee success in the accomplishment of this task.

He had also received a mandate to prepare for armed insurrection. At the same time, he had not been given any clear indication of when the time would come for passing over from preparation to action. Since China was presumed to be standing at the beginning of a new revolutionary wave, it was not unreasonable to construe any sign of weakness on the part of the enemy — any falling out between the Kuomintang and other military cliques, any economic crisis, any unrest in town or country, or any "contradiction" among imperialist powers — as a symptom of the new wave and a signal to action. If Li Li-san failed to act when such opportunities arose, he might well be accused of opportunist passivity. If he acted and failed, he could be accused of "putschism," of premature judgment in calculating the arrival of the new wave.

He had been given a mandate to prepare for an "initial victory in one or several provinces," but had been warned that "unless the conditions of a new revolutionary high tide already exist, such a victory cannot be realized." [1]

If we are to understand the frantic behavior of Li Li-san during his period of leadership, we must consider it in the light of these slippery directives. He may have indeed been ambitious to become the "Stalin of China," he may have indeed been unspeakably ruthless and unscrupulous in his dealings with others as Li Ang charges, but there can be little doubt that he attempted to realize his ambitions within the framework of the Comintern line.

Immediately after his return from Moscow, however, he was confronted with the same hard fact which had shattered the leadership of Ch'ü Ch'iu-pai: the indifference of the urban proletariat. In spite of the Comintern's postulations, the mood of the Chinese working class had not changed. What is more, the mandate Li Li-san had received to "prepare for armed uprisings" merely served to aggravate the isolation of the party from the working class. It is possible, as Trotsky and Ch'en Tu-hsiu have suggested, that if the party had made itself the mouthpiece of the economic needs of the proletariat, it might have succeeded in weaning away segments of the workers from the "Yellow Unions." However, while the Sixth Congress "Resolutions" exhort the party to combine attention to the economic demands of the workers with preparations for armed uprisings,[2] the fact remains that one cannot prepare for armed insurrection aimed at the overthrow of the state in the same manner in which one prepares for a purely economic struggle.

Throughout the latter months of 1928 and the early months of 1929, the Li Li-san leadership stubbornly bent its efforts to the task of recapturing its proletarian base. A "Report on the Sixth Congress" of October 1928 states that "the Congress recognized that there is a danger that the bases of our party may shift from the working class to the peasantry and that we must make every effort to restore the party's working-class base." [3] A party circular issued in November adds that "the main object of our activities among the masses must be the broad laboring masses in the city — particularly the industrial workers. Without the leadership of the workers, there is little prospect of victory in the village. Thus, the restoration of our urban activities, particularly within the workers movement, is now the party's most urgent task. Unfortunately, our union organizations have been reduced to a minimum, our party units in the cities have been pulverized and isolated. Nowhere in China can we find one solid, industrial cell . . . Therefore, the Central Committee has now decided to concentrate its main strength in such industrial and political centers as Shanghai, Wuhan, Nanking, T'ientsin, Dairen, Harbin, etc. In every province we must concentrate our main strength in the important political and industrial centers . . . We must not go to extremes and simply abandon rural activities in order to carry on exclusively in the cities. Activities in the village should not be ignored. Relatively speaking, however, greater emphasis must be placed on urban activities." [4]

This theme runs through almost every circular issued by the party until the Second Plenum of the Central Committee of June 1929. Yet Chou En-lai, Li Li-san's faithful lieutenant at this time, is forced to report in April that "at the time of the Sixth Congress, the proletariat still constituted ten percent of the party membership. Now their proportions have been reduced to three percent . . . Labor union activities are tending to revive but we have been unable to gain control of the spontaneous activities of the workers." [5] The revival mentioned here was indeed a fact. One hundred and twenty strikes had occurred in Shanghai alone during 1928 and this fact is often cited in Communist literature as a symptom of a rising revolutionary wave. Unfortunately, most of these strikes were carried on under the direction of the "Yellow Unions" and five-sixths of them were fought for better wages and shorter hours.[6] Whatever strength the "Red Unions" still had was rapidly being dissipated by the attempts to force political strikes. And yet, if the leadership had confined its attention to economic strikes, there were any number of ambitious zealots within the party and in Moscow ready to seize upon such action as an evidence of "reformism" and "Trotskyism."

In the face of this desperate situation, Li Li-san attempted to defend his position by pointing to the difficulties inherent in the objective situation. The workers, he maintained, were not simply paralyzed with fear of the government's "white terror" but were being lured away by the false promises of the "reformists," by the deceptions of the Kuomintang "Yellow Unions," and by such groups as Wang Ching-wei's "Reorganizationists" and T'an P'ing-shan's Third Party. "Among the combination of forces now impeding the revolution," he said, "the most important is the influence of the reformist mottos of the bourgeoisie." [7] A circular of February 1929 complains that "the recent increase in activities of various bourgeois groups, particularly of the Wang Ching-wei-Ch'en Kung-po group has had considerable influence on the broad masses . . . The influence of reformist deception has become the most serious problem in the struggle of the masses." [8]

Li even bolstered this defense by placing it within a theoretical framework. The Comintern line maintained, it will be recalled, that the feudal classes and the bourgeoisie were now united in a reactionary alliance under the hegemony of world imperialism. At the same time, it had been pointed out that this alliance was not a stable alliance and the basic contradictions between these two classes still existed. Li Li-san took advantage of this "dialectic formula" to stress the element of contradiction between the bourgeoisie and the feudal classes. The compradore-landlord class, represented by such groups as the Kweilin military clique, was tied in with British and Japanese imperialism. While "a momentary peace has been achieved between these classes, the basic contradictions between the national bourgeoisie and compradore-landlord classes remain. The bourgeoisie has little prospect of gaining the upper hand within the anti-revolutionary camp." [9] Hence, "in its war against the feudal militarists, the bourgeoisie must rely not only on its system of winning over warlords but also on the support of the masses. This type of reformist propaganda has won a broad influence among the masses since the failure of the revolution." [10] Furthermore, he went on, American financial imperialism, which was peculiarly subtle, was quite willing to countenance a program of sham reform in China on the part of its bourgeois puppets.[11]

The Comintern, however, was in no way inclined to accept this theoretical alibi. A letter from the ECCI to the Chinese Communist Party dated February 9, 1929, censures this whole line of reasoning. The world line of the Comintern, at this time, tended to conceive of "imperialism" as a monolithic abstract force and was little inclined to regard with favor attempts to draw distinctions between one "imperialist power" and another. "Circular No. 65 of the Central Committee of the CCP," it complains, "states that the policies of the British and Japanese and the policies of the Americans are entirely opposed. This is incorrect. The American policy toward China, like that of the British and Japanese, is an imperialistic policy. The difference lies only in the method of application. The American 'open door' policy is not designed to remove China from a colonial status. It is a liberal hypocrisy meant to prettify imperialist aggression. America is unable to adopt the same methods as the British and Japanese only because of present objective conditions." [12] If it was incorrect to draw overfine distinctions between imperialists, it was, of course, equally incorrect to overstress the contradictions in the camp of the Chinese reactionaries. "The Chinese Communist Politburo has incorrectly stated that 'the bourgeoisie is now planning to administer a death blow to the gentry-landlord class.' This is an exaggeration. Since 1927, the bourgeoisie has been in the anti-revolutionary camp . . . There can be no talk of China developing along a Kemalist path!" [13]

The ECCI letter thus refused to allow the Li Li-san leadership to cover its failures with this excuse. At the same time, the Comintern was still patient. It was still willing to concede that "the revolutionary wave is only at its beginning and we must not exaggerate the weakness of reaction." It warned, however, that "the high tide is coming and unless the Chinese Communist Party can strengthen its own ranks in advance; unless it can strengthen its influence among the industrial proletariat and guarantee the leadership of the peasantry by the industrial proletariat, we shall not be able to take advantage of these objective conditions . . . We must wipe out the isolation of the party from the masses . . . Unless we have a solid base in the working class, unless we have a broad organizational base in various industries and labor unions, the Chinese Communist Party will never win a position of hegemony in the Chinese revolution." [14]

Thus, Li was saddled more firmly than ever with the impossible tasks imposed by the Sixth Congress and allowed no opportunity for evasion. What is more, the Comintern's refusal to allow the Chinese party to differentiate between various forms of "imperialism" made it difficult for the party leadership to exploit the rising tide of anti-Japanese resentment. On the contrary, in a confession of errors which appeared in a party circular of April 1929, the leadership is forced to state that "we must encourage the masses to oppose imperialism, particularly American imperialism, for while the masses can rather easily grasp the evils of Japanese and British imperialism the crafty policy of the United States might easily lead the masses astray, particularly since they have been subject to bourgeois reformist deception. We must therefore stress the aggressive policies of the United States which wishes, as it were, to suck the marrow of our bones and which is a hundred times worse than Great Britain or Japan." [15] The Chinese party was thus hopelessly caught in the scissors between Comintern policy and Chinese realities.

Its difficulties were further aggravated by Li Li-san's highhanded behavior within the party, in his efforts to control directly through his own machine all party organizations (the Youth Group, Red Unions, etc.).[16] It must be observed, however, that while such behavior may in large measure reflect Li's despotic temperament, it was also partly a function of the situation in which he was involved. The local party cells and union apparatus, closely involved as they were in concrete activities, were only too acutely aware of the unreality of the Comintern estimate of the situation. They were thus peculiarly inclined to disaffection. Chou En-lai complains in his report of April 1929 that "the party branch organizations are indulging in all sorts of deviations, sectarianisms and extreme democratic tendencies." [17] The heterodox tendencies which had arisen under the leadership of Ch'ü Ch'iu-pai were now more prevalent than ever. "Responsible comrades in T'angshan," Chou reports, "have demanded that the Shunchih provincial committee called a conference of party members and that representatives be elected in proportion to the number of party members per county . . . At times, comrades demand the right to discuss all questions with superior organs or demand that the leading cadres be elected by the masses." [18] The Kiangsu Committee leadership continued in its unruly tradition and frequently took issue with the Li Li-san leadership.[19] Finally, Ch'en Tu-hsiu, who still held his party membership, was clamoring for the right of free discussion within the party. His constant contention that the policy of "preparing for armed uprisings" was sheer folly [20] must have seemed most plausible to many party members. In the face of this situation, Li Li-san, who was a much more energetic and capable politician than his predecessor, could maintain his power only by a constant and close control of all party organs. He could not afford the luxury of even a semblance of local autonomy.

The Second Plenum of the Central Committee

The Second Plenum of the Central Committee of the Chinese Communist Party summoned in June 1929 was evidently called for the express purpose of confirming the Li Li-san leadership in its position in the face of this most unpromising situation. Every effort is made to show the complete identity of the policies pursued by Li Li-san with the Comintern line. The Resolution of the Second Plenum "is of the view that the Central Committee has correctly applied the policies decided upon by the Sixth Congress." [21] The "Resolutions" do indeed reaffirm all the directives and views of the Sixth Congress as well as the corrections and amendments of the February letter of the ECCI. They still announce in a spirit of official optimism that "the whole revolutionary movement is on the upswing." In proof, they point to the revival of the workers' struggle, to the fact that "certain Soviet areas as well as the Red Army under the command of Chu and Mao are still in existence," [22] to revolts of troops, etc. At the same time, the Li Li-san leadership attempts to protect itself against future difficulties by announcing that "it is equally incorrect to maintain that the surge of the revolutionary wave is very remote or that it is imminent." [23]

The Plenum reasserts its acceptance of the Comintern's mandate "to consummate the agrarian revolution" but also reaffirms the necessity of proletarian hegemony. "Unless the party has a solid foundation in the working class, particularly among the workers in important industries and unless there are unions led by the party, the party will not obtain the leadership of the revolution." [24]

Also, in keeping with Comintern policy as decided at the Sixth Congress the "Resolutions" state that "we should not limit ourselves to the slogans of the daily economic struggle but advance resolutely from minor struggles to large-scale insurrection, from economic struggle to political struggle." [25] Any concentration on economic struggles would be a deviation in the direction of the policies advocated by Ch'en Tu-hsiu.

Finally, like the Sixth Congress, the Second Plenum is ready to take full advantage of the guerrilla activities in the Soviet areas provided that the party's proletarian bases are assured. "We must lead the guerrilla warfare, expand the Soviet areas and organize the Red

Army." [26] It is now hinted, however, that henceforth the central organs will play a more active role in controlling these activities. "The Plenum is of the view," states the resolution, "that there has been a lack of positive direction from the Central Committee concerning these activities." [27]

Thus, the Second Plenum reconfirms Li Li-san in his position of leadership and underlines the absolute identity between his policies and the Comintern line. It does not, however, provide him with an escape from his difficulties. The futile attempts to win away the workers from the Yellow Unions or to control these unions by infiltration and to force street demonstrations and political strikes were to continue as in the past with less and less promising results.

Nor was the Kremlin content to allow Li Li-san to rest in this unpromising situation. We have no way of knowing whether the stream of letters which the Chinese party received during this period from the Executive Committee of the Comintern were inspired in the highest quarters or whether they were prompted by circles of Chinese and Russians in Moscow hostile to the Li Li-san leadership. Whatever may be the case, the fact remains that Li Li-san was subjected to unremitting pressure during his whole period of leadership, in spite of the fact that China had receded from the central focus of the Kremlin's interest. Thus, in October 1929, the Central Committee again received a letter from the ECCI calling for action. "The Chinese crisis is deepening," it proclaims. "This is proved by new wars among the militarists, contradictions among the imperialists, the rise of Wang Ching-wei's 'reorganization' movement, adventurism against the USSR, the deepening of the agrarian crisis, etc. . . There is a new tide swell in the labor movement. This marks the beginning of the new revolutionary tide." [28] Thus, in the view of the Comintern, the trough had finally come to an end and the new wave had finally begun. "We cannot of course predict at what tempo the national crisis will assume a revolutionary form, but we must certainly prepare the masses and take steps to overthrow the landlord-bourgeois regime and set up a dictatorship of peasants and workers of the Soviet type. We must energetically promote a revolutionary class struggle (in the form of political strikes, revolutionary demonstrations, partisan warfare, etc.)." [29]

The letter takes due note of the unexpected dynamism of the

soviet movement in Kiangsi. "The Soviet areas have been able to maintain themselves and even to extend and consolidate their activities of late . . . All these peasant activities have become an important side-current in the revolutionary wave, which will grow and merge into the national revolutionary movement." [30] Having taken note of this development, however, the letter adds "that the most correct and most important sign of the rising revolutionary wave is still the rebirth of the labor movement. The labor movement has finally extricated itself from the depression it entered after the severe failures of 1927. The economic struggles of the proletariat in the form of strikes are now showing signs of passing over into political struggles . . . Our most vital task at present is to take over the leadership of the spontaneous economic and political struggles of the proletariat. This task is still unsolved." [31] The task was unsolved and was to remain unsolved. It can readily be seen, however, how letters of this type which proclaimed the arrival of new high tides and called for visible signs of success goaded the Li Li-san leadership into frantic quests for new expedients.

Li Li-san and the Rise of the Soviet Areas

The latter months of 1929 were, however, marked by the emergence of two new dynamic factors within the Communist movement: the Soviet areas and the Red Army. In his history of the Red Army, Chou En-lai states that "the descent of the armies of Chu and Mao from Chingkanshan on the thirteenth of January, 1929, marks the beginning of a spectacular historic development." [32] It was not until autumn of the same year, however,[33] that the Red Army began to win striking successes. The forces of Chu and Mao had been reinforced by those of P'eng Teh-huai in the winter of 1928 and later by the troops of Ho Lung and others. The new strategy had begun to reap results. While figures regarding the expansion of the Soviet areas and the growth of the Red Army and partisan bands are notoriously unreliable, there can be little doubt that during the latter months of 1929 and the early months of 1930, "Soviet China" began to emerge as a major dynamic force in the Chinese Communist movement.

In considering the relations of the Comintern and of the Central Committee to this new dynamic development, I think that we can dismiss at the outset any notion that the success of Mao Tse-tung and Chu Teh was the result of directives devised in Moscow or Shanghai. It is of course impossible to bring forth documentary proof that their activities were *not* guided directly by the Central Committee, but the nature of the circumstances argues strongly against such a view. The movement operated in hinterland areas of a country which enjoys only the poorest means of communication. It operated in an area surrounded by enemy territory. Furthermore, the type of partisan warfare which was leading the movement to ever new successes was a type of warfare which demanded spot decisions based on an intimate knowledge of local conditions and local terrain. It thus could not be directed from the suburbs of Shanghai or the offices of the Kremlin. Nor could the "Front Committee" simply proceed according to the mechanical directives of the Sixth Congress in implementing its agrarian reforms in local areas with all their peculiar agrarian conditions.

The remoteness of the Kremlin from the rising Soviet movement and its amazing lack of information is graphically illustrated by the fact that an *Inprecorr* bulletin of March 1930 carries a long obituary on the death of Mao Tse-tung who is alleged to have died of consumption! [34] A similar amazing bit of ignorance is displayed in Stalin's report at the Sixteenth Congress of the Communist Party of the Soviet Union held in June 1930. "It is said," Stalin states, "that a Soviet government has already been created there! I think that if this is true, there is nothing surprising in it." [35] Trotsky seizing upon this statement exclaims: "There is nothing surprising in the fact that in China a Soviet government was created about which the Chinese Communist Party knows nothing and about whose political physiognomy the highest leader of the Chinese revolution can give no information!" This bit of hearsay which Stalin repeats may be based on the establishment of the Kiangsi Provincial Soviet Government in February 1930. Whatever may be the case, however, one hardly derives from this statement the impression that Stalin was sagaciously directing the partisan warfare in Hunan and Kiangsi.

We can therefore assume, I think, that the new power arising in Hunan and Kiangsi owed little to the direction of Shanghai or Moscow. It is equally important to note that this movement was developing independent power bases of its own. As a result of its control of an army, the control of territorial bases, and the control of a peasant population from which it could levy revenues, the power of the "Front Committee" did not rest solely on the capricious mandates of Shanghai and Moscow. It is no wonder that the Chu Teh, Mao Tse-tung group were later to be known within the Communist party as the "Real Power Faction." [36]

The very fact, however, that the leaders in the hinterlands enjoyed independent sources of power could not but produce doubts and suspicions in Shanghai. It is safe to assume that the tensions which were to arise between Front Committee leaders and Shanghai were based not simply on ideological considerations but also on sheer power conflict. The two elements were, to be sure, inextricably tied together.

In general, Li Li-san's attitude was predicated on the Comintern line. Guerrilla activities in the hinterlands were legitimate and "could merge with the national revolution." [37] The growth of the Red Army and of the Soviet areas was to be welcomed *so long as they were actively led by the urban proletariat.* Until the movement began to show signs of unusual dynamism in the latter months of 1929, Li Li-san neither exaggerated nor underestimated its importance. In a letter of November 1928 to the party he points to the error of ignoring the peasantry but warns that "as a result of the particular development of the struggle in the countryside during the past year; and the fact that peasants now constitute seventy to eighty percent of our party membership, the peasant mentality is now reflected in our party . . . The Communist Party acknowledges that the peasantry is an ally of the revolution. At the same time, it recognizes that the peasantry is petty bourgeois and cannot have correct ideas regarding socialism; that its conservatism is particularly strong and that it lacks organizational ability. Only a proletarian mentality can lead use onto the correct revolutionary road. Unless we proceed to correct the dangers involved in this peasant mentality, it may lead to a complete destruction of the revolution and of the party." [38] Here Li stands, of course, on the grounds of complete orthodoxy.

After the October letter of the ECCI had announced the arrival of the new revolutionary wave, Li Li-san was, of course, forced to seek signs of its approach. The swelling "side-current" of the Soviet movement was, however, the only sign to be noted. It was thus his problem to take full advantage of this "side-current" and use it for the purposes of the national revolution without falling prey to "peasant deviationism" or without subordinating the power of the Central Committee to the power of the Front Committee.

It is against this background, I think, that we must view the decision to call the "Conference of Delegates from Soviet Areas" held in the suburbs of Shanghai on May 30, 1930. Developments had proceeded so rapidly that on February 7, 1930, a Provincial Soviet government was already established in Kiangsi [39] and similar regimes were soon established in Fukien and Kwangsi. These developments could constitute both an opportunity and a danger. If Li Li-san could control them firmly, they could be used to further the establishment of the type of Soviet regime which both he and the Comintern envisaged — namely, a regime with a given territorial base controlled from urban, proletarian bases within that base or, if necessary, outside of it. Uncontrolled by the urban proletariat, however, such a regime might degenerate into a petty bourgeois regime uncontrolled by the cities. Such was both the ideological and political danger.

Current party literature concerning the question of the Soviet government made this point amply clear. Li Li-san writes in the *Red Flag* of March 29 that "simply to rely on the Red Army to take one or several provinces in order to set up a national revolutionary regime would be a most serious error. Not only is such an idea preposterous but it might even lead us to neglect our most vital activity — the organization of the workers' struggle and the organization of political strikes by armed workers' units. The villages are the limbs of the ruling class. The cities are their brains and heart. If we cut out their brains and heart, they cannot escape death; but if we simply cut off their appendages, it will not necessarily kill them." [40] Li refers bitterly to a growing deviation in the party based on the feeling that "forces of the peasantry, particularly of the Red Army, have far outstripped the forces of the workers." Li Li-san firmly opposes this deviation which he attributes to a "lack of faith in the strength of the working class." [41]

We are somewhat surprised to find that at this time Li even rejected the very strategy he was later to sanction in the attack on Changsha. The thought had already occurred to many that the obvious way of wiping out the "uneven development" between the countryside and the city was to use the power of the Red Army to capture urban bases. In April 1930, Li still emphatically opposed such suggestions. "Unless we have the industrial cities and industrial zones," he states, "we shall never gain a victory in one or several provinces. All talk of 'encircling the city with the country' or of relying on the Red Army to take the cities is sheer nonsense!" [42] The implication that the proletariat must be rescued by a peasant army is monstrous derogation of the leading role of the urban proletariat.

These views were further amplified in a reply to a letter from a correspondent to the *Red Flag* printed a few days before the opening of the Conference of Delegates from the Soviet Areas. The correspondent had naïvely suggested that "rather than continuing to expend our strength in the cities we ought to apply it in the country where we shall certainly be more effective. After we have consolidated our positions in the country we can then surround the cities and besiege them." Li Li-san replied with great heat. He refused to consider any assumption that the urban proletarian movement was lagging behind the peasant movement on the ground that such an assumption was "incorrect on principle . . . It is not that the revolutionary spirit of the proletariat is more backward than that of the peasantry but that in the cities the workers have to contend with more formidable reactionary forces . . . You seem to think that the struggle of the peasants can be isolated from the struggles of the city proletariat." He then proceeded to demonstrate that the Soviet movement in Hupeh could survive only because "the growing acuteness of the workers' struggle in Wuhan has not allowed the Wuhan militarists to divert large sectors of their army from Wuhan . . . All talk of encircling cities is so much hollow bluff." Finally, "the leading role of the proletariat in the revolutionary struggle is not simply a basic principle in the line of any proletarian party but is, in fact, the only guarantee of the success of the revolution. The Proletariat is the leader of the revolution — the peasantry is its ally. No strategic line can ever depart from this principle." [43]

What then was the attitude in Moscow at this time? An article by Pavel Mif, Russia's most eminent "China expert" and a man destined to play an important role in unseating Li Li-san, printed in the *Pravda* issue of April 28, differs on no essential point from Li

Li-san's views. Mif lays great stress on the rising wave of strikes in China and claims without any factual basis that "the role of the red unions is growing." He does indeed point to the spread of the partisan movement and to the fact that "a certain centralization of leadership" has taken place in the Soviet areas. He hastens to add, however, that these partisan wars are still inadequate and still display a "lumpen proletariat basis." "What is most important, the proletarian hegemony of the growing partisan movement has still not been adequately assured . . . It is true that in most cases, Communists stand at the head of the fighting troops. It is true that in these detachments there are proletarian layers although not in any significant number. It is true that the party is sending advanced workers into the combat areas of the partisan troops in order to help organize a Soviet structure. We cannot, however, ignore the fact that the partisan movement is developing in areas far removed from the basic industrial centers and that the problem of the leadership of the peasant movement by the workers is still far from solved." [44]

In a discussion of the forthcoming Conference of Delegates from the Soviet Areas which appears in *Inprecorr* on May 22, Ivin states that that the main problem of the conference will be "to establish the closest connections between the partisan actions and the activities of the industrial proletariat . . . Powerful as the partisan movement already is at present, the counterrevolution which stands under the protection of the imperialists in the industrial and trading centers cannot be finally crushed with the partisan forces of the Chinese village and the small districts alone. Without being burst from within, without the revolt of the industrial proletariat which must have the hegemony of the revolutionary movement not only in the town but also in the village, the main stronghold of the counterrevolution cannot be captured." [45]

It is thus evident that among the main objectives of the Conference of Delegates from the Soviet Areas were the establishment of a closer coördination between activities in the cities and activities in the Soviet areas and, above all, the achievement of a greater degree of "proletarian hegemony" within the Soviet areas. It is significant that the "Joint Call for a Conference of Delegates from the Soviet Areas" of February 25, 1930, was issued jointly by the Central Committee and the all-China Labor Federation, thus underlining the proletarian origin of the invitation. The conference drew up preliminary plans for the establishment of a Soviet government and enacted a series of land laws and labor laws.[46] The land laws were particularly radical in tone and even contemplated the establishment of collective farms within the Soviet areas.[47] The inclusion of this "socialist" measure was later to be part of the bill of accusation against Li Li-san. At the time, however, it undoubtedly seemed to be one of the ways of assuring "proletarian hegemony" within the Soviet areas. Was not Stalin assuring proletarian hegemony in the countryside by similar methods? Did not all Comintern resolutions on China contemplate a "growing over" into socialism?

The *Red Flag*, in its account of the accomplishments of the conference, states that "it stressed the importance of proletarian leadership and emphasized the importance of preparing for armed uprisings in the cities . . . At the same time, it repudiated the incorrect line of neglecting the leadership of the city and concentrating exclusively on the 'encirclement of the city by the country' through attacks on the cities by Red Army forces." [48]

We shall consider in a later chapter the extent to which Li Li-san was actually able to make his will effective within the Soviet areas. The conference itself, however, did not bring him a whit closer to the establishment of a Soviet regime as he conceived of such a regime. The urban proletariat simply did not rise.

The month of June thus found the Li Li-san leadership straining every nerve to find new expedients in the face of constant Comintern pressure. The famous Politburo letter of June 11, which finally set the stage for the attack on Changsha, accurately reflects their mood of desperation. Bearing the title "The New Revolutionary Wave and the Initial Victory in One or Several Provinces," it marks a decided shift in Li Li-san's attitude on the question of Red Army attacks on urban centers. Ostensibly, Li had not changed his previous views regarding the relations of city and countryside. The letter still explicitly attacks the notion of "enveloping the city from the country," and the idea that the "cities can simply be captured by the Red Army." [49] It still insists on the necessity and even the priority of armed uprisings by the proletariat within the cities. Having made all these concessions to consistency, however, the letter significantly adds that "in view of China's peculiar political and economic conditions, a rising wave in the proletarian struggle unaccompanied by peasant risings, army rebellions, and *powerful offensives of the Red Army* [emphasis my own] and lacking a proper disposition of every type of revolutionary force, cannot lead to a revolutionary victory." [50] For the first time we find the Red Army mentioned as a vital factor in the revolution. It may be true that the revolutionary wave must begin with armed uprisings in the cities, but is there any reason why such uprisings should not be supported by Red Army attacks? "It must be the Red Army's aim to create a proper coördination with armed uprisings in important urban centers, capture them, and establish a national revolutionary government." [51] From here one can, if necessary, proceed a step further. It may, after all, not be absolutely necessary for the Red Army attack to *follow* insurrections in the cities. Since a revolutionary situation exists, since the urban proletariat is ripe for insurrection, an assault by the Red Army may itself provide the spark to ignite an insurrection. It would thus be not so much a case of capturing the cities with the Red Army as using Red Army attacks to set in motion the insurrectionary forces already existing within the cities. The priority of urban insurrections need not necessarily be a priority in point of time.

Unfortunately, however, the concepts of strategy which had developed among the Red Army leaders were an obstacle to the most effective use of the Red Army forces. "One of the main obstacles we face," complains the letter, "is the 'guerrilla conception' which has prevailed in the Red Army — the notion that cities should be attacked but not taken, and the lack of determination to set up a Soviet regime in the cities. This is a reflection of peasant mentality which has nothing in common with our present line." [52]

The full measure of Li Li-san's desperation, his frantic need for new expedients, can best be observed in the rather novel attempt he makes to link the destiny of world Communism to the destiny of the Chinese revolution. "China," states the letter, "is the world's greatest colony . . . China is the weakest link in the chain of world capitalism . . . All the contradictions of imperialism are concentrated in China." [53] It thus follows that any revolution in China is bound to act as a spur to world revolution. Since by the Comintern's own postulation, the world revolution had now entered onto its third, final stage, the Chinese revolution could play a vital role in bringing about the final world socialist revolution. Conversely, however, since the imperialists were likely to throw their full forces against any Chinese revolution which had won a victory in one or several provinces, it would be difficult to maintain this victory without the support of the world proletariat and of the already victorious proletariat of the Soviet Union." [54]

Basically, of course, this theoretical analysis, which was later to win Li such thorough condemnation, was designed to justify an appeal for aid from the Soviet Union and the forces of world Communism: since the Chinese revolution was so vital to the whole world picture, it deserved the aid of the Soviet Union and of world Communism. What Li probably contemplated here was perhaps something in the nature of the aid later received by Republican Spain.

While this appeal may not have met with any great enthusiasm in Moscow at the time, there is little evidence that it was regarded as the monstrous error which it was later to become when the time came to remove Li Li-san from power. At most, it may have been regarded as an empty bit of revolutionary rhetoric such as can be found in the literature of all communist parties.

Far from condemning the June 11 Politburo letter, an ECCI letter of July 23 actually endorses its basic strategic suggestion. "The new upsurge in the Chinese revolutionary movement," the Comintern communication proclaims, "has become an indisputable fact . . . In the initial stages there is a certain weakness, namely the fact that the fighting masses cannot at the very beginning occupy the industrial centers." Having pointed out this difficulty, the letter goes on to suggest that the Red Army be strengthened so that "in the future, according to political and military circumstances, *one or several political or industrial centers can be occupied*" (emphasis my own). [55]

The Comintern thus clearly endorses Li Li-san's new conception of Red Army attacks on cities. All that was now necessary was to await the most favorable political and military circumstances for such attacks.

X CHANGSHA AND THE "LI LI-SAN LINE"

Changsha

Favorable circumstances soon presented themselves. Chiang Kai-shek and Feng Yü-hsiang were at this time involved in bitter conflict and Ho Chien, the Kuomintang chairman of the Hunan provincial government was forced to send part of his own forces to help Chiang in his battles. Thus, Changsha, a city located close to the Soviet areas, where an "initial victory" was most likely, suddenly found its defenses greatly weakened.

The Fifth Red Army of P'eng Teh-huai attacked Changsha on July 28 only to be driven out a few days later. Li Li-san did not realize his ambition to become "Chairman of the Hunan-Kiangsi Soviet Government" and his subsequent demand for an attack on Wuhan was simply ignored by the Red Army.

The failure of Changsha, like the Canton Commune, received a world press and was an event which Moscow could not ignore. It was undoubtedly this event above all else which set in motion the process which was to lead to Li Li-san's final disgrace.

Nevertheless, the event did not produce an immediately violent reaction in Moscow. On the contrary, the first news of the capture of Changsha by the Red troops was greeted with great enthusiasm. The August 7 issue of *Inprecorr*, evidently printed before the news of Changsha's recapture, carries a rhapsodic article entitled "The Occupation of Changsha," by Chieh Hua. "With the capture of Changsha," it triumphantly proclaims, "there has commenced a new chapter in the history of the Chinese revolution. It is the first time since the Canton Soviet revolt in December 1927 that a great industrial town is in the hands of the revolutionary workers. In the midst of the Soviet village and small towns there now stands a big town as the main point of support of their power. The leadership of the city proletariat in the whole revolutionary movement is strengthened by this victory." [1] Even though the same Chieh Hua was forced to announce the fall of Changsha a week later, he still spoke of it as a "great step forward in the Soviet movement." [2]

As late as August 10 an article in the *Kommunisticheskii Internatsional* still states that "the Soviet movement must by the very logic of its struggle direct itself to the capture of the industrial administrative urban centers. Only on this condition can we achieve a thoroughgoing and organized union between the proletarian and peasant movement guaranteeing a leadership of the peasant millions by the party of the proletariat." [3]

We find here no awareness that Changsha was a monstrous strategic error resulting from Li Li-san's "semi-Trotskyism." There was no haste whatsoever in Moscow to condemn a strategy which it had itself endorsed as late as July 23.

In China, however, Li Li-san's enemies were only too eager to take advantage of his failures and only too eager to unseat him. His own despotic personality combined with the costly failures that the movement was suffering at his hands won him new enemies daily.

The Opposition Factions

Most formidable among Li Li-san's enemies was still the party's elder statesman Ch'en Tu-hsiu. As a result of Ch'en's enormous prestige Li had been forced to tolerate his presence within the party until the very end of 1929 when he finally found an adequate pretext for ridding himself of Ch'en's bold and annoying criticisms.

The occasion was furnished by the attempts by Chang Hsüehliang, the young warlord of Manchuria, to seize the Chinese Eastern Railroad in the spring of 1929. In line with its general propaganda policy, the Kremlin chose to regard this act as a sign of approaching war against the Soviet Union and called upon all world Communist parties to protect the Soviet Union. The Chinese party under Li Li-san's leadership adopted the slogan "Protect the Soviet Union" without the slightest hesitation.[4]

This slogan, however, provided the Nationalist Government with an excellent propaganda weapon against the Communists. The Soviet Union's interest in the Chinese Eastern Railway was, after all, a special privilege of the old imperialist type. Chang, whatever his failings, was, after all, a Chinese leader defending Chinese sovereignty against a foreign power. By calling upon its followers to protect the Soviet Union, the Communist Party was asking the Chinese people to protect the special interest of a foreign power.

Bearing all this in mind, on August 3, 1930, Ch'en Tu-hsiu addressed an open letter to the Central Committee in which he frankly criticized the slogan. As far as the average Chinese was concerned, he contended, the slogan "Protect the Soviet Union" was too abstract. It might easily be misunderstood and might eventually strengthen the hand of reaction. In its place, he suggested that the party adopt the slogan "Oppose the Kuomintang's Mistaken Policy." Here, the emphasis would lie on the errors of the Kuomintang rather than on the notion of protecting a foreign power.[5]

It is not impossible, of course, that beneath these openly stated reasons there lurked a growing coolness on Ch'en's part toward the Soviet Union itself and perhaps a suspicion that its claims were not without imperialist taint.

Whatever may have been the case, however, this letter provoked a furious retort from the Central Committee. This in turn led to spirited rebuttal on Ch'en's part in which he laid bare all his grievances against the party leadership and the party line.

It was now no longer possible for Ch'en to continue within the party and Li Li-san was finally provided with the opportunity of ridding himself of his inveterate enemy. This was to prove a questionable gain, however, for Ch'en was soon able to gather about himself a group of disgruntled oppositionists, more or less committed to a Trotskyist line (some of them had but recently returned from the Sun Yat-sen University in Moscow). While many of the more dogmatic young Trotskyists regarded Ch'en with some suspicion as the former executor of Moscow's "opportunist" policy, they nevertheless united with him in December 1929 to issue a manifesto which was to exercise a strong pull on disaffected elements still within the party.

The manifesto, entitled "A Statement of Our Views" [6] is strongly influenced by Trotsky's current line on the Chinese situation. The fact, however, that it is written by Ch'en Tu-hsiu — a man of great historic stature in the Chinese movement — and that it is written with considerable knowledge of the concrete conditions in China, gives it a relevance which it certainly would not have had if it had merely been another Trotskyist tract.

Like Trotsky, Ch'en insists that Chinese society is now under the sway of capitalism rather than of feudalism. Feudalism, in fact, has not existed in China for centuries since free alienation of land is incompatible with feudalism. The Kuomintang is now simply the party of the bourgeoisie.[7]

The coming socialist revolution can be consummated only by the proletariat at the head of the nonproletarian masses and not by any "dictatorship of workers and peasants."[8] This revolution, however, still lies well in the future. At the present time China finds itself in a protracted revolutionary trough. The imminent new revolutionary wave postulated by the Comintern is a fantastic mirage.[9] During this trough period, the party must bend all its efforts to the recapture of its proletarian bases. It can do this, however, only by associating itself with the daily economic struggles of the workers and by demanding from the victorious bourgeoisie a greater degree of political democracy in the form of a democratically elected national assembly. All talk of uprisings must be eschewed.[10]

Like all Trotskyist literature of this period, this pamphlet shows a belated appreciation of the value of "inner party democracy" but fails to explain how such democracy can be achieved in a party in which unlimited effective power is concentrated at the center.[11]

The most effective appeal of the "Statement" undoubtedly lay in its attack on Li Li-san's policy of political strikes and "preparation for uprisings." It was this attack which made it immediately relevant to the situation in which the party was involved. "The worker comrades in our party feel more and more," it complains, "that the party's policies and practices are absolutely unsuited to the present needs of the masses . . . The party's ties to the proletarian masses are nonexistent . . . We must associate ourselves with the economic struggles of the masses."[12]

The influence of this type of criticism on the party ranks was evidently so great that the Politburo letter of June 11 speaks of "rightist tendencies" as the most serious obstacle to the "implementation of the Comintern line."[13] It seems to have evoked a deep response particularly in those circles of the Communist Party most closely associated with labor activities and most familiar with the real problems of the workers.

It was precisely in these circles that there emerged a distinct faction during the latter months of 1930.[14] Led by Ho Meng-hsiung, the chairman of the traditionally rebellious Kiangsu Provincial Committee, and Lo Chang-lung, a veteran labor leader, this group was particularly embittered by the effects of the official policy on the Red Unions, as well as by Li Li-san's complete elimination of every vestige of labor-union autonomy. Deeply committed as they were to the struggle to win the worker away from the Yellow Unions, how could they help but view with consternation the total disintegration of Communist influence among the urban workers? Unlike Ch'en Tu-hsiu, however, this group was not inclined to break with the party or with its Stalinist loyalties. Since the fault, in its view, lay solely with the Li Li-san leadership, all would be well once it had managed to gain control of the party apparatus.

Subsequent events were to show that there was little inner cohesiveness among these people and that they were motivated in no small measure by private ambition. The group never seems to have developed a distinct "theoretical analysis" of its own, but until Li Li-san's fall from power it was held together by its opposition to his suicidal labor policies.

The most formidable and aggressive threat to Li Li-san's power, however, came from quite another source: the "Returned Student Clique." [15] This group of young men, known also among the party veterans by other ironic appellations such as the "Twenty-eight Bolsheviks," [16] was led by Wang Ming (Ch'en Shao-yü) and included such men as Ch'in Pang-hsien (Po Ku), Shen Tze-min, Wang Chia-hsiang, Ho Tse-shu, and Chang Wen-t'ien (Lo Fu). It had spent all the years since 1926 in study at the Sun Yat-sen Academy in Moscow far from the stormy crises in which the Chinese party had been embroiled. At the academy, the group had distinguished itself, above all, by the ardor with which it had defended the Stalinist cause against all signs of heterodoxy among the academy's student body and by its doglike devotion to the academy's director, Pavel Mif.[17] They were, in effect, Mif's protégés. Since Mif was at this time the most eminent Stalinist "China expert" his patronage was a matter of considerable weight.

Thus we find that when Mif was appointed Comintern Delegate to China in the spring of 1930, his young protégés accompanied him back to China. Li Ang's portrayal of the attitude of the experienced party veterans toward these young "Bolshevik" newcomers has a genuine ring of psychological authenticity. "These fellows," he says, "were all young students who, needless to say, had made no contribution whatsoever to the revolution. While we were carrying on the revolution they were still suckling at their mothers' breasts . . . These men who were infants in terms of their revolutionary background were now sent back to be the leaders of the Chinese Revolution!" [18]

In spite of their unpopularity, however, their special connections with the Comintern Delegate soon won them high positions in party councils.

In accounting for their hostility to Li Li-san, primary weight must be attributed, I think, to their youthful ambitions, to their exuberant assurance that, having but recently returned from the center of world revolution, they could "do things better." Considerable weight must also be ascribed, I think, to the Comintern Delegate's resentment of Li Li-san's determination to keep the reins of party control in his own hands.

We have no evidence that any of them had previously represented any strikingly new points of view in the Communist movement. On the contrary, the few writings of Wang Ming which we have from the period before Li Li-san's fall differ in no essential point from what was later to be known as the "Li Li-san line."

Thus in a pamphlet entitled *Armed Uprisings*,[19] written as early as May 1928, Wang Ming turns in fury against all those who doubt the feasibility of armed insurrections in China. In his conception of the relations of the urban proletariat to the partisan movement in the countryside, he does not depart by a hair from the later Li Li-san policies which were, after all, the policies of the Comintern itself. "Partisan warfare," he insists, "must be tied in with industrially based uprisings . . . We must closely tie in this type of warfare (guerrilla warfare) with the highest form of class struggle — the armed uprising of the proletariat." [20] "In carrying out our task of arming the masses we must pay greatest attention to the proletariat of the industrial cities and must certainly not regard armed uprisings of the proletariat as simply a reflection of or supplement to partisan warfare in the village. Whoever fails to realize that only the industrial cities can form the organized centers of revolution, whoever fails to realize that only the proletariat can provide the directing force in our uprisings, simply has no understanding of the Marxist strategy of insurrection." [21] He quotes Lenin to the effect that "the party of the proletariat must never consider partisan war as its only or most important tool. This tool must be subordinate to other tools and must tally with those other tools." [22]

Long before Li Li-san, he recommends the strategy of Red Army attacks on urban centers. One of the main tasks of the Red Army, he states, is to "occupy cities and unite with the revolutionary forces in the city." [23]

Lest we think that he may have later introduced striking modifications into his views, we should note that he asserted as late as May 15, 1930, that "the establishment of the Soviet government must, without a doubt, begin with the capture of Wuhan." [24] In the same article we find him attacking all "those who harbor doubts regarding the rising tide of revolution on a world scale or in China in particular." [25]

If Wang Ming's writings can be considered indicative of the views prevalent among the "Twenty-eight Bolsheviks" (he was the undisputed leader of the group), we may assume that the general "line" of this group differed little, if at all, from the views which guided the actions of Li Li-san.

Some sources claim that Wang Ming vigorously opposed the Politburo letter of June 11.[26] Unfortunately, we have no access to materials which would throw light on the content of his opposition or inform us whether it concerned any major points of strategic policy. If he favored an attack on Wuhan as late as May 15, the presumption is strong that he did not oppose the letter's recommendation of Red Army assaults on major cities. In general it is safe to assume, I think, that this faction's opposition did not have its roots in the ideological sphere.

Some Japanese accounts of the inner party frictions of this period mention the "Real Power Faction" — that is, the leaders of the Soviet areas — as yet another faction hostile to the Li Li-san leadership. The relations of the Soviet areas to the Li Li-san leadership will be discussed in greater detail in a later chapter. At present it will suffice to point out that if these leaders represented a faction hostile to the Central Committee, they were a silent faction quite content to sabotage the leadership's policies in act rather than in word. We have no evidence to indicate that the "Front Committee" leaders played any important role in factional conflicts of the latter months of 1930 or that they made any serious attempt to capture the Central Committee apparatus.

Such, in brief, were the main forces of the opposition to Li Li-san's leadership. None of these forces, however, constituted an important threat until the failure of Changsha and the ignominious failure to goad the Red Army into an attack on Wuhan had greatly reduced Li's prestige and occasioned a grievous loss of "face." After July, the tide of opposition began to mount steadily.

Toward the end of the summer of 1930, Mif, the patron of the "Returned Student Clique," was finally able to impress the Kremlin with the fact that all was not well in China. The result was the despatch to China of Ch'ü Ch'iu-pai, who had managed to recover in Moscow some of the prestige lost during his period of party leadership. By his unswerving loyalty to Stalin, he had managed to win for himself something of a reputation as a Stalinist authority on the colonial question.[27]

Ch'ü was sent back to China for the express purpose of summoning a meeting of the Central Committee to review the actions and policies of the Li Li-san leadership. Presumably, this represented something of a triumph for him. Unlike the young men of the "Returned Student Clique," he was no callow youth without revolutionary experience; unlike the Ho Meng-hsiung, Lo Chang-lung faction, he was not without influence in Moscow. Armed as he was with the mandate of the Kremlin, there was every reason to assume that he would recapture a position of leadership in the Chinese party.

Instead, we find to our astonishment that the Third Plenum of the Central Committee, held in Lushan in late September 1930, actually reconfirmed the Li Li-san group in its position of leadership, that Ch'ü's attack on this leadership proved halfhearted and ineffectual, and that none of the opposing factions were able to make any headway against the Li Li-san machine.

The Third Plenum

It is perhaps in the very divided nature of the opposition that we must seek the main reason for its failure to unseat Li at this time. Whatever may have been the failures of Li's policies, he had managed to build about himself a tightly knit machine completely loyal to himself. He had also managed to retain the loyalty of Chou En-lai, who is said to have had his own following particularly among certain former Whampoa military elements in the Soviet areas.[28] Against this machine, neither the "Twenty-eight Bolsheviks," aided and supported as they were by the Comintern delegate, nor the labor-union faction could hope to prevail. The Soviet area leaders, the "Real Power Faction," simply held themselves aloof.

Ch'ü Ch'iu-pai's failure to avail himself of the opportunity provided by Moscow has been explained on many grounds. Li Ang maintains that Ch'ü was of a somewhat timid nature, easily intimidated by the overpowering personality of Li Li-san and by the strength of his machine.[29] It is also possible that Ch'ü felt little affinity with either the young men of the "Returned Student Clique" or the "Labor Union Faction."

I would suggest, however, that more important than all these considerations was the dilemma in which Ch'ü and the opposition factions found themselves. Ch'ü, it is true, had been empowered to criticize the Li Li-san leadership, but which elements of Li's policy could he criticize without criticizing the basic theoretical and strategic recommendations of the Comintern itself? The Kremlin had not, after all, announced any new shift in its line on China and any attack on Li Li-san's theoretical pronouncements or even on his overt acts might easily expose Ch'ü to the charge of "right opportunism," Trotskyism, or "Social Fascism."

Li Li-san and Chou En-lai were quite conscious of this dilemma and determined to exploit it to the full. Li could not, of course, deny his past failures. Instead, he seized the bull by the horns and admitted certain past errors "in the spirit of Bolshevik self-criticism." At the same time, he staunchly maintained that these errors had all simply been errors of timing and tactic — *and not* basic errors of theory or strategy. "Is there any disagreement between the Comintern and the Central Committee on basic line?" asks Chou En-lai in his report on the Third Plenum. "Absolutely not! There are no discrepancies in basic line!" [30] Whether such a separation of tactic and line was legitimate is, of course, open to serious doubt. Yet Li's formula is extremely shrewd in that it thrusts onto the shoulders of the opposition responsibility for finding discrepancies between his policies and the Comintern line. It was probably this awful responsibility coupled with the strength of the Li Li-san machine which sufficed to frighten Ch'ü into ineffectuality.

Chou En-lai's report on the Third Plenum [31] gives a clear account of the strategy adopted by the Li Li-san leadership at this time. In dealing with general theoretical questions, Chou defends Li Li-san's thesis that a world revolution is imminent and that the Chinese revolution will play an important role in it. Had not Stalin proclaimed the end of capitalist stabilization? Had he not pointed to the Depression as a portent of a new world-wide revolutionary upsurge? Had he not further stated that the world crisis would extend to the backward agrarian countries as well as to the industrial countries of the West? Hadn't the July letter of the ECCI proclaimed that "the existence of a revolutionary surge in China was indisputable?" [32] The Central Committee had perhaps underestimated the "unevenness" of the development of the revolutionary situation in China but its contention that an initial success in one or several provinces could not be realized without the presence of a general revolutionary situation throughout the country was entirely in accord with the analysis of the Sixth Congress.[33]

As for the attack on Changsha, it might have been ill-timed but the fact that the Red Army was able to take and hold the city demonstrated its strength and pointed to better things in the future.[34]

In its strategy in the labor movement, the Central Committee had acted in entire accord with the policy of the Comintern which had called for a transformation of the economic struggle into a political struggle. "Economic conflicts and political strikes are inseparable." [35] The Central Committee may have been a bit "mechanical" in applying the policy but "any doubt that this policy can be implemented must be regarded as a rightist deviation." [36]

In the past, the Central Committee had thought, in accordance with Comintern directives, that a Soviet government could not be established until the party had occupied large urban centers. Now, however, it would proceed with preparations for the formation of a Soviet government without awaiting the capture of large cities.[37]

In sum then, Chou En-lai's whole report was designed to prove that whatever errors the Central Committee might have committed, "were not due to any disagreement with the Comintern's basic line, but to errors of tactic and timing." [38]

Having proved the complete identity of views between the Central Committee and the Comintern, Chou was now free to take the offensive against the opposition. Since the Ho Meng-hsiung faction was the most vociferous at this Plenum, he turned his full fire on them.[39] It was precisely these opportunists, clamoring for a greater emphasis on purely economic struggles, who were at variance with the basic line of the Comintern. By casting doubts on the imminence of a new revolutionary tide, by underestimating the role of the Soviet areas and of the Red Army, and by questioning the wisdom of the policy of "preparing for uprisings," the opposition had simply succeeded in unmasking its rightist deviations.[40]

As a result of the use of the clever strategy outlined in this report and of the strength of its party machine, the Li Li-san leadership was able to postpone the day of reckoning. Ch'ü Ch'iu-pai was effectively silenced and the opposition groups were kept away from the seats of power. The *Red Flag* of October 4, 1930, was complacently able to report the success of the Third Plenum and the defeat of "right opportunism." [41]

There can be little doubt that this unexpected turn in events infuriated the Comintern delegate Mif. According to remarks which appear in the Resolutions of the Fourth Plenum one gathers that the Third Plenum had been carried on behind his back and that Chou En-lai's report had been drawn up entirely without his consent.[42] We are thus not surprised to find him redoubling his efforts to unseat Li Li-san after the Third Plenum. To do this was no easy task. It would be necessary to prove: (1) that Li Li-san's errors had not merely been picayune errors of tactic but fundamental errors of principle; (2) that these errors of principle later to be subsumed under the phrase "the Li Li-san line" were in direct contradiction to the principles laid down in the Comintern line.

Luckily for Mif and the "Returned Student Clique," the Kremlin had at this time actually begun to reconsider its strategic policy in

China. The contrast between the repeated failures of the Communist Party in the regions outside the Soviet areas and its successes within those areas was raising many new questions among the Kremlin loaders themselves.

On the one hand, Moscow was extremely eager to take full propaganda advantage of the successes in the Soviet areas. On the other hand, it was by no means anxious to reveal the weakness of the Chinese party's proletarian base. The existence of an armed force, a territorial base, and even a state power all operating under a Stalinist banner was at the time a unique phenomenon within the world communist movement. On the other hand, the Trotskyists and the "liquidationists" in China had already begun to point to the heretical implications of a peasant partisan movement operating in complete isolation from the urban proletariat. As has already been pointed out the Kremlin could not afford to treat such accusations lightly since they involved the very bases of authority of the Communist Party.

By the end of 1930, however, it would appear that the former consideration was beginning to outweigh the latter. The propaganda value of the Soviet areas was beginning to outweigh considerations of orthodoxy (but not to cancel them). It was thus decided that at least for the immediate future the Soviet areas should be allowed to develop along the lines which were proving so successful, and that a state power should be established within the area without awaiting the capture of large urban centers. At least temporarily, the attitude toward the Soviet areas was to be one of laissez faire.[43]

At the same time, as I hope to indicate, there is no evidence whatsoever that this was meant to imply a shift of supreme party power to the Communist leaders within the Soviet areas. On the contrary, there is every indication that Moscow intended to keep the reins of power in the hands of a Central Committee of its own choosing to be located in urban, proletarian Shanghai. Nor was it meant to imply that this Central Committee could abandon its main task, the recapture of its urban proletarian bases.

It is, however, this shift in strategy which forms the hard core of reality in the whole attack on the "Li Li-san line." The previous strategy, which had been just as much Moscow's as Li Li-san's, had failed and someone had to bear the responsibility for this failure.

Actually, Chou En-lai's report demonstrates that the Li Li-san leadership was aware of the new shift in the wind from the Kremlin and was quite willing to make all the necessary changes in strategic policy. Moscow, however, needed its scapegoat while Pavel Mif and the opposition factions in China were only too eager to aid the Kremlin in converting Li Li-san into such a scapegoat.

It need hardly be added that in carrying on its attack on Li Li-san, the Kremlin was in an entirely different position from the opposition factions at the Third Plenum. It could ignore and reinterpret its own past statements and directives with reckless abandon.

The Attack on the "Li Li-san Line"

The opening shot of the attack on Li Li-san was fired by the Comintern itself in its letter of November 16.[44] The attack was so devastating and all-inclusive in nature, that Li could not survive in his position of leadership. His power within the party was completely undermined. A Politburo meeting of November 25 held under the auspices of the opposition factions declared its complete solidarity with the directives of the Comintern letter and forced Li Li-san to resign after he had made an abject confession of past errors.[45]

Armed with the Comintern letter, the "Returned Student Clique" with the support of Mif made an open bid for power. The only obstacle in their path was the Ho Meng-hsiung, Lo Chang-lung faction which was equally eager to take advantage of Li's disgrace. It was, however, an uneven battle. In his capacity as Comintern Delegate, Mif was able to assume the responsibility for interpreting Moscow's new directives. It was thus comparatively easy for him to interpret these directives in such a way as to turn them against the "Labor Union Faction" as well as against Li Li-san. The battle, he contended, was to be a battle "on two fronts" against the Li Li-san line and against the "right opportunists." [46]

Li Li-san soon left for Moscow where he made his humble recantation. The fact that the Kremlin in its heart of hearts did not regard him as disloyal to its will was amply proved when he returned to Manchuria with the Red Army several years later.

The basic features of the "Li Li-san line" can be found in the November 16 letter and in the later interpretations and elaborations of this letter by Mif and the "Returned Student Clique."

The strategic errors of Li Li-san had, it was contended, flowed inexorably from certain basic theoretical errors. These theoretical errors were most clearly illustrated in the Politburo letter of June 11 previously discussed. It is strange, of course, that Moscow had failed to perceive the monstrous nature of Li's errors at the time. Ignoring this difficulty, however, the November 16 letter and the Resolutions of the Fourth Plenum of the Central Committee direct their fire primarily at this document.

This Politburo letter, it will be recalled, had emphasized the organic connection between the Chinese revolution and the world revolution. It had pointed to the imminence of a rising wave in the world revolution and asserted that the Chinese revolution could not be culminated without the support of the world revolution. Conversely, it had maintained that, since China was "the world's greatest colony," a successful consummation of the Chinese revolution could not help but precipitate the collapse of world capitalism. We have suggested that the motive underlying this analysis may have been the desire to enlist the active aid of the Soviet Union and of the world communist movement in the Chinese party's struggles.

This analysis now became the main focus of attack. In making it, Li had "ignored the uneven development of the world revolutionary crisis." [47] He had thus committed the Trotskyist error of denying "the possibility of victory in the Chinese revolution independently of a victory in the world revolution." [48] In this he had displayed his "opportunist passivity." On the other hand, by stressing the importance of the Chinese revolution to the world revolution, he had laid bare his "petty bourgeois chauvinism," his "velikokitaism" (literally, greater China-ism).[49]

Now, in the first place, with the spread of the world-wide Depression in 1930, there had arisen in Moscow itself a growing tendency to stress the perspectives of a "world-wide revolutionary upsurge" rather than the perspective of the "uneven development of the revolutionary wave." As Chou En-lai points out in his report on the Third Plenum, the speeches of both Molotov and Stalin at the Sixteenth Congress of the Soviet Communist Party had been rather sanguine about the possibility of a world-wide revolutionary upsurge.[50] Furthermore, "unevenness" did not imply disconnectedness, as is clearly illustrated by the Comintern's attack on certain elements in the American Party who preached the doctrine of American "exceptionalism." [51]

In the second place, the emphasis on China as an important focal point of world imperialism can be found throughout Comintern literature. Long after the disgrace of Li Li-san, Manuilsky was to proclaim at the Seventeenth Congress of the Soviet Communist Party that "the struggle around China is one of the principal elements of imperialist antagonism." [52]

Yet, even if it were granted that Li Li-san had here committed a grave theoretical error, even if his comparison of China's role to the role of Russia in the October Revolution was displeasing in Moscow's eyes, how had this "theoretical" error affected his concrete behavior? How could he be charged with passively waiting for the revolution when hardly a day passed without some attempt on his part to foment revolutionary insurrections in China? On the other hand, how had his "chauvinism" affected his behavior? Had he not gone as far as any Communist leader in disassociating himself from Chinese nationalism at the time of China's Eastern Railway affair?

A parallel charge against him is that in his domestic policy he had "subordinated the perspectives of an initial victory in one or several provinces to the perspectives of the nation-wide, revolutionary wave." [53] It is, of course, true that in his pronouncements on this subject, Li had constantly stressed the fact that no regional victory was possible without the presence of a nation-wide revolutionary situation. It may be that, in part, his motive in stressing this point had been the desire to counterweigh the growing power of the Soviet area leaders by stressing the necessity of activities in the non-Soviet areas. Whatever may have been his motive, however, his position was in entire harmony with the Resolutions of the Sixth Congress, which explicitly state that "under the conditions of a new revolutionary high tide, the revolution may well win an initial victory in one or several provinces. Unless such a revolutionary upsurge does exist, however, such a victory cannot be realized . . . In this connection, the cities and the upsurge of the proletarian masses will play a decisive role in determining victory or defeat." [54]

Furthermore, how had this supposed "theoretical" error influenced Li Li-san's behavior? Had the attack on Changsha been a proof of his failure to appreciate the uneven development of the revolution? The exact reverse is true. The choice of such places as Changsha, Kian, and Wuhan as points of attack was based squarely on the fact that these urban centers were in close proximity to the Soviet areas — that is, precisely in those areas where an "initial victory" was most likely.

Another accusation, more to the point, was that Li had failed "to appreciate the uneven development of the workers' and peasants' struggle." [55] Here, of course, we are closer to the core of reality in the Comintern's attack on Li, for this attack reflects the actual shift in the Comintern's views on strategy already described above. It must be emphasized, however, that Li's unwillingness to recognize this "uneven development" had been in entire harmony with Comintern policy. The Ninth Plenum of the ECCI had already noted this uneven development but had deplored it as an obstacle to be overcome rather than as a situation to be accepted. How could a proletarian party acquiesce in such a situation? Ch'ü Ch'iu-pai had been condemned for failing to coördinate uprisings in the countryside with uprisings in the city while the Sixth Congress of the Chinese Communist Party had insisted time and time again that the peasant struggle must be led by the workers' struggle.

Addressing himself precisely to this problem, Losovsky had stated in July 1928 that "the present moment is characterized by a separation between the workers' and peasants' movement. The workers' movement lags behind that of the peasants and this is fraught with tremendous dangers to the further development of the Chinese revolution. Therefore, the question of organizing the Chinese trade unions and of attracting the industrial and artisan proletariat to activity acquires exceptional importance to the Chinese revolution because it offers the only way for the straightening out of the difficulties which may arise in the future if the peasant movement will be far ahead of that of the proletariat." [56] We shall find that in spite of their attack on Li Li-san's error, neither Mif nor Wang Ming were later able to abandon the attempt to bring the labor movement abreast of the peasant movement.

One of the main points of attack, however, is Li Li-san's policy of "adventurism" or "putschism." [57] As has already been pointed out, an adventurist or "putschist" policy is a policy which encourages acts of organized violence at a time when objective conditions preclude the success of such acts.

Now there can be little doubt that Li's policy was adventuristic. There can also be little doubt however, that his actions were predicated on a description of Chinese objective conditions which had been made in Moscow. The Ninth Plenum of the ECCI, the Sixth Congress of the Chinese Communist Party, and the Sixth Comintern Congress had all announced that the "Chinese revolution was at the beginning of a new revolutionary upsurge" while the ECCI letters of February and July 1930 had actually announced the arrival of the new wave.[58] In a period of revolutionary upsurge it can always be assumed that the strength of the reactionary forces is declining and that the masses are ready to rise in desperation. As Li Li-san had himself stated, "When a revolutionary wave begins to rise, a mass organization can grow with lightning speed from an organization of small groups to an organization of several millions." [59] If Li Li-san had in a time of revolutionary upsurge turned aside to engage in humdrum efforts to win a large party membership or to engage in purely economic struggles, he might easily have exposed himself to the charge of "right opportunism."

Li Li-san's accusers could not deny, of course, that the Comintern had clearly announced a new revolutionary upsurge. Instead, they resorted to an ingenious linguistic quibble. Li, it seems, had misinterpreted the Russian word *pod'em* (upsurge). "A revolutionary *pod'em*," states Wang Ming, "is not the same thing as a 'direct revolutionary situation.' A 'direct revolutionary situation' is the highest point of development of the revolutionary *pod'em*, but the revolutionary *pod'em* is the whole process of the development of the revolution . . . What must the party do during the period of *pod'em*? It must do everything in its power to strengthen and broaden our party organization, union organization, young Communist League, etc." [60] Ingenious as this distinction is, however, we find no such clear-cut distinction in previous Comintern literature. Pavel Mif himself, the moving spirit of the anti–Li Li-san movement, had written in September 1929 that "with the present upsurge [*pod'em*] of the strike movement it should be easier to capture the masses of the Yellow Unions than it is to capture the workers of the reformist unions of the capitalist countries." He adds that, in view of the rising wave, "the economic struggle of the Chinese proletariat can rapidly be converted into a political struggle." [61] We find no evidence here of any clear distinction between a *pod'em* and a "direct revolutionary situation." It is easy enough to create spatialized images of this type but somewhat difficult to see how they can be applied to concrete political situations.

Having made this new *ad hoc* distinction, however, Li's enemies were able to attack him freely on the basis of a definition of which he could not have been aware in advance. They could now condemn him for failing to emphasize the economic struggles of the masses and the day-to-day tasks of mass organization.

At the same time they could not proceed too far in this direction for fear of lending comfort to Trotsky, to the "liquidationists" (Ch'en Tu-hsiu), and to the "Labor Union Faction." Even while emphasizing the importance of the daily economic struggles of the masses, the Comintern letter of November 16 warns that "we must tie in these day-to-day demands with the demands of the proletariat as a whole." [62] The demands of the proletariat as a whole, however, are nothing less than the destruction of the whole prevailing regime! Thus, the Chinese Communist Party finds itself once more in the exact position in which it had found itself immediately after the Sixth Congress of 1928 — at the beginning of a revolutionary wave. The time has not yet come for uprisings and insurrections but the party must still prepare for such uprisings. There must be no concessions to the "right opportunists"!

In order to demonstrate the "semi-Trotskyist" nature of Li Li-san's errors, certain phrases of his concerning the "growing order of the revolution into socialism" were fully exploited. In Li's own words in his well-rehearsed recantation, "I maintained that the victory of the bourgeois democratic revolution directly passes over into a socialist revolution. This point of view is semi-Trotskyist." [63]

Actually, Comintern literature is itself replete with phrases which could easily have led Li to this error. Alongside of emphatic statements concerning the bourgeois democratic nature of the Chinese revolution we constantly find phrases concerning the possibility of a "noncapitalist" development in China. It was constantly being pointed out that, since the Chinese revolution was taking place after the great October Revolution in the epoch of the world socialist revolution, it would not necessarily follow previous paths in its march toward socialism. In 1931, after Li Li-san's disgrace, Mif was to write an article entitled "The Chinese Revolution and the Noncapitalist Path of Development" [64] in which he stressed the possibilities of such a development in China. At the Seventeenth Congress of the Soviet Communist Party, two years after Li Li-san's disgrace, at a time when the Chinese Communist Party had completely abandoned its urban bases, Manuilsky proudly announced that "the Soviet government (in China) is carrying the bourgeois democratic revolution to its completion and carrying out a number of measures of a socialist character in the process. All this, taken together, ensures the rapid growing over of this revolution into a socialist revolution provided that the power of the soviets is extended to the industrial centers." [65]

Li's accusers are, however, able to point to one concrete instance of the manner in which this premature expectation of socialism had affected Li Li-san's strategy. At the Conference of Delegates from the Soviet Areas of May 1930, he had suggested that large land holdings be collectivized rather than divided among the peasants.[66] On the face of it, as we have just seen, there was no reason why "measures of a socialist character" might not be inaugurated even in a period of bourgeois democratic revolution. It is, however, true that this particular measure had not been authorized by the Comintern or the Sixth Congress.

We are somewhat struck to find that Li was accused simultaneously of exactly the opposite error — that of an overgenerous attitude to rich peasants.[67] No attempt was made to show how Li Li-san came to commit both these errors at once, except for reference to Stalin's cliché about rightist acts lurking behind leftist phrases. It is not impossible, of course, that Li is here being held responsible for policies actually pursued by the leaders inside the Soviet areas.

It is difficult to see, however, how this particular "Trotskyist" error affected any of Li Li-san's other acts. What relation did it have, for instance, to his attack on Changsha? How could that attack be considered "Trotskyist" when the basic strategy underlying it was endorsed by the ECCI letter of July 23?

It has already been pointed out that the *theoretical* distinctions between Trotsky's "permanent revolution" and the Comintern's "democratic dictatorship" had become utterly nebulous in their application to China. On the other hand, the *strategic* policy pursued by Li Li-san during his period of leadership had been diametrically opposed in almost every respect to the strategy currently advocated by Trotsky.

Such, nevertheless, were the main lines of the attack directed against Li Li-san. It was by means of such arguments that the Comintern and the "Returned Student Clique" attempted to prove that the "Li Li-san line" had "had nothing in common with the Comintern line or the teachings of Marxism-Leninism." Because of his dependence on the prospects of world revolution he had been guilty of "opportunist passivity." Because of his exaggeration of the role of the Chinese revolution, he had been guilty of "petty bourgeois chauvinism." Because he had taken literally the Comintern's postulation of a new revolutionary upsurge, he had been guilty on the one hand, of "adventurism" and on the other hand of "opportunist passivity" in the field of organizational activities and of economic struggle. He had furthermore not understood the peculiar meaning of the word "upsurge" (*pod'em*) as used by the Comintern. His use of phrases about the imminent transformation of the revolution into a socialist revolution and his attempts to force a premature collectivization had proved his Trotskyist proclivities. This had not prevented him, however, from harboring rightist inclinations toward the rich peasantry. He had underestimated the importance of the injunction to seek an "initial victory in one or several provinces" even though his attack on Changsha had been directly based on this injunction. Because of his failure to take into account the uneven development of the revolution in the country and in the city — a failure he had shared with the Comintern — he had incorrectly insisted on the possession of urban bases as a prelude to the establishment of a Soviet government.

XI

THE WANG MING LEADERSHIP

While Li Li-san had been decisively defeated, the victory of Mif and his young protégés was not easily won. The followers of Ho Meng-hsiung and Lo Chang-lung determined to prevent these "callow Bolsheviks" [1] from gaining control of the party. Insofar as their hostility was not simply based on personal resentment and political ambition, it probably reflected their fear that the "Returned Student Clique" would never effect the changes in policy desired by them.

Unfortunately, most of the literature produced by this faction is simply not available. We do, however, have one small pamphlet written by Ho Meng-hsiung after the Third Plenum. The pamphlet, entitled *A Statement of the Views of Ho Meng-hsiung*, is essentially an attempt on the part of Ho to defend his position against the then victorious Li Li-san leadership. It also serves to illuminate certain basic features of Ho's own thought. He takes pains to demonstrate that he is a loyal follower of the Comintern line, that he accepts the perspective of armed uprisings and all the other directives of the Comintern.[2] Having paid his respects to orthodoxy, however, Ho goes on to lay bare his real grievances. "We must admit," he states, "that the relations between the party and the masses are extremely weak . . . The party is not leading the strike movement. The Central Committee claims (1) that it has already won over the working class, and (2) that even in the advanced countries of the west it is difficult to win over the working masses." [3] Such views, in Ho's opinion, represent a denial of the leading role of the proletariat. The first and paramount duty of the Communist Party is to win back its proletariat base. To do this "more emphasis must be placed on strikes of an economic nature. We must not simply confine ourselves to political strikes . . . Our Red Unions have failed but our cure has been worse than the disease. We have not allowed unions to maintain separate organizations but have governed by edict through party delegates. This has widened the rift between the party and the masses." [4] In such complaints, I think, we can find the authentic voice of whatever labor union elements still remained within the party.

It is quite evident that this faction expected little improvement under the leadership of young amateurs from the Sun Yat-sen Academy who had little concrete knowledge of conditions in China and who were quite as eager as Li Li-san to condemn this faction's views as "right opportunism" and to accuse it of compromising with Ch'en Tu-hsiu's "liquidationists."

The Ho Meng-hsiung faction was not the only stumbling block, however. Now that Li Li-san had been removed from the seat of authority, Ch'ü Ch'iu-pai was once more prepared to make a bid for leadership. At the beginning of December 1930 he wrote a Letter to Our Party Comrades in which he gave his own account of the errors of Li Li-san. [5] Since this document is not available we cannot compare his version of those errors with the Mif, Wang Ming version. Later, however, when Wang Ming's victory was assured, Ch'ü's letter was severely condemned for its "compromising" nature and its failure to consider Ch'ü's own ignominious role at the Third Plenum. [6]

Finally, the lower echelons of Li Li-san's machine regarded the upstarts from Moscow with sullen resentment. [7]

Mif's authority as Comintern delegate, however, proved sufficient to overcome all these obstacles. The fact that at the Fourth Plenum of the Central Committee held on January 7, 1931, Ch'ü Ch'iu-pai, Chou En-lai, and others were forced to make abject confessions of error would indicate that Mif had managed to secure the active support of the Kremlin itself, for neither Chou nor Ch'ü had particularly respected his own authority in the past. Ch'ü was forced to speak of his own "cowardly rotten opportunism" while Chou En-lai was forced to condemn *in toto* his own report on the Third Plenum. [8] However, while Ch'ü was sent off to the Soviet areas, Chou En-lai was able to rehabilitate himself to such an extent that he won a high post on the new Central Committee. The Ho Meng-hsiung, Lo Chang-lung group was thoroughly routed. Mif was able to use the November ECCI letter as a double-edged sword against them. However well grounded their opinions may have been, Mif was easily able to impugn their orthodoxy. Simply by pointing to their lack of enthusiasm for political strikes, he was able to insinuate a tendency to compromise with "liquidationism." [9]

Wang Ming and the "Twenty-eight Bolsheviks" were thus completely victorious. Yet the same Fourth Plenum which marks their accession to power carries a step further the process of disintegration in the Communist Party outside of the Soviet areas. The constant shift in Comintern line, the enormous "scissors" between the Comintern line and the Chinese realities, and finally the imposition of the "Twenty-eight Bolsheviks" as leaders of the party had simply undermined the faith of party members. Thus we find that the Ho Meng-hsiung, Lo Chang-lung faction simply refused to accept the decisions of the Fourth Plenum or the authority of the new Central Committee even though this leadership was directly imposed by Moscow itself. Instead of bowing to party discipline, Ho Meng-hsiung, Lo Chang-lung, Wang K'o-ch'uan, Hsü Hsi-ken, and others formed an "Emergency Committee" to consider further steps. [10] As a result, they were all expelled from the party.

On January 17 a meeting of the committee was discovered by the British police. The members of the committee present were all arrested and on February 7, Ho Meng-hsiung and twenty-four others were executed by the Kuomintang. Hostile sources have strongly intimated that Wang Ming was implicated in this event; that the Emergency Committee represented such a danger to the authority of the new Central Committee, that its existence could not be tolerated. [11]

After this event, the Emergency Committee, which was itself riven by personal animosities, rapidly disintegrated. Some of its members broke with the party entirely and sought refuge among the followers of Ch'en Tu-hsiu. Others drifted back into the party. [12]

To judge from references in Communist literature of the period it would appear that "Lo Chang-lungism" in the ranks of the labor unions continued to exist for some time to come. This is particularly significant in view of the fact that Lo had been a leader of the maritime union, one of the last strongholds of Communist influence among the urban proletariat. As late as December 1931, a *Red Flag* article is forced to complain that most of the leaders of the maritime union "are still deeply influenced by Lo Chang-lung . . . They have only paid lip service to the new line." [13] The article goes on to complain of the indifference of both the leadership and the rank and file to the directives of the party. The party, it seems, was calling for the maritime union to concentrate its activities among the boatmen on the Yangtze since "it is only by means of such a shift that we can carry on our central task at present — namely, to support the activities of the Red Army and the Soviet areas." [14] The maritime union leaders, it seems, continued to look down their noses at the river boatmen. Furthermore, they strongly resented the notion that in a communist party the proletariat should act as auxiliary force to peasant partisans.

With the alienation of these union leaders, the Communist Party can be said to have lost its last concrete link of any consequence with the urban proletariat.

The demoralization in Communist ranks outside the Soviet areas was to continue throughout Wang Ming's period of leadership. A contemporary Japanese account sums up the general situation as follows: "What we do know is that in every province and every county the struggle between the Mif faction, the Li Li-san faction, and the Compromise faction (Ho Meng-hsiung, Lo Chang-lung faction), taken together with the pressure of the Kuomintang, has greatly reduced the party's ability to act." [15]

The Fourth Plenum Line

The Fourth Plenum did not confine its attention to the elimination of the opposition. It also set the line for the future.

The main features of the Comintern's theoretical line remained unchanged. The Kremlin was not inclined to change any of its basic analyses until the shift to the "United Front" policy at the Seventh Comintern Congress finally forced a change. The Kuomintang was still a coalition of feudal classes and bourgeoisie. The revolution was still a bourgeois democratic revolution and the main "content" of that revolution was still the agrarian problem. The "democratic dictatorship of workers and peasants" remained the political form of the revolution and the soviets were still the vehicle for the realization of the dictatorship. The proletariat would continue to exercise hegemony within the dictatorship, and the peasantry was to remain unrepresented by a party of its own. There was to be no coalition with other political groups and the party's unchanging aim was the overthrow of the national government. In accordance with the new definition of the word *pod'em* the Chinese revolution was now in a period of revolutionary upsurge but had not yet reached a "direct revolutionary situation." [16] Or, to use the older terminology, the revolutionary wave was still at its beginning and had not yet reached a crest. We thus find that in the field of theory nothing new had been added. [17]

In the field of strategy, however, it had now become possible to recognize the "uneven development of the workers' and peasants' struggle." Henceforth, the spectacular developments in the Soviet areas would be allowed to continue without interference. Thus, the Comintern letter of November 16 calls for: (1) the organization and training of a consolidated Red Army of Peasants and Workers; (2) the immediate establishment of a solid Soviet regime capable of action; (3) the organization of the masses in the Soviet areas under the banner of Bolshevism; (4) the organization of the economic and political struggles of the masses in non-Soviet areas; (5) the organization of the anti-imperialist struggle. [18]

The Comintern was now willing to contemplate the establishment of a Soviet government without the possession of urban proletariat bases. We must therefore once more raise a question which has been raised before. Does this mean that the Comintern and the Fourth Plenum had sanctioned the total shift of power to the Soviet areas — that they had underwritten Maoism?

I would suggest that even at this late date the Kremlin anticipated no such development, that it did not — and could not — take the initiative in divorcing the Chinese Communist Party from its supposed urban proletarian bases, and that it did not thrust the mantle of leadership onto the shoulders of the Front Committee leaders in Hunan and Kiangsi. We have every reason to believe, in terms of the experience of the Soviet Union, that the Kremlin naturally assumed that any Soviet government which might arise would be controlled by the party. The party, however, would continue to have its central organs in the city and would continue with its task of recapturing its proletarian bases.

Thus, while the ECCI letter of November 16 placed considerable weight on activities in the Soviet areas, it by no means neglected the urban proletariat. The uneven development between town and country was henceforth not to be remedied by using the Red Army to capture urban bases, but a remedy was still to be sought. Henceforth, this situation was to be remedied by bringing the workers' movement abreast of the peasants' movement rather than by willfully wrecking the Red Army. As a matter of fact, the November 16 letter evinces considerable optimism on this subject. "At the present time," it states, "the organization of activities among the workers in the Yellow Unions, the increase of membership in the Red Unions, and the increase in party membership can proceed more rapidly than in the past because the victories in the Soviet areas as well as general political and economic conditions have all served to intensify the struggles of the workers." [19] It goes on to assert that once the workers have been won over "we shall be able to prepare uprisings in large urban industrial centers, and by coördinating the uprisings of the workers in the cities with the action of the Red Army we shall be able to take those cities." [20] This is simply a return to the position of Li Li-san before the Politburo letter of June 11. It hardly forecasts the circumstances under which the Communists were actually to occupy the cities several years later.

The Resolutions of the Fourth Plenum call for an improvement of tactics in mass activities "particularly in labor unions . . . We must pay particular attention to our work in factories." [21]

The November letter and the Resolutions of the Fourth Plenum both pay considerable attention to the "leadership of the anti-imperialist struggle in the cities." [22] With the growing penetration of Japanese power in China there was now less inclination in Moscow to insist that all "imperialists" be opposed equally. Moscow was now much more ready to take advantage of the anti-Japanese sentiments current among the urban masses of China. We can, in fact, detect a considerable note of urgency behind the injunction to "increase the struggle against imperialism tenfold." [23] The struggle against imperialism at this time, however, was primarily an urban struggle. The urban masses were the ones most directly exposed to the humiliations of the imperialists and so most responsive to anti-imperialist propaganda.

The fact that the Kremlin anticipated no abandonment of the cities is conclusively proved by an article of Mif in *Bol'shevik* for July 15, 1931. Mif, the main architect of the anti–Li Li-san line, had been the moving spirit of the Fourth Plenum. He was thus eminently qualified to interpret the results of that assembly as well as the will of the Kremlin.

Mif points to frequent complaints in the Soviet press concerning "the huge scissors between the workers' movement and the peasants' movement" in China.[24] He deplores such statements on the ground that they lend comfort to "right and left opportunism." At the same time, he adds that "all this is said not in order to excuse theoretically the present level of the labor movement in the main centers of China . . . Without a further development of the labor movement on the basis of day-to-day struggles particularly in areas where the working class is concentrated; without a rise in the movement to a higher stage we shall not be able to win a victory in the Chinese revolution. *A maximum of the efforts of the Chinese Communist Party must be applied to the task of overcoming the relative weakness of its organization in the main industrial centers of the country* [emphasis my own]. The party must disassociate itself from the tendency among certain Communists to underestimate the importance of the problem of organizing the strike struggle, to underestimate labor union activities as a whole and activities in the Yellow Unions in particular. It is indisputable that the problem of carrying forward the struggle of the working class in the industrial centers is a problem of paramount importance." He goes on to claim that under its new leadership (which he had himself imposed on the party) "the party has already achieved certain successes, albeit elementary ones, in the matter of organizing and leading the strike struggle of the workers in basic industrial centers." [25]

Nor was Mif alone in expressing such views. In an article entitled "The Struggle for the Bolshevization of the Communist Party of China" printed in a *Communist Internationale* issue of March 1931, Kuchumov discusses the errors of the Li Li-san line. "On the basis of such an anti-Leninist line," he states, "the party could not liquidate the backwardness of the workers' movement as compared with the peasant war which exists at present — a backwardness which has to be liquidated at all costs so as to assure a really victorious advance of the revolution." [26]

On November 4, 1931, on the eve of the formation of the provisional Soviet government, Yolk states in Pravda that "the founding

of a central Soviet government and a permanent territorial base require the reinforcement of the proletarian nucleus in the Soviet
movement, but this, in turn, presupposes a further development of
the proletarian struggle in the strong industrial centers of China." [27]

The most concrete and incontrovertible proof of the Kremlin's
intentions is, first, the fact that the Central Committee — the highest
organ of the Communist Party — continued to maintain its headquarters in proletarian Shanghai long after the Fourth Plenum and
abandoned these headquarters only under pressure; and, second, the
fact that the control of the party was entrusted not to the experienced leaders of the Soviet areas but to a group of urbanized students
fresh from their lessons in Marxist-Leninist dogma at the Sun Yat-
sen Academy.

In addition to the ideological factor — the inability of Moscow
to overlook the basic dogma that a communist party must have
urban proletarian connections — there were also, I think, considerations of a power nature which militated against the bestowal of
leadership on the leaders of the Soviet areas. There was a growing
tendency in Moscow at this time to eliminate from the leadership of
Communist parties everywhere all those in the Communist world
who had derived their prestige from sources other than the authority
of Stalin himself.[28] The imposition of the "Twenty-eight Bolsheviks"
on the Chinese party must be viewed, in part, in the light of this
tendency.

Unlike Li Li-san, who had achieved a reputation of his own in
the May Thirtieth period, or Ch'ü Ch'iu-pai, who had played a role
of his own at the August Seventh Conference, and unlike the leaders
in the Soviet areas who had built their power on the basis of a
strategy of their own making, the "Twenty-eight Bolsheviks" had
no history in the Chinese Communist Party and represented nothing.
They had, in fact, been directly imposed on the party by the Comintern delegate Mif and could be expected to be more dependent on
the Kremlin than any other group within the party.

How, then, are we to account for the eclipse of the Communist
movement in the cities after 1931, for the total shift of power to the
Soviet areas, and the emergence of Mao Tse-tung as the leader of
the movement?

XII

THE TRIUMPH OF
MAO TSE-TUNG

Victory Within the Soviet Areas

In treating the history of the Chinese Communist Party thus far, we have focused our attention on the Central Committee in Shanghai and treated the Soviet areas from the point of view of their impact on the party leadership. Most available histories of the movement have, of course, focused their attention on the Soviet areas and treated the activities in Shanghai as peripheral. Inasmuch as the Soviet movement was to emerge as the unique dynamic force in Chinese Communism, this is only natural. Unfortunately, however, the very fact that most histories have been written from the point of view of its most successful protagonists tends to cast a mist over many of its aspects, particularly in the earlier period. There is much in the early history of the Soviet areas and in the history of the relations of the Soviet areas to the Central Committee that remains particularly obscure in such accounts as Mao Tse-tung's autobiography (as related to Edgar Snow).

We do, of course, have nonofficial Chinese and Japanese sources. Some of these, however, are written from a distinctly hostile point of view and hence are also open to suspicion of tendentiousness. Nevertheless, it is only by comparing such sources with each other and against the official accounts that we can hope to arrive at even a tentative judgment.

Thus Mao Tse-tung's own account sheds little light on the circumstances of his own rise to undisputed leadership within the Soviet areas unless we are willing to accept the easy assumption that leadership naturally and painlessly gravitated into his hands. That Mao is a man of great leadership ability, a man of "charismatic" personality, is a matter beyond dispute. At the same time, there is room for doubt whether he was able to establish his leadership by the sheer force of his personality.

While Mao may have been the chief exponent of what we have chosen to call the "Maoist strategy," he was by no means the only exponent. We know, of course, that partisan groups had sprung up in various separate areas — in western Fukien, northeastern Kiangsi, Anhwei, etc.[1] Mao's own ability to maintain his position in Ching-kanshan was itself due in no small measure to the reinforcements he had received from Chu Teh and later from P'eng Teh-huai.[2] While many of these partisan-military leaders, Chu Teh in particular, may have been willing to subordinate their own ambitions out of loyalty to the cause, there is ground for suspecting that others were by no means willing to subordinate their own ambitions to the authority of Mao Tse-tung.

The tension between military and civilian power seems to have been a particularly serious source of conflict in the early days of the Soviet movement. Mao Tse-tung had early shown keen awareness of this problem. In part, this awareness may have been due to his own realization that he was not essentially a great military leader. Essentially, however, it was probably due to his awareness that the conception of a communist party demanded a disciplined subordination of the military to the civilian, as well as to his determination to prevent the Soviet movement from becoming the plaything of ambitious generals as had happened in the case of so many movements in China. As early as the period of the Autumn Harvest uprisings we find him identifying himself with the civilian party authority and resigning the leadership of the armed forces to Yü Sha-t'ou.[3] When Mao Tse-tung and Chu Teh combined forces in May 1928, it was definitely decided that Mao Tse-tung would remain the civilian leader of the movement.[4] Thus, in fighting to maintain his power position, he was at the same time fighting to maintain the subordination of the military to the civilian, of the army to the party.

The Soviet areas depended for their very existence, however, on the skill of the military leaders and the latter were not unaware of their own importance. Japanese sources speak quite definitely of the existence of a "military faction" and a "party faction" within the Soviet areas.[5] While this division may oversimplify the complexity of the power relations within these areas, the writings of Mao Tse-tung prove beyond a doubt that such a conflict did exist. In his report on the Resolutions of the Ninth Conference of the Fourth Army held at

Chiht'ien in Fukien in February 1929, Mao speaks at some length of the "purely military point of view" within the Fourth Army, the army in which Mao himself held the position of commissar. Mao notes a tendency "to see a conflict between military affairs and political affairs, a failure to understand that military power is merely one tool designed to fulfill certain political tasks." [6] He complains of the tendency to say that "if military developments go well, political developments follow suit. If military developments do not go well, political developments do not go well . . . From this, it is just a step to saying that military affairs have priority over political affairs." [7] He further complains that "some comrades responsible for military affairs forget that they must accept party directives and report to the party . . . In the organizational sphere, they subordinate political organs to military organs." [8]

In the Edgar Snow account, Mao adds that the tendencies described above "were very serious and were utilized by a Trotskyist faction in the party and the military leadership to undermine the strength of the army." [9] Now, inasmuch as whatever Trotskyists existed in China at this time repudiated *in toto* the Soviet movement and all its works, it is difficult to see what particular stake they could have had in this conflict. It is thus probably safe to assume that we are dealing here with a conflict of power intertwined with a conflict of strategic policy rather than a conflict between Trotskyism and Stalinism.

Li Ang and other hostile sources enumerate long lists of military commanders eliminated by the Mao machine during the course of 1930 and 1931,[10] while both he and other sources speak of definite rivalries between Mao Tse-tung and certain top military leaders (P'eng Teh-huai in particular).[11]

Both official and nonofficial sources agree that as the Soviet movement grew in strength during the 1930–1931 period, all sorts of tensions developed within the Soviet areas. In the official sources we find constant references to such factions as the Trotskyists, the Anti-Bolshevik (A.B.) faction, Social Democrats, Li Li-sanists, etc. To what extent do these ideological labels represent realities? We are of course aware that it is part of standard procedure in the Communist tradition to attribute all opposition in the first instance to ideological errors and ultimately to the tainted class background of those involved in these errors. If a sheer conflict of power exists, the official account is not likely to mention it. It is not probable that all the conflicts within the Soviet areas were simply naked conflicts for power, but it is just as unlikely that they were all conflicts of an ideological nature fomented by landlords and rich peasants. The hostility of expropriated landlords and mistrustful peasants and the presence of Kuomintang agents undoubtedly played a role. We must also consider the tensions between Mao and his rivals for power, the tensions between the military and party authorities, and the tensions between the Central Committee and the Front Committee leaders.

Thus, if we consider the famous Fut'ien incident of December 1930 in the light of all the available sources, I think that we can discern the presence of a whole complex of elements. The Fut'ien incident was an affair of such gravity that, in the words of Mao, "to many it must have seemed that the fate of the revolution depended on the outcome of this struggle." [12]

According to Mao's account, the "Fut'ien incident was a manifestation of the Li Li-san line in the Soviet areas: "The Twentieth Army led by Liu Ti-ts'ao rose in open revolt, arrested the chairman of the Kiangsu Soviet, arrested many officers and officials, and attacked us politically on the basis of the Li Li-san line." [13]

We have, however, other more detailed versions of this incident. According to Hatano, certain Communist officials in south Kiangsi deeply resented Mao's imposition of members of his own personal machine as leaders of the Kiangsi Soviet government.[14] Tseng Shan, who according to Li Ang was the actual manager of Mao Tse-tung's machine within the party, had been selected chairman of the Kiangsi Soviet. Embittered by this imposition, a group of Kiangsi leaders including T'uan Liang-pi, Chin Wan-pang, and Li Po-fang formed a small anti-Mao faction. In opposing Mao they also opposed his policies. Thus, their opposition soon assumed an ideological coloration. According to Hatano's account, they raised these slogans: "Oppose the practice of dividing land on the basis of the possession of tools and labor power!" "Oppose the rich peasants!" "Divide the land equally!" "Oppose the capture of the government by landlords and rich peasants!" [15] To judge from the general tenor of these, it would appear that Mao's own agrarian policies were extremely moderate in nature. (It may well be, as has been suggested, that when Li Li-san was accused of undue moderation in his attitude to rich peasants he was actually being held responsible for the policies of Mao Tse-tung.)

Mao acted swiftly to meet this challenge. On December 7, 1930, he had some seventy members of the Kiangsi Soviet arrested. It would appear, however, that the anti-Maoist faction had sympathizers within P'eng Teh-huai's Third Army. Liu Ti-ts'ao, the Commander of the Twentieth Corps, was so incensed by this mass arrest that he led his unit of four hundred men in an attack on Fut'ien prison and managed to liberate Li Po-fang and some twenty other men. Li Po-fang immediately summoned a "people's conference" which called for the overthrow of Mao Tse-tung.[16] Some one hundred of Mao's supporters were killed. Mao soon managed, however, to dislodge Li and his followers from Fut'ien and forced them to flee to Yungyang in Kian county. Li Po-fang thereupon set up a rival provincial soviet in Kian. The revolt was finally quelled, however, at the cost of considerable bloodshed. Its leaders were arrested and liquidated.[17]

Ch'eng Sheng-ch'ang, in his "Fut'ien Incident and Internal Divisions in the Red Party," quotes the following version of the incident from a letter written by Wen Tse-tung, one of Li Po-fang's ardent supporters: "The Fut'ien incident was entirely a plot on the part of Mao Tse-tung to kill off the southwest Kiangsi leadership and to bring about his own personal counterrevolution." [18]

When we consider these various versions of the incident, I think it becomes possible to discern various crosscurrents of conflict. First of all, it becomes impossible, I think, to deny the presence of a hard core of naked political rivalry between the Mao machine and the southwest Kiangsi leadership. Secondly, the participation of a unit of P'eng Teh-huai's army in this incident suggests that the rivalry between the military and party leadership may also have been involved. In the Edgar Snow account, Mao specifically absolves P'eng of all implication in the incident.[19] Other sources have strongly suggested, however, that the relations between Mao and P'eng were not happy.[20] Wen Tse-tung's letter, cited above, implies that relations between Mao Tse-tung and the Central Committee were also involved. The Central Committee, according to this version, favored the southwest leadership. This might seem to lend color to Mao's own assertion that Fut'ien was essentially a conflict with Li Li-sanism. Actually, however, we know that, by December 1930, Li Li-san was no longer in control of the Central Committee. Finally, the slogans of the anti-Mao faction would suggest that a genuine difference of opinion on questions of agrarian policy was also involved. The anti-Mao faction seems to have adopted a much more radical approach on agrarian issues than the Mao leadership. Was this a manifestation of the "Li Li-san line"? As we have seen, the charges against Li Li-san had stressed both his leniency toward the rich peasants and his call for collectivization. The slogans mentioned above make no mention of collectivization and call for a severe policy toward the rich peasantry. It is interesting to note that the Fourth Plenum, which is supposed to have liquidated the errors of the Li Li-san line condemns Li for favoring the rich peasants and calls for a more vigorous policy against them.[21] Can we then assume that the Fut'ien incident was a manifestation of the Mif, Wang Ming line?

It is interesting to note that a document included in the official Stalinist publication *Soviety v Kitae* attributes the Fut'ien incident not to the Li Li-sanists but to the Anti-Bolshevik faction.[22]

The complexity of the elements involved in the Fut'ien incident lead one to suspect that the other sanguine conflicts mentioned in Soviet documents of this period were equally complex. The phrase "Anti-Bolshevik League" is used time and time again to describe the source of opposition to the Maoist leadership within the Soviet areas. While Li Ang's contention that no such organization existed may be an exaggeration,[23] it was certainly easy enough for the GPU within the Soviet areas to use this label to cover the most diverse sources of opposition.

Soviet documents also devote a great deal of attention to the activities of the "Third Party" and to Teng Yen-ta's "Social Democrats" in the Fukien Soviet area during 1930 and 1931.[24] We need not doubt that these non-Communist political groups did make some headway within the Soviet areas. At the same time, the glib assertions that these groups merely represented rich peasants or landlords should be treated with considerable skepticism. It is not at all unlikely that political rivalry and even regional jealousies played a larger role than the ideology of the Second International.

It is thus clear even from official sources that Mao Tse-tung did not achieve his position of preëminence in the Soviet areas without harsh and bloody conflict. We would also suggest that all attempts to view these conflicts as simple conflicts of ideology or "class conflicts" should be regarded with suspicion, that sheer political rivalry intertwined with conflicts on major questions of strategy played a decisive role, and that Mao Tse-tung was not able to impose his leadership without the aid of a party machine loyal to himself.

This view of Mao's rise to unchallenged preëminence within these areas may contrast with the general image of him as a man of compromise and conciliation. Mao's inclination to compromise with rather than destroy possible rivals for power has often been noted by foreign correspondents and others. Such has indeed been his general inclination since the establishment of the Provisional Soviet Government at the end of 1931. This may be due in no small measure, however, to the fact that Mao's major struggle to achieve a position of relative superiority within the Soviet areas took place *before* the end of 1931, and before foreign correspondents had begun to observe the movement. Having achieved a position of leadership, precarious though it might be, he chose to absorb potential rivals into the Soviet structure rather than to destroy them.

By the end of 1931, Mao's position of leadership within the Soviet areas was sufficiently strong to win him the position of chairman of the newly established Soviet Provisional Government.[25]

Victory Within the Communist Movement

It is not easy to find documentation dealing with the question of the relations of Mao Tse-tung and the other Soviet area leaders to the highest organs of party authority in Shanghai.

In attempting to ascertain their attitude, we must first of all bear in mind the fact that they regarded themselves as sincere Communists. As such, they could not take lightly the symbols of party authority and party hierarchy. Mao could not openly flout the authority of the Central Committee without further ado or openly contradict its directives. At the same time, his deep conviction that the peasantry could by itself provide the necessary driving force to effect a complete revolution in China, a conviction which he had expressed so crassly in his "Report on the Peasant Movement in Hunan" [26] and which he later learned to express with all the necessary Marxist-Leninist rationalizations, was not easily moved by shifts in Comintern line concerning this point. He himself informs us that after the Autumn Harvest uprising "I was dismissed from the Politburo and also from the party front committee. The Hunan committee also attacked us, calling us the 'rifle movement.' We nevertheless held our army together at Chingkanshan, feeling certain that we were following the correct line." [27] In other words, Mao was willing, at this point, to carry forward his movement in the very face of the Central Committee's disapproval. At the same time, he was probably much more comfortable when the Sixth Congress of the Comintern granted his movement a legitimate, albeit modest, place in the total Communist program.[28]

Whatever may have been his desire to see his activities "legitimized," however, evidence would indicate that from the very beginning of the experiment on Chingkanshan, he resented attempts on the part of the Central Committee to direct the Soviet movement from Shanghai or to sacrifice the movement for other ends.

As early as November 1928, in a Report from the Chingkanshan Front Committee, we find Mao lecturing the Central Committee in the following vein: "Henceforth, in issuing directives, we earnestly request that you study our reports and not simply rely on the one-sided reports of your inspectors. The report of inspector Tu Hsiuch'ing was completely erroneous in its point of view [e.g., in its implication that the Red militia could hold its border area base with two hundred more guns, its charges concerning the "conservatism" of the Red Army, etc.]. The Provincial Committee based its actions on this report and suffered failure. In issuing directives concerning military actions we beg you, by all means, not to be too dogmatic. The letters of the Central Committee must consider the conditions in which we are operating. It must leave us some room to maneuver." [29] The same report points again and again to conflicts between the Front Committee and the special representatives of the Central Committee. This document, couched as it is in the restrained language befitting a report to a higher organ, undoubtedly points to conflicts deeper than the official language suggests.

At the heart of the relations between the Soviet areas and the Central Committee, it seems to me, there lay a question of power closely related to a question of strategy. To what extent would the

Front Committee be master within its own domain? To what extent would the Soviet movement be allowed to develop along the lines of the strategy adopted by Mao and others and to what extent would it be used for ends lying outside itself? In discussing the policies of the Li Li-san leadership, we have already suggested that that leadership was determined to assert its power within the Soviet areas and to dominate any "Soviet government" which might emerge. It has also been pointed out that neither the Comintern line nor the policies of the Central Committee which were based on that line contemplated an autonomous and isolated development of the Soviet movement in the countryside. The Comintern line insisted on the contrary, that this movement be "coördinated" with the movement in the cities.[30]

How did Mao Tse-tung and the "Real Power Faction" react to this pressure? The evidence of his own writings would indicate that he resisted it with every means possible.

It is true that in the Edgar Snow account Mao states that, after the Sixth Congress, all disharmonies disappeared. "From that time on," he says, "differences between the leaders of the party and the leaders of the Soviet agrarian districts disappeared. Party harmony was reëstablished." [31] This is, of course, entirely in keeping with the orthodox school of history writing with its emphasis on harmonious continuous development. This statement does not prevent Mao, however, from attacking Li Li-san a few pages later even though Li Li-san was the leader of the party after the Sixth Congress.[32] It also does not prevent him from making the astonishing statement that "the Li Li-san line dominated the party then *outside the Soviet areas* and was sufficiently influential to force acceptance, *to some extent*, in the Red Army *against the judgment of its field command*" (emphasis my own).[33] Thus we learn that, at a time when the "Li Li-san line" was the line of the Central Committee, some time before Li had been driven from power, Li Li-san's policies were dominant only outside the Soviet areas, were accepted only to some extent in the Red Army, and were furthermore contrary to the judgment of the Army's field command! Mao is informing us here, in essence, that the policies of the Central Committee were largely being sabotaged within the Soviet areas.

The Politburo letter of June 11, it will be recalled, complains about the guerrilla concept of warfare prevalent within the Soviet areas, and calls upon the Soviet armies to consolidate all its military forces into a well-organized Red Army.[34] Mao Tse-tung informs us, however, that "the Red Army refused to immobilize its partisan groups and open up its rear to the enemy during these adventures" (the attack on Changsha).[35]

It would be an error, of course, to assume that the Central Committee was completely powerless within the Soviet areas. As has already been pointed out, it was difficult for the Front Committee openly to flout its directives. Furthermore, the Central Committee was able to take advantage of the factionalism existing within the areas themselves. We thus know that Chou En-lai, at this time Li Li-san's close ally and head of the department of military affairs, had connections within the Red Army with generals whom he had known since the early days at the Whampoa academy. Ch'en Tu-hsiu, in his "Statement of Our Views," refers to "Chou En-lai's Whampoa clique in the Soviet Areas," [36] while Hatano refers to Hsü Hsi-ch'en, Commander of the First Army, Chou I-chün, and others as close adherents of Chou En-lai within the Soviet areas.[37]

While factionalism in the Soviet areas may have had local causes it is not surprising that it soon came to involve the relations between the Soviet areas and the Central Committee. It would appear that disaffected elements within the Soviet areas attempted to strengthen their positions by leaning on the authority of the Central Committee and that the "delegates" of the Central Committee were particularly influential among such groups. Thus a Report on the Struggle for Soviets in Southern Kiangsi states that "under the banner of Li Li-sanist slogans" attempts were actually made in Kiangsi to found collectives on the basis of the Resolutions of the May Conference of Delegates from the Soviet Areas.[38] Another account states that in southwest Kiangsi, the "A.B. League" attempted to embarrass the Mao leadership by implementing Li Li-san's agrarian policies, opposing the redivision of land, and calling for the establishment of collectives.[39] Here again, whatever may have been the nature of the opposition group involved, the implication is clear that Mao Tse-tung himself was consciously flouting the agrarian policies adopted at the Conference of Delegates from the Soviet Areas.

The attack on Changsha is of course the most direct evidence of

Li Li-san's ability to carry out his will in the Soviet areas. Yet even here we are confronted with puzzling circumstances. It is known that Li Li-san's plans envisaged the attack on Changsha as one in a long series of attacks which would include assaults on Nanchang, Wuhan, and even Nanking. According to the document just mentioned, the "A.B. League . . . led the agitation for an attack on Nanchang" on the basis of Li Li-san's policy, thus again implying that the Mao leadership did not favor such an attack.[40] The order for an attack on Wuhan was simply ignored. According to Li Ang, Mao Tse-tung openly refused to commit the Red Army to an attack on Wuhan after the failure of Changsha.[41] Mao himself tells us that "this failure [Changsha] helped to destroy the Li Li-san line and saved the Red Army from what would have been a catastrophic attack on Wuhan which Li was demanding." [42] Since over a month elapsed between the attack on Changsha and the abandonment at the Third Plenum of the policy of attacks on large cities, it would appear that, in the intervening period, the Red Army simply ignored the Central Committee's directive to attack Wuhan.

The fact that the "Red Army refused to immobilize its partisan groups and open up its rear to the enemy during these adventures" [43] proves quite conclusively that the Front Committee refused to stake its existence on Li Li-san's policy in spite of Li Li-san's call for a total mobilization of forces in an all-out effort to capture the cities.

All this leads to the suspicion that the attack on Changsha may itself have involved considerations other than the directive of Li Li-san. It may well be that P'eng Teh-huai, who had once before undertaken an attack on Changsha,[44] was more favorably disposed toward Li Li-san's views on attacking cities than Mao Tse-tung. One hostile source hints that Mao Tse-tung was only too willing to have P'eng Teh-huai's forces engaged in this huge undertaking.[45] At least one Comintern source does indeed state that P'eng Teh-huai had not been adequately reinforced by other Red Army units. In an article entitled "The Red Army of the Chinese Revolution," Sinani states that "at the moment when P'eng Teh-huai was making his attack, the Fourth Corps was inactive although it could have rendered effective assistance at this juncture." [46] All sources agree that one positive result of the attack on Changsha was the capture of large stores of arms, ammunition, and supplies and the recruitment of "three thousand workers" for the Red Army.[47] Thus, from the point of view of the Soviet areas, the attack represented a net gain. It is therefore not inconceivable that the capture of these much needed supplies was itself a consideration in leading the Soviet area leaders to comply with Li Li-san's directives. Guerrilla attacks on small cities for the capture of supplies and recruitment of men were not unknown phenomena in the Soviet areas. Thus, in a report on the attack against the town of Kian carried out in October 1930, Ch'ü Ch'iu-pai complains that the attacking army confined itself to the "recruitment of new soldiers." [48]

Whatever may have been the case, however, Mao's own account as well as other sources all suggest that his general relations to the Li Li-san leadership are probably most succinctly described in the Chinese phrase used by Li Ang: "outward obedience — inner disobedience" (*Yang feng yin wei*).[49] He did not openly disobey the directives of the Central Committee, but he did everything possible to prevent the Committee from deflecting the Soviet movement from the main lines of the strategy which had been adopted on Chingkanshan.

The November 16 letter of the ECCI and the Resolutions of the Fourth Plenum mark, as has been pointed out, a victory for this strategy. As a result of the spectacular expansion of the Soviet areas during the course of 1930, the Kremlin had now adopted a policy of noninterference in the military affairs of the Soviet areas. The uneven development of the workers' and peasants' struggle was henceforth to be overcome by bringing the proletarian struggle abreast of the peasant struggle.

It has also been pointed out, however, that while the Soviet areas may have won a victory on the question of strategy, the question of power still remained. There is no ground for believing that the Kremlin intended to surrender supreme power in the Chinese Communist movement to Mao Tse-tung and the leaders of the Red Army. The new Central Committee, controlled by the loyal "Twenty-eight Bolsheviks," was to remain in Shanghai and to exercise supreme authority from there. While a Soviet government was to be established as soon as possible, there was every reason to assume that the relation of government organs to party organs would be based on the model of the Soviet Union.

The realities of the Chinese situation were, however, pointing in quite another direction. The contrast between the growing solidity of the actual power of the leaders in the Soviet areas and the growing hollowness of the titular power of the Central Committee in Shanghai was becoming so obvious that it was soon bound to affect the course of events.

While Li Li-san had been able to exert pressure within the Soviet areas, the young men of the new Central Committee had few connections within the area. Mao Tse-tung had little reason to respect the authority of these callow Bolsheviks. A fact of even greater importance, however, was the growing financial dependence of the Central Committee on the Soviet areas. As a result of the drastic decline in party membership and the loss of its urban mass basis, the party's sources of revenue had been greatly reduced. Edgar Snow reports that at the trial of the Noulens in 1932 it was revealed that the Soviet Union, at the time so deeply involved in domestic concerns, was allotting a total of some fifteen thousand dollars for all its activities in the Orient.[50] Li Ang adds that most of the funds supplied to China were earmarked for labor-union activities. The only other remaining source of funds was from the revenues of the Soviet areas. According to Li Ang, "most of the party's operating funds were supplied by the Soviet areas." [51]

Another debilitating factor was the recrudescence in 1931 of an active "white terror" campaign on the part of the national government. The growing strength of the Soviet movement had thoroughly aroused the fears of the national government, calling forth the first unsuccessful "extermination campaign" in November 1930 and the second in April 1931. On the assumption that the root of Communist authority lay in Shanghai, the government police began an active campaign in 1931 to ferret out Communists in Shanghai.

In the spring of 1931 Ku Shun-chang, the chief of Li Li-san's dreaded "special affairs unit" (GPU) who had managed to retain his position under the new leadership, had gone to Wuhan on a special mission (according to Li Ang he had gone for the purpose of obtaining funds from the Soviet areas) [52] and had been arrested there by the Kuomintang police. After his arrest he had voluntarily turned traitor and had been able to furnish the police with the addresses of most of the prominent Central Committee leaders. While most of them were warned in time, Hsiang Chung-fa, the "puppet" chairman of the Central Committee, was seized in his home and shot on June 21, 1931.[53] (After his death, Wang Ming, the real head of the Central Committee, also became titular head of the Committee.) [54] After this event, however, the Central Committee operated in an atmosphere of growing insecurity.

The First All-China Conference of the Soviets, finally called in the new Soviet area capital, Juichin, on November 7, 1931, for the purpose of establishing a "Provisional Central Government of the Chinese Soviet Republic," [55] cast a glaring light on the abyss which lay between the actual power of the government leaders in Juichin and the titular power of the Central Committee leaders. While all the Central Committee leaders won positions as members of the Central Executive Committee of the new government, they shared this honor with hosts of obscure party members. Real power remained concentrated in the hands of the Soviet area leaders.

The complete victory of the Mao-Chu leadership within the Chinese Communist movement can be said to have been achieved during the 1932–1933 period when the Central Committee was finally forced to move its headquarters from Shanghai to Juichin.[56]

According to the rather detailed account of Li Ang, this move was the direct result of pressure from within the Soviet areas. After the establishment of the Provisional Government, according to Li Ang, Mao felt himself in a position to assume control of the Chinese Communist movement as a whole. He accordingly decided to adopt the strategy of Ts'ao Ts'ao in his favorite Chinese novel, *The Romance of the Three Kingdoms*, the strategy "of capturing the Emperor in order to control the lords." [57] He sent a series of telegrams to the Central Committee urging it to transfer its headquarters to Juichin because of the danger of the "white terror" in Shanghai, because of the necessity of calling a Fifth Plenum of the Central Committee in which the Front Committee might participate, and because the Soviet government suffered from a lack of capable leading cadres.[58] Li Ang adds that the Central Committee showed little inclination to comply with these suggestions. After these polite suggestions had failed, Mao sent a telegram in which he implied that it might henceforth be impossible to supply funds from the Soviet areas because of the difficulties of communication.[59] This threat, Li Ang claims, combined with the growing insecurity of its position in Shanghai, finally forced the Central Committee to move to Juichin.[60] Other hostile sources support this account.[61] It is, of course, also possible that the "white terror" and the Central Committee's own sense of futility were themselves sufficient to force this move without the aid of pressure from within the Soviet areas. However, the fact that the Central Committee did not leave Shanghai until several months after the murder of Hsiang Chung-fa would suggest that some factor other than sheer terror was involved.

Whatever may have been the case, with its removal to Juichin the Central Committee became totally subordinated to the Soviet government leadership. Some of the "Twenty-eight Bolsheviks" — Shen Tse-min, Ch'in Pang-hsien, Chang Wen-t'ien, Yang Shang-k'un, and others — were, it is true, to win for themselves honorable positions within the Soviet government structure,[62] while Chou En-lai, who had had previous connections within the Soviet areas, again displayed his amazing powers of adjustment by becoming Commissar of Military Affairs.[63] All this was, of course, in entire keeping with Mao Tse-tung's tendency to absorb rather than eliminate rivals. It is significant, however, that Wang Ming, the erstwhile Chairman of the Central Committee, won no position for himself in the new government. Instead, he was sent back to Moscow as delegate to the Comintern.[64]

There are those who have maintained that Wang Ming continued to be a leading force in the Chinese Communist movement after his return to Moscow in 1932.[65] He had, after all, held what was presumably the highest post within the Communist hierarchy and his departure from that post had evidently not resulted from any loss of favor in Moscow. We find no evidence of laborious attempts to construct an "anti–Wang Ming line." Furthermore, after his return to Moscow he was to achieve a world-wide reputation in the international Communist movement as an interpreter of Chinese affairs and as one of the much publicized architects of the "United Front" policy at the Seventh Comintern Congress.[66]

Nevertheless, while Wang may never have lost the favor of Moscow, I would suggest that his return to Moscow was more in the nature of an exile from the sources of power in the Chinese Communist movement than a climb to new heights of power. Had not Ch'ü Ch'iu-pai also become a delegate to the Comintern after his loss of power in the Chinese Communist movement and had he not won fame in the Communist world as a Chinese "theorist"? It must again be emphasized that the power of the Chinese Communist leaders after 1931 did not derive solely from the mandate of Moscow, but was solidly based on the control of a military force, a territorial base, and a governmental apparatus. Wang had no access to this "real power" at the Hotel Lux in Moscow.

It would go beyond the scope of this book to consider the role actually played by Wang Ming in the formation of the "United Front" after 1935. I think that it is sufficient to point out, however, that since his return to China in 1938 he has held no position of consequence in the Chinese Communist movement. He is not even mentioned in the various speculations concerning Moscow's candidate for strong man behind the throne. On the contrary, his erstwhile bitter enemy, Li Li-san has figured most prominently in such speculation. There is thus every reason to assume that his return to Moscow in 1932 marked a real and lasting loss by him of power in the Chinese Communist movement.

What role, then, did Moscow play in establishing the Mao Tse-tung leadership? One cannot here speak in tones of dogmatic finality. Secret documents may exist in the archives of the Kremlin which prove conclusively that Moscow directly bestowed upon him the mantle of leadership.[67] On the basis of the documentation available to us, however, we cannot but conclude that Mao established his leadership within the Chinese Communist movement by dint of the real military, financial, and mass power which had been created by his own successful strategy; that the gravitation of power into the hands of Mao Tse-tung and Chu Teh was the result of circumstances and power relations existing within the Chinese Communist movement rather than of any decision made in Moscow. We have, indeed, attempted to demonstrate that it would have been most difficult for Moscow to take the initiative in granting the leadership of the movement to men who were quite satisfied to see Chinese Communism completely isolated from its supposed urban proletarian bases. We must therefore conclude that Moscow's recognition of the Mao Tse-tung leadership was essentially in the nature of an acquiescence to a *fait accompli.*

In the apt phrase of Li Ang, "Moscow itself had to buy 'face' through Mao Tse-tung." [68] The existence of a dynamic Soviet regime operating under a Stalinist banner was a propaganda asset which Moscow could not relinquish no matter what the ideological price.

By the time of the Fifth Plenum of the Central Committee, held in Juichin in 1933, the Maoist strategy had become the strategy of the Chinese Communist movement.

ESSENTIAL FEATURES OF
THE MAOIST STRATEGY

It is not the purpose of this book to treat the history of the Soviet period or of the New Democracy period which followed it. If I nevertheless presume to discuss the essential features of Maoism at this point it is because of my conviction that these features lie not in the sphere of theory but in the sphere of strategy and that the basic elements of this strategy were already formed by the time Mao Tsetung had achieved a position of leadership within the Chinese Communist movement. While this strategy does indeed have profound implications for Marxist-Leninist doctrine, they are implications which are never made explicit in theory. On the contrary, every effort is made in the theoretical sphere to conceal these implications.

The Maoist Strategy

Essentially, the Maoist strategy involves the imposition of a political party organized in accordance with Leninist principles and animated by faith in certain basic tenets of Marxism-Leninism onto a purely peasant mass base.

While this is the heart of the strategy, more specific features were evolved in the course of the experiences in Hunan during the 1926–1927 period and the experiences of the autumn harvest uprising. It can, however, be stated that the basic features are already present in a report written by Mao as early as 1928. In his Report of the Chingkanshan Front Committee to the Central Committee,[1] Mao enumerates the conditions necessary for the maintenance and development of "separate armed Soviet bases." The first condition is the existence of "a strong mass base." Although it is not specified, the mass base is, of course, to be a peasant mass base. These peasant masses are to be won by a program of land reform designed to satisfy the basic grievances of the bulk of the peasantry within the areas under Communist control. The second condition is the existence of a strong party, that is, of a party leadership organized along the lines prescribed by Lenin. The third is the existence of a strong Red Army for, in an environment in which military power was decisive, a Soviet base could survive only by possessing its own military force. The fourth condition is the control of a strategically located territorial base, and the fifth condition is that the area in question be self-sufficient enough to maintain its population. Remembering his experiences in the autumn harvest uprising, Mao lays particular stress on the possession of a "central, solid base" and repudiates charges of the Central Committee that the insistence on the maintenance of such a base is an expression of "conservatism." [2]

Another peculiar feature of the Maoist strategy already mentioned in the report is the preference for "border area" bases; that is, bases from which it would be possible "to influence both provinces." [3] "The Red Army must resolve to carry on its battles in border areas where it must have sufficient fortitude to carry on sustained warfare . . . If the Red Army is able to sustain itself in these border areas its reputation will spread throughout the surrounding countryside and even among the troops of the enemy. This will create a favorable atmosphere for its advance into the surrounding areas." [4]

Thus we see that the Maoist strategy was based not only on an insight into the revolutionary potentialities of the peasantry but also on the realization that in a country where centralized authority had been destroyed and only precariously reëstablished, state power was weakest in the vast swamplike countryside, in those areas furthest removed from centers of administrative and military power.

The main tasks of the Red Army within the context of this strategy were succinctly summarized by Mao in his interview with Edgar Snow. "The main tasks of the Red Army," he said, "were the recruiting of new troops, the Sovietization of new rural areas, and above all, the consolidation under thorough Soviet power of such areas as already had fallen to the Red Army." [5]

Such, I think, are the main lines of the strategy which, *in conjunction with favorable external circumstances*, was finally to lead the Chinese Communist movement to victory.

What, then, are the implications of this strategy for Marxist-Leninist dogma?

The Maoist Strategy and Marxist-Leninist Dogma

Officially, of course, there was no break whatsoever between the Comintern line, as fixed in the November 16 letter of the ECCI and in the Resolutions of the Fourth Plenum, and the theoretical line of the Chinese Communist movement during the whole Soviet period. Actually, however, the gravitation of power into the Soviet areas marked almost the total severance of the Chinese Communist party from its supposed urban proletarian base. It was the beginning of a heresy in act never made explicit in theory. Chinese Communism in its Maoist development demonstrates in fact that a communist party organized along Leninist lines and imbued with a sincere faith in certain basic Marxist-Leninist tenets can exist quite apart from any organic connection with the proletariat. The experience of Chinese Communism thus casts a doubt on the whole organic conception of the relation of party to class.

This is, however, a doubt which neither the Chinese Communist movement nor the Kremlin can tolerate, for it is a doubt which strikes at the very heart of the legitimization of power within the Leninist framework. The extraordinary and total power which the Communist Party arrogates to itself and the infallibility which it ascribes to itself are justified entirely on the ground that it is the head of a social organism the body of which is the proletariat, the class destined by history to inherit the earth as well as to grasp ultimate absolute truth. In the words of the Hungarian Communist theoretician, Lukacs, the activity of the Communist Party "is not an activity representing the class but the focalization of the activity of the class itself." [6] Elsewhere, he states that the Communists are "the class consciousness of the proletariat which has taken on visible form." [7] It has, however, always been considered a minimum guarantee of the identity of a communist party that it stand in some concrete relationship to a visible proletariat. Otherwise, it might easily lose its identity as a communist party. Most Communist literature suggests in fact, that the Communist Party is a peculiarly sensitive organ highly susceptible to infection from nonproletarian classes, even when its base is secure. The implication is clear that in isolation from the proletariat the Communist Party must lose its very identity.

If the ties between the Communist Party and its proletarian base are weak then it is the first and paramount duty of the party to strengthen these bonds lest the party lose its basis of existence. Nowhere in the whole body of Lenin's writings do we find a hint that the Communist Party can exist as an entity apart from its proletarian base.

We thus find that after 1931 it became one of the basic concerns of the Kremlin as well as of the Chinese Communist Party to conceal by every device possible the actual severance of the Chinese party from its proletarian base.

The process of devising such concealment devices had actually begun before Mao Tse-tung's final victory. While the Comintern and the Chinese leadership were straining every nerve to win back the urban proletariat, the "scissors" between the movement in the city and the movement in the country had of course become a fact long before the final victory of Mao. In his Report on the Third Plenum, Chou En-lai is forced to admit that the party has no more than two thousand proletarian members [8] (probably an exaggerated figure). Seizing upon this fact — and ignoring the intentions of the Comintern — Trotsky had as early as 1928 begun to flay the Comintern for the anomaly of supposedly Communist elements operating in a completely peasant environment in isolation from the urban proletariat.[9] In China, Ch'en Tu-hsiu had taken up the refrain. We have already seen how unhappy the Comintern and the Chinese leadership themselves had been about this state of affairs. They could not, however, allow Trotsky's accusation to go unanswered. Thus we find Manuilsky stating at the Sixteenth Congress of the Soviet Communist Party that "the third peculiarity [of the Chinese revolution] is that the Chinese revolution even before the final victory of the workers has at its disposal a Red Army. It is in possession of a considerable territory. At this very moment it is creating in this territory a Soviet system of workers' and peasants' power in whose government the Communists are in a majority. And this condition permits the proletariat to realize *not only an ideological but also a state hegemony over the peasantry*" (emphasis my own).[10] This phrase was to be repeated over and over again in subsequent Chinese Communist literature as a defense against the charge that the movement lacked a proletarian base.

What does this phrase mean in essence? It can only mean that since the leaders of the Soviet areas are convinced Communists, since the Soviet areas are under the control of the Communist Party, that is in itself a guarantee of proletarian hegemony. Trotsky answers this claim most incisively from the solid ground of orthodoxy. "In what way," he asks, "can the proletariat realize state hegemony over the peasantry when state power is not in its hands? It is absolutely impossible to understand this. The leading role of isolated Communist groups in the peasant war does not decide the question of power. *Classes decide and not parties*" (emphasis my own).[11] This is the very crux of the matter. Manuilsky's phrase assumes that a political group held together by common convictions and organized as a communist party can initiate fundamental historic changes. Such a proposition strikes at the heart of even the most "sophisticated" versions of Marxism-Leninism. Was this not one of the issues which had divided Marx from the utopian socialists? It was not simply that the utopian socialists thought that socialism could be implemented when objective conditions were not ripe for socialism, but also their belief that small groups of men with benevolent ideas could realize these ideas when actually only economic classes could act as the instruments of history. Neither Marx nor Lenin could in the nature of things deny that well-intentioned men of nonproletarian origin could become identified with the proletariat but both would have strenuously denied that they could become identified simply by an act of faith in the absence of any actual ties to the proletariat. To believe that the "vanguard of the proletariat" can exist without a main force in the rear is to grant political power a role in human history which Marxism-Leninism cannot allow.

Discussing this problem in her book *Inside Red China* Nym Wales remarks that "the Chinese Communists seem to consider their party itself equivalent to direct participation by the proletariat." [12] This, of course, is another version of the Manuilsky formula. Is the subjective conviction of the Chinese Communist leaders that they are the bona fide representatives of the proletariat sufficient proof in terms of Marxist-Leninist doctrine of the validity of their claim? How then are Communist subjective convictions to be weighed against those of Social Democrats or Syndicalists? To those standing outside the tradition, it may well seem that it is nothing more than such a subjective conviction (or pretense) which lies at the heart of the Communist faith everywhere. A Marxist-Leninist, however, cannot admit this. Theoretically, he must be able to show at least a minimum relationship between the Communist Party and the urban proletariat and must at all times make every effort to strengthen such relations.

Manuilsky's phrase is, however, not the only concealment device used to disguise the true state of affairs. Another common device is the equation of the "rural proletariat" with the proletariat proper. It has already been pointed out that while Lenin and Trotsky had advocated the absorption of the "rural poor" into the Communist Party, they had advocated it only on the condition that the "rural poor" be tied to a strong urban-based party. "Only the industrial proletariat," Lenin insisted, "led by the Communist Party, can liberate the toiling masses of the countryside from the yoke of capital." [13] The "rural proletariat" in isolation from the urban proletariat is essentially "petty bourgeois" in mentality, bitter against those with land but consumed by the desire to win for itself a foothold in landed property.

The constitution of the Soviet government drawn up at the All-China Soviet Conference in November 1931 contains an imposing series of labor laws, including ordinances regarding working hours, child and female labor, etc.[14] Many of these laws were obviously designed for the industrial proletariat. Under the conditions of the Soviet areas, they could only have a propaganda value by helping to create the impression of a proletarian base where none existed.

The Soviet government did indeed make strenuous efforts to establish labor unions based squarely on the "rural proletariat." In fact, most of the references to labor unions in the Soviet period refer to such unions. The peculiar difficulties which these unions confronted are graphically illustrated in a "Circular of the Standing Committee of the General Labor Federation" which appears in *Red Flag* of November 15, 1932.[15] The circular is essentially an attack on local union organizers who tend to set overstringent qualification requirements for union membership. Many of these organizers had formerly been organizers of industrial labor and were finding it most difficult in terms of their Marxist-Leninist precepts to classify large groups of the "rural poor" as bona fide proletarians. For one thing, many of these rural poor possessed their own tools, while one of the prime marks of the proletarian in the Marxist definition is his alienation from his means of production.[16] Furthermore, most of the rural proletarians worked on an individual basis now with one employer and now with another; in the view of the organizer, "independent laborers who sell their labor from house to house are not qualified to enter a labor union." [17] What was even more serious, the very land reforms effected by the Soviet government had served to "deproletarianize" many of the rural poor. The circular itself admits that 90 per cent of the workers in Hunan and Hupeh were landholding peasants who worked in their spare time.[18]

The Standing Committee of the General Labor Federation is not inclined, however, to lose its *raison d'être* without further ado. "To set such requirements for entry into labor unions," it complains, "is simply to liquidate labor unions in the Soviet areas." [19] The mere possession of tools should not disqualify a candidate since the tools are not being used by these men for their own enterprise but in order to perform work for others. (In the view of Marx, the possession of tools by a producer whose labor is exploited by others is actually characteristic of precapitalist modes of production.) While their work may be independent and allotted among several employers, it is still exploited by others. (In the view of Marx, all presocialist systems — except of course primitive Communism — are characterized by exploitation.) Finally, workers should not be debarred simply because they own a plot of land. The land will merely serve to measure their loyalty to the revolution! [20]

Now, while the labor-union form has been adopted throughout the world by occupations which are not strictly proletarian in the Marxist sense, in Chinese Communist literature the existence of labor unions in the Soviet areas is often cited as proof of the existence of a genuine proletariat in these areas. The factual data adduced in this "Circular" prove quite clearly that the rural workers with their fluid and nondescript economic status possessed few of those attributes which account for the revolutionary potentialities of the proletariat in the Marxist scheme.

Another device of concealment frequently used during the Soviet period was the constant emphasis on the "soviet" as a genuine proletarian political institution. After the abandonment of the soviet form in the "New Democracy" period, this earlier fetishism of the soviet was to prove a source of embarrassment. At the time, however, it was used as yet another proof of "proletarian hegemony" within the Soviet areas. The very fact, it was argued, that the Soviet government operated within the framework of the soviet was a visible sign of proletarian hegemony since the role played by that institution in the Soviet Union, the land of proletarian dictatorship, proved its fundamentally proletarian nature. "The very form of the soviet is a conquest of the Chinese proletariat" [21] states the introduction to the book *Soviets in China*. By focusing the history of the Chinese Communist movement on the institution of the soviet, it is possible to begin with the Canton Commune, an eminently proletarian phenomenon, and to pass imperceptibly as it were to the purely peasant soviets of the 1931–1935 period, thus casting a mist over the actual shift which has taken place. Thus we read in the introduction to *Soviets in China* that "the Soviet power in Canton in the December days of 1927, the Soviet republic in Hailufeng, the Soviets in Liling, and the victorious wave of the Soviet movement occupying the important provinces of south and central China were all organized and led by the Communists." [22]

Actually, of course, Lenin had not always thought of the soviets as an eminently proletarian institution. During the July days of 1917 he had even thought of abandoning the soviets. "The power can be seized henceforth," he declared, "only by armed insurrection. We must obviously rely in this operation not on soviets demoralized by compromisers but on factory committees." It was only after the Bolsheviks had won control of the soviets that they took on their sacred "proletarian" character. We know, however, that even after the revolution, Lenin had speculated on the possibility of applying the form of soviets to "backward" lands of Asia where the proletariat was presumed not to exist at all. [23] The soviet was a form, he felt, which could be adapted to the psychology of a backward peasant society. It is somewhat curious to note that, in his polemics against Trotsky at the Eighth Plenum of the ECCI, Stalin had used this passage from Lenin in a rather sophistical attempt to prove that China did not need soviets. "Lenin," he said, "did not have in mind countries like China and India where a certain minimum of industrial proletariat exists . . . He rather had in mind other backward countries like Persia." [24] It is thus clear that there is no warrant in Communist tradition for considering the soviet form itself a proof of "proletarian hegemony." After the abandonment of the soviet form, of course, the Chinese Communists themselves were to bend every effort to prove that the soviet form was not a necessary vehicle of proletarian hegemony.

One of the most effective devices of all, from the point of view of its appeal to the emotions, is the use of Lenin's own polemical tactic of offense rather than defense. The Trotskyists, Social Democrats, and others who were raising embarrassing questions concerning the Chinese Communist Party's lack of a proletarian base did this, it was maintained, only in order to deliver China over to the bourgeoisie "because they wish to create a rift between the world proletariat and the Chinese proletariat. They wish to hide from the European proletarian the heroic history of the struggle of the Chinese proletariat for hegemony in the national movement of liberation." [25]

Now, however sinister the motives of the Trotskyists and Social Democrats might be, the question they raised still remained unanswered. The fact that the Chinese Communist Party carried on a truly heroic struggle against overwhelming odds in the hinterlands of Hunan and Kiangsi, and later in the northwest areas, might prove its heroic qualities of leadership. It does not, however, prove that the party had an urban proletarian base.

We thus find that the hard fact of the isolation of the Chinese Communist Party from the urban proletariat during all the years of its rise to power emerges, naked and irreducible, from behind all the devices of concealment used to hide it.

At present, of course, the Chinese Communist Party can once more claim a proletarian base. It is once more in contact with the urban industrial proletariat. Yet, the very circumstances under which the Communists finally achieved power throw a glaring light on the lack of relationship between the urban proletariat and the Chinese Communist Party. The Chinese urban proletariat — whatever its sympathies may have been — waited inertly and passively for the peasant troops to occupy the cities. It certainly played a much less active role than the students.

The fact that the Chinese Communist Party has existed for some twenty years without any significant connections with the industrial proletariat, and the fact that the industrial proletariat played no actual role in the consummation of the revolution, are circumstances which cannot be erased by the belated reunion of head and body. It has already been demonstrated that a communist party can exist quite apart from any real connection with the urban proletariat.

If the concealment devices used by the Kremlin and the Chinese Communists cannot bear scrutiny, what can be said of the Trotskyist interpretation of the development of Chinese Communism? There can be no doubt that from the point of view of Marxist-Leninist orthodoxy the Trotskyist position is unimpeachable. By severing itself from its urban proletarian base and tying itself to the peasantry, the Chinese Communist Party has ceased to be a party of the proletariat, for a political party can have no autonomous life of its own. In the words of Isaacs, "the Communist Party tried to substitute itself for the proletariat as a class. In the process, however, it was transformed into a peasant party." [26]

To what extent, however, does this allegation correspond to fact? Did the Chinese Communist Party indeed become a party of the peasants in the sense in which that word is used by Trotsky, Isaacs, and Ch'en Tu-hsiu? Such a view, I think, falsifies realities no less than the camouflage of the official line. There is no evidence that the aspirations and ambitions of the Communist Party leaders were at any time circumscribed by what Marxist-Leninists consider to be the peasant mentality or that they at any time aspired to achieve the "peasant socialism" advocated by the Russian *narodniki* who were considered the very archetype of the peasant party.

I would suggest that Chinese Communism in its Maoist development can simply not be understood within the narrow framework of Marxist-Leninist premises; that both the official and the Trotskyist interpretations obscure rather than illuminate the nature of the movement since 1931. The Chinese Communist Party under the leadership of Mao Tse-tung has not been the party of the industrial proletariat nor has it been the party of the peasantry in the Marxist-Leninist sense. It has rather been an elite corps of politically articulate leaders organized along Leninist lines but drawn on its top levels from various strata of Chinese society. In her study of the background of seventy Chinese Communist leaders in the New Democracy period, Nym Wales finds that only seventeen per cent are proletarians. This percentage is probably obtained by stretching the meaning of the word "proletarian" well beyond its legitimate Marxist limits. She finds, however, that seventy per cent are *hsüeh-sheng* or "students from families of small farmers, professionals, merchants, and even aristocratic official families." [27] Under the leadership of Mao Tse-tung this elite group had come to realize in the face of Marxist-Leninist dogma that the peasantry could itself provide the mass basis and the motive power for a revolutionary transformation. This realization may owe much to the peasant background of such leaders as Mao Tse-tung. It would, however, be a grave error to assume that once having achieved power, the aspirations or intentions of the Communist leaders would necessarily be determined by their peasant background or by the interests of the peasantry. On the contrary, we have every reason to believe that these men had thoroughly absorbed the Leninist abhorrence of "backwardness" as well as the extravagant Marxist-Leninist belief in the potentialities of industrialization even when circumstances forced them to lurk in the hinterlands. Chinese Communism in its Maoist development can only be understood when — to modify Trotsky's phrase — we realize that parties *as well as* classes decide. The Chinese Communist Party under the leadership of Mao Tse-tung has been, I would suggest, neither "the vanguard of the proletariat" in the Marxist-Leninist sense, nor a "peasant party" in the Marxist-Leninist sense, but an elite of professional revolutionaries which has risen to power by basing itself on the dynamic of peasant discontent.

The Maoist Strategy and the Party Line

We have chosen to draw a distinction between vital core presuppositions of Marxism-Leninism and the transient superficial elements of the shifting party lines. It has been suggested that the Maoist strategy represents a heresy in act toward one such vital presupposition. We should now like to consider briefly the relations of this strategy to the shifting party lines after 1931.

The shift of the center of power from Shanghai to Juichin was not accompanied by any change in party line on the part of the Kremlin. On the contrary, the Kremlin was most concerned to obscure the change which had taken place. Everything was done to maintain the appearance of a smooth continuity. On the other hand, the Mao leadership seemed quite content to pursue its strategy within the framework of the theoretical line formulated at the Fourth Plenum. We find little evidence at this time of any ambition on the part of Mao to create theoretical innovations within the Marxist-Leninist tradition.

The result was, of course, an utter lack of relation between theory and practice. Presumably, the political form of the bourgeois democratic revolution during the whole Soviet period was still the "democratic dictatorship of workers and peasants." We have already noted that this formula had already lost a great deal of its relevance as early as 1928 when it was decided that the proletariat — that is, the Communist Party — would exercise exclusive political hegemony within the dictatorship and that the peasantry would not be represented by a political party of its own.[28] With the establishment of the Soviet Provisional Government, the formula became completely meaningless. We have in the Soviet Republic a "democratic dictatorship of workers and peasants" in which the peasantry is allowed no political expression of its own and in which the party of the proletariat has no mass basis of its own.

While it would go beyond the scope of this book to consider the party line of the New Democracy period, it should nevertheless be pointed out that the shift to the New Democracy line involved no change in the basic Maoist strategy outlined above. I would suggest that the actual strategic shifts made in 1935 were more in the nature of shifts in "foreign policy" than shifts in basic strategy. At no time during the New Democracy period do we find any inclination on the part of the Yenan leadership to renounce its territorial base, its actual control of its own armed forces, or its tendency to infiltrate "border areas." The changes in agrarian policy do not contradict this contention for it has nowhere been implied that a fixed agrarian policy was a basic feature of the Maoist strategy. The change from the "soviet" to the "assembly" with its allotment of representation to other parties is overridden by the basic fact that fundamental decisions of policy were made by neither the "soviets" nor the "assemblies" but by the Communist Party itself. The fact that the New Democracy period is marked by a statesmanlike regard for local initiative and by a marked decline in the use of force as an instrument of policy represents a refinement in strategy rather than a basic modification of it.

While the New Democracy period marks no change in the basic Maoist strategy, it does, however, add many new and significant features. As a result of its role in the war against Japan, the Chinese Communist Party was finally able to harness nationalist sentiment to its own cause. The period also marks a profound change in the psychology of the Communist leadership which may itself spring in no small measure from nationalist sentiment. Having taken the initiative in the field of strategy in the early thirties, having exercised actual state power during the Soviet period, and having led the movement through the vicissitudes of the Long March, Mao was now sufficiently self-confident to take the initiative in the field of theoretical formulation. He was no longer content to explain his strategy in terms of the general theory of the "United Front" as promulgated in Moscow, but was intent on proving that developments in China represented a unique and original development in the course of human history and that he himself was a theoretical innovator in the line of Marx, Lenin, and Stalin. It is here, I think, that we must seek the unique significance of the whole "New Democracy" theory. For a time, at least, Mao Tse-tung has received Moscow's acquiescence in this also.

Abiding Elements of Marxism-Leninism

How far can a historic movement, based on certain beliefs, drift from basic original premises and still maintain its identity? This is, of course, one of the most perplexing questions in the history of human thought. To some extent this may be a question of semantics, for our ultimate judgment may depend in no small measure on our evaluation of the relative importance of various premises of the movement at its beginnings. What, for instance, are the essential premises of early Marxism? To what extent is Lenin still a true Marxist? To what extent is Stalin a good Marxist-Leninist? To what extent has Mao Tse-tung been a faithful Stalinist? Our answers to each of these questions will depend, of course, on where we seek the crucial elements of Marxism-Leninism-Stalinism respectively. The general view underlying this study is that the general trend of Marxism in its Leninist form has been toward disintegration and not toward "enrichment" and "deepening" as its orthodox adherents would have us believe. Thus we would maintain that the Maoist heresy *in action* on the matter of the relations of party to class represents yet another major step in this process of disintegration. In spite of this movement toward disintegration, however, we would nevertheless maintain that other core elements of Marxisn -Leninism still remain integral living elements of Chinese Communism.

In the first place, we must not overlook the abiding conviction of the Chinese Communists themselves that they are unswerving Marxist-Leninists. Just as Lenin had thought of himself as a monolithic Marxist, so are the Chinese Communists convinced that they are monolithic Marxist-Leninists. Such a subjective conviction is no guarantee against heresy in action, but is a historic force which must be considered in its own right, for the feeling of solidarity of belief is a force which must not be underestimated. At the same time, however, whether such solidarity of belief is as important in the long run as certain factors working in an opposite direction, is open to doubt.

Second, all evidence would indicate that the basic Hegelian faith which underlies and animates Marxism-Leninism, has been thoroughly assimilated by the Chinese Communists — the Hegelian-Marxist faith in a redemptive historic process and the Leninist faith that the Communist Party is itself the sole agent of historic redemption. Chinese Communist literature is genuinely imbued with this faith, however doubtful may be the party's credentials as the party of the proletariat. However immersed they may have been in a peasant environment, the leaders of the party never for a moment doubted that they were the chosen instruments of History, destined to lead China on the road to an industrialized socialism. While the concept "socialism" has undergone strange transformations since Stalin chose to proclaim its existence in the Soviet Union, and while it may yet undergo even stranger metamorphoses in China, this faith has definitely precluded the possibility of the party becoming "a peasant party" and wedded it — for good or ill — to the ideal of the industrialized power state. It also undoubtedly sustained the party's spirits during its darker days.

Third, as has been stated, the party is the agent of historic redemption; thus, the Leninist theory and practice of party organization has remained a hard unchanging core in the midst of change. The basic Leninist formula of a tightly organized elite which strives toward power by identifying itself with the dynamism engendered by the immediate needs and discontents of the masses [29] has, without a doubt, played a large role in accounting for the success of Chinese Communism. The experience of China has simply demonstrated that a mass basis can be provided by the peasantry and other strata of society, and that the industrial proletariat need play no role in this formula.

Fourth, totalitarianism is a tendency inherent in the Leninist conception of the party. As the sole agent of a unified historic process, the party must be the ultimate arbiter in every sphere of human life. This tendency inherent in Marxism-Leninism has, of course, been reinforced to the ultimate degree by the concrete example of the Soviet Union itself. A reading of the writings of Mao Tse-tung and of "The Documents on the Correction of Tendencies" would suggest, I think, that this totalitarian tendency is part of the vital core of Chinese Communism inhibited only by the force of external circumstances and softened until recently by the party's sparing use of force. This is true in spite of the fact that the Chinese Communist Party has not yet claimed to have attained socialism. By stressing "the hegemony of the proletariat" even in this presocialist era, it is able to preserve for itself the right of ultimate decision in every sphere of human experience. Thus, Mao Tse-tung's own writings on literature demonstrate the extent to which he has arrogated to himself the position of arbiter in that sphere. Totalitarianism will, I think, be inhibited in a Communist China only by limits imposed by external circumstances.

Finally, the Leninist doctrine of imperialism, which so strongly attracted the founders of the Chinese Communist Party in the days of the May Fourth movement, still plays a vital role in Chinese Communism. It has been suggested at the beginning of this study that it was this element above all which first seemed to give Marxism-Leninism its burning relevance to the situation in which the Chinese intelligentsia found itself involved. Quite apart from the truth or falsehood of Lenin's interpretation of imperialism, the fact that he *had* a theory of imperialism (derived largely, to be sure, from others), and the fact that he turned his attention to the hatreds and resentments aroused by nineteenth- and twentieth-century western imperialism, and had included them as a factor in his calculations, differentiated him sharply from both the liberals and the Marxists of the West who continued in their complacent belief that all the central problems of mankind would be solved in the West and by the West. This political insight may itself have been more a function of his Russian background than of his Marxism; it may itself have reflected his own ambiguous relationship to what he regarded as the smug self-centered West. Whatever the case, however, this political insight made it possible for him to establish a rapport with the politically articulate intelligentsia of Asia. The Leninist theory of imperialism thus became the binding link between Marxism-Leninism and Asiatic resentments. So widespread has been the acceptance of the Leninist theory of imperialism in China, for instance, even in circles far removed from the Communist Party, that wherever imperialism was discussed the Leninist interpretation came to be taken for granted.

Whether living experience will ever teach the Chinese Communists to doubt the Leninist theory that imperialism is a phenomenon peculiar to a certain stage of "capitalism" is a question which only the future and their own interests can decide.

In sum, then, while Chinese Communism did conclusively demonstrate *in fact* the utter lack of any necessary, organic relation between Communist parties and the industrial proletariat, the movement still retains certain fundamental elements of Marxist-Leninist tradition.

A CHRONOLOGY OF KEY EVENTS, 1918–1933

The following is based on the chronology compiled by Mr. K. C. Chao for the forthcoming volume, *A Documentary History of Chinese Communism*, by Brandt, Fairbank, and Schwartz.

1918   Spring: Marxist study groups formed in Peking University under the leadership of Professor Li Ta-chao.

1919   March 2–6: Communist International organized and First World Congress held in Moscow.

         May 4: May Fourth Movement begins.

1920   Spring: Voitinsky arrives in China. A Chinese Communist Youth Corps branch formed in France.

         July 19–August 7: Second World Congress of the Communist International held in Moscow and Petrograd.

1921   June 22–July 12: Third Congress of the Communist International, Moscow.

         July 1: First National Congress of the Chinese Communist Party held at Shanghai and Chiaing (Kashing); party formally established.

1922   January 12: Hong Kong seamen's strike begins; successfully concluded March 5.

         May 1–6: First Congress of the All-China Labor Federation at Canton, attended by some 170 delegates from more than 100 unions.

         May–July: Second Congress, CCP, convenes at Canton.

         August: Special Plenum of the Central Committee meets at Hangchow.

         November 5–December 5: Fourth World Congress of the Communist International calls for a Kuomintang-Communist alliance.

1923   January 26: Sun Yat-sen and A. Joffe issue Joint Manifesto in Shanghai.

         February 7: Peking-Hankow Railway workers' strike, partly led by the CCP; scores of workers killed by soldiers of Wu P'ei-fu.

         June: Third Congress, CCP, at Canton with about twenty delegates; manifesto issued resolving to coöperate with the Kuomintang.

September: Michael Borodin arrives at Canton on invitation of Sun Yat-sen.

1924　January 20: First Congress of the Kuomintang held at Canton.

May: Whampoa Military Academy founded with Chiang Kai-shek as President.

1925　January: Fourth Congress of the CCP held at Canton (some sources say Shanghai).

May 30: May 30 Movement begins when concession police at Shanghai under command of a British sergeant fire on demonstrators, killing thirteen.

Summer: Mao Tse-tung and others begin to organize peasant movement in Hunan.

Sun Yat-sen University founded in Moscow with Radek as president and Pavel Mif as vice president; a number of young Communists are sent from China as students.

1926　March 20: Chiang Kai-shek's coup against the CCP at Canton. A resolution of the Executive Committee of the Kuomintang of May 15, 1926, bars Communists from top posts in Kuomintang organizations.

July: The Northern Expedition begins.

November: National Government moves from Canton to Wuhan.

November 29–December 16: Seventh Enlarged Plenum of the Executive Committee of the Communist International, Moscow, discusses new strategy in China.

1927　April 5: Ch'en Tu-hsiu and Wang Ching-wei issue a joint declaration at Shanghai favoring continued Kuomintang-Communist collaboration.

April 12: Anti-Communist coup launched by Chiang Kai-shek. Leftist organizations are disbanded in Shanghai and Nanking and thousands of Communists and leftists are executed.

April 27–early May: Fifth National Congress of the CCP, Hankow.

April 28: Li Ta-chao and other CCP leaders executed in Peking by Chang Tso-lin. USSR Embassy in Peking raided.

May 20–26: Eighth Plenum of the Executive Committee of the Communist International held at Moscow. Stalin defends his line on China against Trotsky's attacks.

July 13: CCP orders members to withdraw from Wuhan Government (but not from the Kuomintang).

August 1: Nanchang Uprising led by Yeh T'ing and Ho Lung (who joins the CCP after the insurrection); Chu Teh and Chou En-lai also participate.

August 7: Emergency Conference of the CCP. Ch'en Tu-hsiu, whose policy is condemned as opportunistic, is replaced by Ch'ü Ch'iu-pai as Secretary-General of the CCP.

September 5–18: Autumn Harvest Insurrection in Hunan. After its failure Mao is reprimanded by the Central Committee but continues to organize the peasant movement.

September 25: Yeh T'ing and Ho Lung, joined by Chou En-lai and T'an P'ing Shan, occupy Swatow for a week.

October 4: First Chinese Soviets organized by P'eng Pai at Hai-lu-feng, Kwangtung. Last until February 28, 1928.

November 10–14: The "November Plenum" held at Hankow.

December 11–14: Insurrection in Canton, commonly known as the Canton Commune.

1928　February 9–25: Ninth Plenum of the Executive Committee of the Communist International, held at Moscow, announces a new line on China.

May: Mao Tse-tung and Chu Teh join forces at Chingkanshan.

July–September: Sixth National Congress of the CCP held in Moscow.

The Sixth World Congress of the Communist International convenes during the same period.

1929　June: The Second Plenum of the Central Committee of the CCP meets in Shanghai.

November 15: Ch'en Tu-hsiu and other oppositionists dismissed from the CCP.

1930　May: Conference of Delegates from the Soviet Areas meets in or near Shanghai.

May: Ch'en Shao-yü (alias Wang Ming) and the "Returned Students" return from Moscow to China; Mif also comes to China as Comintern representative.

August–September: Third Plenum of the Central Committee of the CCP convenes in Lushan.

November 16: Letter from the Comintern to the CCP condemns the Li Li-san line.

November 25: Li Li-san resigns from the Political Bureau.

December: The Fu-t'ien Incident.

1931   January 8: Fourth Plenum of the Central Committee of the CCP convenes in Shanghai and formally abandons the Li Li-san line.

February 7: Ho Meng-hsiung and twenty-two others executed by the Kuomintang in Shanghai.

June 21: Hsiang Chung-fa, Secretary-General of the CCP, is arrested and executed by the Kuomintang in Shanghai.

June: Ch'en Shao-yü (Wang Ming) elected acting Secretary-General.

November 7: First All-China Congress of the Soviets convenes at Juichin.

The Chinese Soviet Republic is established with Mao Tse-tung as Chairman.

1932   February: Chinese Soviet Republic declares war on Japan and calls on all groups and classes in China to resist Japanese aggression.

October 15: Ch'en Tu-hsiu, P'eng Shu-chih, and other Communist oppositionists are arrested by the Kuomintang in Shanghai and sentenced to imprisonment.

Autumn: Ch'en Shao-yü (Wang Ming), Chang Wen-t'ien, Ch'in Pang-hsien, Liu Shao-ch'i, and other members of the Central Committee proceed to Juichin, Kiangsi. Ch'in Pang-hsien succeeds Ch'en Shao-yü as Secretary-General of the CCP and Ch'en leaves for the Soviet Union as Chinese delegate to the Comintern.

NOTES · BIBLIOGRAPHY

NOTES

I. *The Origins of Marxism-Leninism in China*

1. Names such as Blüntschli and Samuel Smiles appear almost as frequently as those of greater figures. The Japanese who were responsible for introducing the Chinese intelligentsia to many of the thinkers of the West were, in the beginning, quite undiscriminating in their choice of works to be translated.

2. Karl Marx is already mentioned in Ch'en Tu-hsiu's article, "Fa-lan-hsi yü chin-tai wen-ming" (France and Modern Civilization), *Hsin ch'ing-nien*, vol. I, no. 4 (1915), p. 2. His name occurs in the following passage: "In the nineteenth century this doctrine [socialism] was revived by Saint-Simon and Fourier. They advocated that the state or society be the sole proprietor. Several years later the Germans, Lassalle and Marx, developed and expanded their doctrine . . . although the system of private property has not been abolished, the wealthy classes and those in political power have begun to doubt whether excessive contrasts of wealth and poverty are in the interests of society, and are now attempting to bring about harmony between capital and labor to protect labor and limit monopoly." In other words, the merit of Marx and the other socialists lay in the fact that they had helped to make the leaders of industry more socially conscious.

3. Ch'en Tu-hsiu specifically states in reply to a correspondent who advocates socialism that socialism is not at all applicable to an unindustrialized country like China. See T'ung-hsin (Correspondence), *Hsin ch'ing-nien*, vol. II, no. 5 (December 1916).

4. Even Plekhanov, who stood well to the left within the Marxist movement, states in his *Fundamental Problems of Marxism* (New York, 1928), p. 106, "that at the present moment history is preparing in the most advanced countries a revolutionary change of altogether exceptional importance and one which, we may presume, will be achieved by force . . . That is how the historic movement is proceeding, not here in Russia but in the West."

5. Karl Marx, *A Contribution to the Critique of Political Economy* (Chicago, 1904), preface, p. 12.

6. Among Marx's scattered references to this question is the following passage concerning the effects of the discovery of gold in California, which occurs in an article in the *Neue Rheinische Revue*: "Californian gold is pouring in streams over America and over the Asiatic coast of the Pacific, sweeping the unwilling barbarian peoples into the orbit of world trade, into the province of civilization."

7. See Benjamin Schwartz, "Biographical Sketch, Ch'en Tu-hsiu, Pre-

Communist Phase," *Papers on China* (Harvard University, 1948), II, 168.

8. See *ibid.*, p. 193, n. 5.

9. *Ibid.*, p. 195, n. 12.

10. *Ibid.*, p. 196, n. 16.

11. Born in Hopei Province in 1888, he studied political economy at the Peiyang School of Legal Administration. He later studied at Waseda University in Japan, specializing in political economy. Upon his return to China he became librarian at the Peking University library. (In 1918 Mao Tse-tung was one of his library employees.) In 1920 he became Professor of History at Peking University. During these years he helped Ch'en Tu-hsiu and Hu-Shih to edit the *Hsin ch'ing-nien*, and also helped the student body to edit the *Hsin Ch'ao* (Renaissance) review. In the late months of 1920 he collaborated with Ch'en Tu-hsiu in founding the Chinese Communist Party and was later considered the virtual leader of the Communist Party in the northern provinces. In April 1927 he was arrested in the Soviet Embassy at Peking by Chang Tso-lin's troops and summarily executed. He has been venerated ever since as one of the outstanding martyrs of the Chinese Communist movement.

12. Ch'ü Yuan. A minister of the King of Ch'ü (332–295 B.C.), he was the very prototype of the loyal minister. However, as a result of intrigues at court he was impeached and exiled. In a long elegy entitled *Li Sao*, he pours forth his disenchanted views on human destiny and the nature of the cosmos.

13. *Hsin ch'ing-nien*, vol. II, no. 1 (September 1916).

14. *Hsin ch'ing-nien*, vol. IV, no. 4 (April 1918).

15. "Ch'ing-ch'un" (Youth), *Hsin ch'ing-nien*, vol. II, no. 1.

16. *Ibid.*, p. 3.

17. "Ch'ing-ch'un," p. 3.

18. *Idem.*

19. "Chin" (Now), *Hsin ch'ing-nien*, vol. IV, no. 4, p. 307.

20. *Ibid.*, p. 308.

21. Emerson is specifically quoted in many places.

22. "Ch'ing-ch'un" (Youth), *Hsin ch'ing-nien*, vol. IV, no. 4, p. 6.

23. "Shih-hsing min-chih ti chi-ch'u" (Basis for the Realization of Democracy), *Hsin ch'ing-nien*, vol. I, p. 14.

24. See the article, "Tui-te wai-chiao" (Our Policy Toward Germany), *Hsin ch'ing-nien*, vol. III, no. 1 (1917).

25. "Bolshevism ti sheng-li" (Victory of Bolshevism), *Hsin ch'ing-nien*, vol. V, no. 5 (1918). The same issue also carries an article by him entitled "Shu-min ti sheng-li" (Victory of the Masses), which is on the same theme.

26. "Bolshevism ti-sheng-li," p. 443.

27. *Ibid.*, p. 447.

28. "Shu-min ti sheng-li."

29. "K'o-lin-te p'ai" (The Von Ketteler Monument), *Hsin ch'ing-nien*, vol. V, no. 5.

30. *Ibid.*, p. 458.

31. Chinese interest in Russia had manifested itself at a rather early date. Lin Shu, the famous nineteenth-century translator, had already translated Tolstoy into classical Chinese, while the great reformer K'ang Yu-wei had been fascinated by the personality of Peter the Great. Tretiakov, in his *T'an Shih-hua, a Chinese Testament*, gives a vivid account of the hold of Russian literature on many young Chinese of the early years of the twentieth century, while the pages of the *Hsin ch'ing-nien* abound in translations from Turgenev, Tolstoy, and others. This particular fascination was undoubtedly due to certain similarities in the situation of China and Russia. The Chinese intelligentsia, like the Russian intelligentsia, was alienated from the peasant masses and their traditional patterns of life so that many of the psychological conflicts portrayed in Russian literature had for them a most overwhelming immediacy. Moreover, both countries suffered from a multitude of similar political ills. It was thus inevitable that any major political transformation in Russia, whatever its nature, would be studied with intense interest by the intellectually and politically articulate in China.

32. Ch'en Tuan-chih in his *Wu-ssu yün-tung-shih ti p'ing-chia* (An Evaluation of the May Fourth Movement), relates that after the Russian Revolution the archconservative Progressive Party (Chinputang) began to speak in terms of socialism in its attacks on the warlords.

33. Sun Yat-sen had developed an elitist view of government in his theory of political tutelage some time before the Russian Revolution. "The Chinese," he asserted, "having been under tyrannical rule for centuries, are deeply afflicted with a servile mentality which does not admit of an immediate cure. The period of political tutelage is to purge their minds of such antiquated degenerate thoughts." In this period of tutelage the counterparts of Lenin's "professional revolutionaries" are those whom Sun calls the "foreknowers" who initiate and invent. He cites as examples of these the mythical Emperor Yü who dredged the nine rivers, and Shih Huang-ti who built the Great Wall. In the light of these views, there can be no doubt that he watched Lenin's political techniques with rapt attention even before his meeting with the Russian representatives in 1923. Lenin's conceptions of party discipline and his formula of an elitist revolution brought about on a basis of mass support seemed to supply the very elements lacking in his own conception. It would, therefore, not be wrong to assert that he understood Leninism as a method of political organization before either Ch'en Tu-hsiu or Li Ta-chao did. According to Wang Ching-wei, Sun Yat-sen had sent Lenin a message of congratulations immediately following the success of the October Revolution. See Yasushi Okubo, *Chūkyō Sanjūnen* (Thirty Years of Chinese Communism) (Tokyo, 1949), p. 31.

34. Hatano Kanichi, *Saikin Shina Nenkan* (New China Yearbook) (Tokyo, 1935), p. 1597.

35. "Wo ti Ma-k'o-ssü-chu-i kuan" (My Views on Marxism), *Hsin ch'ing-nien,* vol. VI, no. 5, p. 521.

36. In his "Hsüeh-sheng-chieh ying-kai p'ai-su ti Jih-huo" (Japanese Goods Which Our Student Circles Ought to Boycott), *Hsin ch'ing-nien,* vol. VII, no. 2 (January 1920). Ch'en Tu-hsiu specifically rebukes the nationalistic students for their excessive chauvinism. "Chinese scholars in ancient times and our old-fashioned peasants only knew of the world and the universe and did not understand what a nation was. Now, however, we have a group of half-baked people who preen themselves on their modern learning and who are constantly prating about the 'nation' and 'patriotism.' Some of our students who are returning from Japan are also bringing back this shallow, selfish type of nationalism. At the present time when the cry is being raised in student circles to boycott Japanese goods, ought not our students to boycott this spiritual importation from Japan as well . . . an importation which is even more harmful?"

37. For an account of Bertrand Russell's impressions of China see his *Problems of China.* Many of the advance-guard intelligentsia in China were exasperated by what they regarded as his perverse tendency to find values in traditional Chinese civilization.

38. An impressionistic account of John Dewey's stay in Peking can be found in his *Letters from China and Japan* (New York, 1921). While at Peking he delivered the following lectures: (1) Social Philosophy and Political Philosophy; (2) Philosophy of Education; (3) Ways of Thought; (4) Three Philosophers of Our Times (Bergson, Russell, James); (5) On Ethics.

39. "Shih-hsing min-chih ti chi-ch'u" (The Basis For the Realization of Democracy), *Hsin ch'ing-nien,* vol. VII, no. 1, p. 15.

40. *Ibid.,* p. 17.

41. *Ibid.,* p. 17.

42. Quoted by David Shub, *Lenin, A Biography* (New York, 1948), p. 144.

43. See his *Imperialism, the Highest Stage of Capitalism* (New York, 1939).

44. It would be impossible to overestimate the impression produced in China by Karakhan's proposal. The *Hsin ch'ing-nien* issue of May 1920 (vol. VII, no. 6) carries a translation of the proposal, as well as a large collection of expressions of approval received from various organized groups throughout China; see "Tui-yü Ngo-lo-ssü Lao-nung cheng-fu t'ung-kao ti yü-lun (Expressions of Public Opinion on the Proclamation of the Russian Government of Workers and Peasants). Among the organizations represented are: "The All-China Journalists Union," "The All-China Student Federation," "Deputies of the National Assembly," "The Commercial National Salvation Association," etc. In this proclama-

tion Karakhan states, "We shall not merely aid the workers, but also wish to aid the people of China . . . Every nation whether large or small should have complete autonomy. We proclaim that all secret treaties made before the revolution with China, Japan, or the allies are hereby abrogated." He then specifically enumerates the treaties to be abrogated, all of which are prejudicial to Chinese sovereignty. "We hereby renounce all territory obtained through aggressive means by the former Russian imperial government in China, Manchuria, and elsewhere . . . In short, we hereby renounce all special privileges formerly obtained by Russia in China . . . If the Chinese people as a result of our proposals wish to become a free people and escape the evil fate of becoming a second India and Korea as has been planned for her at the Paris Peace Conference, we fervently hope that the Chinese people will make common cause with the peasants, workers, and Red soldiers of the Soviet Union and fight for their freedom!" The statements from the various organizations are replete with the most fervid expressions of gratitude and all of them, regardless of political coloration, profess to see in this act of the Soviet Union the beginning of a new era.

45. "Sui-kan-lu" (Random Thoughts), "Ko-ming yü tso-luan" (Revolution and Rebellion), *Hsin ch'ing-nien*, vol. VIII, no. 4 (December 1920), p. 3.

46. "Sui-kan-lu" (Random Thoughts), "Kuo-chi-p'ai yü shih-chieh ho-p'ing" (The Extremists and World Peace), *Hsin ch'ing-nien*, vol. VII, no. 1, pp. 115–116.

47. "Wu-chih pien-tung yü tao-te pien-tung" (Material Change and Ethical Change), *Hsin ch'ao* (Renaissance), vol. II, no. 2 (December 1919). The *Hsin ch'ao* review was a short-lived but extremely influential periodical published by a group of students at Peking University. (Its editor at the height of the May Fourth movement was Fu Ssu-nien.)

48. *Ibid.*, p. 207.

49. "Wei-wu shih-kuan tsai-hsien tai li-shih-hsüeh-sheng ti-chia-chih" (The Value of the Theory of Historic Materialism in Modern Historical Science), *Hsin ch'ing-nien*, vol. VIII, no. 4.

50. The *Hsin ch'ing-nien* issue of May 1920 is devoted almost exclusively to a symposium on labor. It carries an article by Li Ta-chao on the history of the May First celebration ("Wu-i yün-tung-shih") and a speech by Ch'en Tu-hsiu entitled "Lao-tung-che ti chüeh-wu" (The Awakening of the Laborer), in which he calls upon labor to realize its own importance in society and to prepare itself to take control of society. The influence of Leninism is thus quite apparent.

51. See *Chieh-fang yü kai-tsao* (The Emancipation and Reconstruction Semimonthly), vol. V, no. 2 (March 1920).

52. See his article, "Wu-chih sheng-huo-shang kai-tsao ti fang-chen" (Program for Reconstructing Our Material Life), *Chieh-fang yü kai-tsao*, vol. II, no. 1 (January 1920). Also "Ching-shen sheng-huo ti kai-tsao" (Reconstruction of Our Spiritual Life), *ibid.*, no. 7 (April 1920).

53. See Edgar Snow's *Red Star Over China* (New York, 1938), p. 151. It would also appear that Mao Tse-tung was at this time very much influenced by the widespread movement for provincial federalism. The "Hsin-min Hsüeh-hui" (New People's Study Society) of Hunan, which he had been active in organizing and leading, had as one of its programmatic aims the "independence" of Hunan. Li Ang in his *Hung-se Wu-t'ai* (Red Stage) states that even as late as 1921, Mao was still a fervent Hunanese patriot and was fond of comparing Hunan's role in China to Prussia's role in Germany.

54. Mao himself acknowledges the decisive influence of Li Ta-chao and Ch'en Tu-hsiu on p. 157 of Edgar Snow's *Red Star Over China* where he states, "Under Li Ta-chao as assistant librarian at Peking National University I had rapidly developed towards Marxism and Ch'en Tu-hsiu had been instrumental in my interests in that direction too . . . Ch'en's own assertions of belief had deeply impressed me at what was probably a critical period of my life."

55. Mao Tse-tung states in his official biography as related to Edgar Snow, "From this time [1920] on I became more and more convinced that only mass political power, secured through mass action, could guarantee the realization of dynamic reforms." Mao omits to mention here only one vital element in the Leninist formula for political action, namely, that the mass action be led by a highly disciplined party elite.

II. *The Founding of the Party*

1. "Tui-yü shih-chü ti wo-kuan" (My Views on the Current Situation), *Hsin ch'ing-nien*, vol. VIII, no. 1 (September 1920), p. 2.

2. "Kuan-yü she-hui chu-i ti t'ao lun" (A Discussion Concerning Socialism), *Hsin ch'ing-nien*, vol. VIII, no. 4 (December 1920), p. 1.

3. *Ibid.*, p. 8.

4. *Ibid.*, p. 4.

5. "Kuo-ch'ing chi-nien ti chia-chih" (The Value of Celebrating the Founding of the Republic), *Hsin ch'ing-nien*, vol. VIII, no. 3 (November 1920).

6. "Tui-yü shih-chü ti wo-kuan," p. 3.

7. Lenin, W. "Demokratie und Narodniktum in China," *Ausgewählte Werke* (Berlin, 1937), IV, 321.

8. Lenine, V. "Thèses sur les questions nationales et coloniales," *Oeuvres complètes* (Paris, 1935), XXV, 342.

9. *Ibid.*, "Rapport de la commission nationale et coloniale," p. 421.

10. *Ibid.*, "Thèses sur les questions nationales et coloniales," p. 342.

11. Fang Lu, "Ch'ing-suan Ch'en Tu-hsiu" ("Liquidating" Ch'en Tu-hsiu), from *Ch'en Tu-hsiu P'ing-lun* (Discussions Concerning Ch'en Tu-hsiu) (Peiping, 1933), p. 66.

12. "She-hui ti kung-yeh chi yü liang-hsin ti hsüeh-che" (Society's In-

dustry and Learned Men with a Conscience), "Sui-kuan-lu" (Random Thoughts), *Hsin ch'ing-nien*, vol. VIII, no. 3 (November 1920), p. 1.

13. Fang Lu, *op. cit.*, p. 66.

14. "Chung-kuo Kung-ch'an-tang chien-ming-shih" (A Short History of the Chinese Communist Party), from the *Su-lien Yin-mou Wen-cheng Hui-pien* (A Collection of Documents on the Soviet Conspiracy), vol. II, fasc. 1, p. 4. These are the documents confiscated by Chang Tso-lin in his raid on the Soviet Embassy in 1927. While it has often been charged that all these documents are forgeries, a close examination of some of them does not confirm this impression. Where it has been possible to check the account of the "Short History" with other accounts, it has proven accurate in every instance.

15. Hatano Kanichi, *Saikin Shina Nenkan* (New China Yearbook), p. 1598.

16. The issues of *Reconstruction* of the years 1919–1920 contain a number of essays on Marxism by both Tai Chi-t'ao and Hu Han-min. We have here the origins of that unique phenomenon of conservative Marxism which is one of the peculiar features of modern Chinese and Japanese thought. Hu Han-min's "Criticism of Criticisms of the Materialist View of History" of November 1919 is a more thorough treatment of the subject than anything we can find in the writings of either Li Ta-chao or Ch'en Tu-hsiu, while his "Study of Chinese History from the Materialist Point of View" of October 1919 is a pioneer attempt to find precedents for Marxism-Leninism in Chinese traditional thought.

17. "Tao Ch'en Ching-ts'un lun-ko-ming ti hsin" (Letter to Ch'en Ching-ts'un on the Question of Revolution), *Chien-she*, vol. II, no. 1 (February 1920), p. 179.

18. See Tai Chi-t'ao, "Tsung ching-chi-shang kuan-ch'a Chung-kuo ti luan-yuan" (The Causes of China's Disorder Viewed from an Economic Point of View), *Chien-she*, vol. I, no. 2 (September 1919), p. 355.

19. Hatano, p. 1598.

20. "T'an cheng-chih" (Speaking of Politics), *Hsin ch'ing-nien*, vol. VIII, no. 1 (September 1920), p. 1.

21. "Chung-kuo-shih ti wu-cheng-fu-chu-i" (A Chinese Brand of Anarchism), *Tu-hsiu Wen-ts'un* (The Works of Ch'en Tu-hsiu) (Shanghai, 1922), II, 118.

22. Snow, *Red Star Over China*, p. 155.

23. Hatano Kanichi, *Ajia Mondai Kōza* (Lectures on Problems of Asia) (Tokyo, 1935), II, 23–24.

24. *Ibid.*, p. 24. Hatano lists the names of Ch'en Kung-po, Pao Hui-seng, Li Han-chün, Li Ta, Chang Kuo-t'ao, Liu Jen-ching, Tung Pi-wu, Ch'en T'an-chiu, Mao Tse-tung, Ho Shu-heng, Chou Fu-hai, Wang Chin-wei, and Teng Yen-ming. In France a party branch was being formed almost simultaneously by Chou En-lai, Ts'ai Ho-shen, and Li Li-san.

25. "Chung-kuo Kung-ch'an-tung chien-ming-shih" (A Short History of the Chinese Communist Party), p. 6.

26. Hatano, *Saikin Shina Nenkan* (New China Yearbook), p. 1598.

27. Teng Chung-hsia, *Chung-kuo Chih-kung Yün-tung Chien-shih* (A Short History of the Chinese Labor Movement) (Yenan, 1943), p. 19.

28. *Ibid.*, p. 46.

III. *Prelude to Collaboration*

1. Hatano, *Saikin Shina Nenkan*, p. 1600.

2. *The Fourth Congress of the Communist Internationale* (London, 1922), p. 221.

3. *Ibid.*, p. 222.

4. See article of Vilensky in *Izvestiya* of October 9, 1920; quoted in Pasvolsky's *Russia in the Far East* (New York, 1922), p. 87.

5. On the interview between Marin and Sun see Okubo Yasushi, *Chūkyō Sanjūnen* (Thirty Years of Chinese Communism), p. 31.

6. Fang Lu, "Ch'ing-suan Ch'en Tu-hsiu," *Ch'en Tu-hsiu P'ing-lun* (Discussions Concerning Ch'en Tu-hsiu), p. 68.

7. "Ti erh-tz'ü ch'uan-kuo tai-piao ta-hui hsüan-yen" (Manifesto of the Second Congress), quoted in Chu Hsin-fan, *Chung-kuo Ko-ming yü Chung-kuo She-hui Ko Chieh-chi* (The Chinese Revolution and China's Social Classes) (Shanghai, 1930), p. 260.

8. *Declaration of the Chinese Communist Party on the Political Situation in China*, translated by Steiner from *Novyi Vostok*, no. 2 (1922), p. 6.

9. *Ibid.*, p. 6.

10. Chu Hsin-fan, p. 278.

11. Ch'en Tu-hsiu, *Kao Ch'üan-tang T'ung-chih-shu* (A Letter to Our Party Comrades), Hoover Library, Chinese Collection, p. 4.

12. *Ibid.*, p. 3.

13. *Ibid.*, p. 4.

14. Hatano, in the compilation by Obikawa Tsunetada, *Shina Seiji Soshiki no Kenkyū* (Tokyo, 1933), p. 88.

15. Since the beginning of the New Democracy period of Chinese Communism there has been an amazing lack of literature on the history of the party's early years.

16. Hua Kang, *Chung-kuo Ta Ko-ming-shih* (History of the Great Chinese Revolution) (Shanghai, 1932), p. 447.

17. "Ch'en Tu-hsiu ti sheng-p'ing chi cheng-chih chu-chang" (Ch'en Tu-hsiu's Life and Political Views), *Ch'en Tu-hsiu P'ing-lun* (Discussions Concerning Ch'en Tu-hsiu), p. 175.

18. "Chin-jih Chung-kuo chih cheng-chih wen-t'i" (China's Present Political Problems), *Hsin ch'ing-nien*, vol. V, no. 2 (July 1918), p. 3.

19. "Shih-hsing min-chih ti chi-ch'ü" (The Basis for the Realization of Democracy), *Hsin ch'ing-nien,* vol. VII, no. 1, p. 15.

20. "Hsin-hai ko-ming yü kuo-min-tang" (The Revolution of 1911 and the Kuomintang), from *Chung-kuo Ko-ming Wen-t'i Lun-wen-chi* (A Collection of Articles on the Problems of the Chinese Revolution) (Shanghai, 1927), p. 271.

21. *Declaration of the Chinese Communist Party on the Political Situation in China,* p. 4.

22. Very few of the major classics of Marxism-Leninism had as yet been translated into Chinese.

23. Lenine, "Discours sur l'adhesion des Communistes au Labour Party," *Oeuvres Complètes,* XXV, 432.

24. Leon Trotsky, *Problems of the Chinese Revolution* (New York, 1932), p. 52.

25. *Ibid.,* p. 52.

26. Ch'en Tu-hsiu, *Kao Ch'uan-tang T'ung-chih-shu* (Letter to Our Comrades), p. 3.

27. To one who does not accept Marxist-Leninist premises, it must seem doubtful whether the Kuomintang was ever simply the superstructure of an economic class or group of economic classes. During the course of its history, Communists have glibly identified the Kuomintang as: (1) a coalition of bourgeoisie, petty bourgeoisie, peasantry and workers; (2) a coalition of petty bourgeoisie, peasants, and workers; (3) the party of the bourgeoisie (Trotsky, Ch'en Tu-hsiu); (4) a coalition of petty bourgeoisie and feudal classes; (5) again a coalition of bourgeoisie, peasantry, petty bourgeoisie, and workers (New Democracy); (6) a coalition of bureaucrat capitalists and feudal elements. During all these shifts of "class analysis" the personnel of the leading circles of the party have remained remarkably stable. There have been, of course, complex and manifold relationships between the officialdom of the Kuomintang and various economic strata of the country. Thus, there can be no doubt that Chiang Kai-shek had established close relations with the bankers and industrialists of Shanghai at the time of the 1927 *coup d'état.* This, however, does not prove that he was a "representative of the bourgeoisie" any more than his previous attempt to harness the mass movement to his ambitions proved that he represented the peasants or proletariat. Viewed in the light of Chinese history, a history in which political power has itself often constituted a real source of economic power and social status, it would probably be more relevant to think of the Kuomintang with all its factions as a socio-political factor in its own right. I would suggest that in China, at least, the bureaucrat and the militarist must be viewed as primary and not secondary social categories.

28. Okubo, *Chūkyō Sanjūnen* (Thirty Years of Chinese Communism), p. 25.

IV. Collaboration

1. *The Fourth Congress of the Communist Internationale*, p. 222.

2. Teng Chung-hsia, *Chung-kuo Chih-kung Yün-tung Chien-shih* (Short History of the Chinese Labor Movement), p. 115.

3. Ts'ai Ho-shen, "Lun Ch'en Tu-hsiu-chu-i" (Concerning Ch'en Tu-hsiuism), from *Ch'en Tu-hsiu P'ing-lun* (Discussions Concerning Ch'en Tu-hsiu), p. 14.

4. "Chung-kuo Kung-ch'an-tang chien-ming-shih" (A Short History of the Chinese Communist Party), p. 15.

5. "Chung-kuo kuo-min ko-ming yü she-hui ko-chieh-chi" (The Chinese National Revolution and the Various Classes of Chinese Society), from the *Chung-kuo Ko-ming Wen-t'i Lun-wen-chi* (A Collection of Articles on Problems of the Chinese Revolution), p. 45.

6. *Ibid.*, pp. 45–46.

7. Ts'ai Ho-shen, p. 16.

8. Li Li-san, *Kung-ch'an Kuo-chi tui Chung-kuo Ko-ming Chüeh-i-an Tai hsü* (A Preface to Comintern Resolutions on the Chinese Revolution), p. 10.

9. *Kao Ch'üan-tang t'ung-chih-shu* (A Letter to Our Party Comrades), p. 7.

10. "Chūgoku Kyōsantō dai-san-kai zenkoku daihyō-taikai" (The Manifesto of the Third Congress of the Chinese Communist Party), from Okubo, *Chūkyō Sanjūnen* (Thirty Years of Chinese Communism), p. 26.

11. *T'an-ho Kung-ch'an-tang Liang Ta-yao-an* (Two Proposals for the Impeachment of the Communist Party), subtitled *Chung-kuo Kuo-min-tang, yüan-wen chi Tsung-li chih p'i-shih* (The Nationalist Party of China; Original Text and Notes of Generalissimo Sun) (Shanghai, 1923), p. 1.

12. "Kokumintō-ni-zentaikai ni-okeru Ōseiei no seiji hōkoku" (Wang Ching-wei's Political Report at the Second Congress of the Kuomintang), Okubo, *op. cit.*, p. 41.

13. *T'an-ho Kung-ch'an-tang Liang Ta-yao-an* (Two Proposals for the Impeachment of the Communist Party).

14. *Ibid.*, p. 15.

15. Even Mao Tse-tung admits in his autobiography as related to Edgar Snow that he had not realized the degree of class struggle among the peasantry until after the May Thirtieth incident. See *Red Star Over China*, p. 160.

16. See Teng Chung-hsia, *Chung-kuo Chih-kung Yün-tung Chien-shih* (Short History of the Chinese Labor Movement), pp. 137–278.

17. "Chung-kuo Kung-ch'an-tang ti-erh-tz'u Chung-yang k'uo-ta chih-hsing wei-yuan-hui i-chüeh-an" (Resolutions of the Second Enlarged Plenum of the Central Executive Committee of the Chinese Communist Party), from the *Su-lien Yin-mou Wen-cheng Hui-pien* (A Collection of Documents of the Soviet Conspiracy), IV, 52.

18. Mandalian, *Wei-shen-mo Chung-kuo Kung-ch'an-tang ti Ling-tao P'o-ch'an* (Why Did the Leadership of the Chinese Communist Party Fail?), translated from the Russian *Pochemu Obankrotilos Rukoved'stvo Kitaiskoi Kompartii* (Moscow, 1927), p. 9.

19. Trotsky, *Problems of the Chinese Revolution*, p. 43.

20. The best known of these pamphlets is his *Sun-wen-chu-i chih Che-hsüeh ti Chi-ch'u* (The Philosophic Foundations of Sun Yat-senism) (Shanghai, 1925).

21. *Kao Ch'üan-tang T'ung-chih-shu* (A Letter to our Party Comrades), p. 9.

22. Mandalian, p. 8. Also Pavel Mif, *Chin-chi Shih-chi-chung ti Chung-kuo Kung-ch'an-tang* (The Chinese Communist Party in Critical Days), translated from the Russian (Moscow, 1928), p. 25.

23. *Kao Ch'üan-tang T'ung-chih-shu* (A Letter to Our Party Comrades), p. 11.

24. "Lun Ch'en Tu-hsiu-chu-i" (Concerning Ch'en Tu-hsiuism), p. 21.

25. Li Li-san, *Kung-ch'an Kuo-chi Tui Chung-kuo Ko-ming Chüeh-i-an Tai-hsü* (A Preface to Comintern Resolutions on the Chinese Revolution), p. 20.

26. "Kei Chiang Chieh-shih ti i-feng-hsin" (A Letter to Chiang Kai-shek), *Hsiang-tao Chou-pao* (Guide Weekly), no. 151 (June 9, 1926).

27. Harold Isaacs, *Tragedy of the Chinese Revolution* (London, 1938), p. 110.

28. See note 25.

29. "Lun kuo-min cheng-fu chih pei-fa" (Concerning the Northern Expedition of the National Government), *Hsiang-tao Chou-pao* (Guide Weekly), no. 160 (June 30, 1926).

30. "Wo-men ti pei-fa-kuan" (Our Views on the Northern Expedition), *Hsiang-tao Chou-pao*, no. 170 (August 10, 1926).

31. "Theses on the Chinese Situation," *International Press Correspondence* (Inprecorr), vol. VII, no. 11, p. 232.

32. *Ibid.*, p. 231.

33. *Ibid.*, p. 231.

34. *Wei Shen-mo Chung-kuo Kung-Ch'an-tang ti Ling-tao P'o-ch'an?* (Why Did the Leadership of the Chinese Communist Party Fail?), p. 9.

35. *Kao Ch'üan-tang T'ung-chih-shu* (A Letter to Our Party Comrades), p. 13.

36. *Ibid.*, p. 15.

37. *Ibid.*, p. 15.

38. Mandalian, p. 12.

39. "Lun Ch'en Tu-hsiu-chu-i" (Concerning Ch'en Tu-hsiuism), p. 37. Li Ang, a former Communist, has written a detailed account of internal political relations among the leaders of the Chinese Communist movement. The book, entitled *Hung-se Wu-t'ai* (The Red Stage), is bitterly anti-Stalinist and its judgments must be treated with caution. It does,

however, contain detailed information regarding aspects of Chinese Communist history untreated elsewhere. Where it has been possible to compare Li Ang's factual account with other sources, it has generally proven accurate.

40. Shinshi Teiichiro, "Kushūhakuden" (The life of Ch'ü Ch'iu-pai), *Kaizō*, vol. XVIII, no. 8 (August 1936), p. 34.

41. P'eng Shu-chih, "Shui shih Chung-kuo Kuo-min ko-ming chih ling-tao-che?" (Who Are the Leaders of the Chinese National Revolution?), from the *Chung-kuo Ko-ming Wen t'i Lun-wen-chi* (A Collection of Articles on Problems of the Chinese Revolution), p. 29.

42. P'eng Shu-chih, "Chung-kuo ko-ming chih ken-pen wen-t'i" (Basic Problems of the Chinese Revolution), quoted in Ch'ü Ch'iu-pai's *Chung-kuo Ko-ming Chih Cheng-lun Wen-t'i* (Controversial Questions of the Chinese Revolution) (Shanghai, 1927), p. 67.

43. "Shui shih Chung-kuo kuo-min ko-ming chih ling-tao-che?" (Who Are the Leaders?), p. 28.

44. "Chung-kuo ko-ming chih ken-pen wen-t'i" (Basic Problems of the Chinese Revolution), p. 77.

45. "Tu-che chih sheng" (The Reader's Voice), *Hsiang-tao chou-pao* (Guide Weekly), no. 160 (June 30, 1926).

46. Mandalian, p. 12.

47. Ch'ü Ch'iu-pai, *Chung-kuo Ko-ming chih Cheng-lun Wen-t'i* (Controversial Problems of the Chinese Revolution), p. 149.

48. Mif, p. 35.

49. N. Bukharin, "An Abrupt Turn in the Chinese Revolution," *Inprecorr*, vol. VII, no. 41 (July 14, 1927), p. 894.

50. "Theses on the Chinese Situation at the Seventh Plenum of the Executive Committee of the Communist Internationale," *Inprecorr*, vol. VII, no. 11 (February 3, 1927), p. 231.

51. Ch'en Tu-hsiu, "Chung-kuo kuo-min ko-ming yü she-hui ko-chieh-chi" (The Chinese National Revolution and the Various Classes of Chinese Society), p. 41.

52. *Ibid.*, p. 41.

53. P'eng Pai, the son of a Kwangtung landlord had begun organizing peasants in the Haifeng area as early as 1921. An account of his experiences can be found in *International Literature*, nos. 2–3 (Moscow, 1932).

54. Snow, *Red Star Over China*, p. 160.

55. At the Fifth Congress of the Chinese Communist Party held on April 17, 1927, Hsü Chien, a left Kuomintang leader, had suggested that, since the Communist Party represented the proletariat, the Kuomintang should be accorded the exclusive right to represent the peasantry. See Mif, p. 22.

56. "Chung-kuo Kung-ch'an-tang ti-erh-tz'u Chung-yang k'uo-ta chih-hsing wei-yüan-hui chüeh-i-an" (Resolutions of the Second Enlarged Plenum of the Central Executive Committee of the Chinese Communist

Party), from the *Su-lien Yin-mou Wen-cheng Hui-pien* (A Collection of Documents on the Soviet Conspiracy), IV, 50.

57. "Theses on the Chinese Situation," *Inprecorr*, vol. VII, no. 11, p. 232.

58. Resolutions of the Second Enlarged Plenum, p. 50.

59. T'an P'ing-shan had participated in the deliberations of the Seventh Plenum of the ECCI and even delivered one of its key addresses. See *Inprecorr*, vol. VII, no. 4, p. 83 (January 12, 1927).

60. The contents of this letter are summarized in Ch'en Tu-hsiu's *Kao Ch'üan-tang T'ung-chih-shu* (A Letter to Our Party Comrades), p. 12. See the discussion of this letter in Isaacs, *Tragedy of the Chinese Revolution* (London, 1938), p. 294.

61. *Kao Ch'üan-tang T'ung-chih-shu* (Letter to Our Party Comrades), p. 10.

62. For a further discussion of this point see the beginning of the next chapter.

63. *Chin-chi Shih-chi-chung ti Chung-kuo Kung-ch'an-tang* (The Chinese Communist Party in Critical Days), p. 22.

64. See Li Ang, *Hung-se Wu-t'ai* (The Red Stage), p. 16.

65. *Chung-kuo Ko-ming Cheng-lun Wen-t'i* (Shanghai, 1927), p. 16.

66. *Chung-kuo Ko-ming chih Ken-pen Wen-t'i*. The original text is not available. Many passages, however, are quoted in Ch'ü's pamphlet.

67. Ch'ü Ch'iu-pai, *Chung-kuo Ko-ming Cheng-lun Wen-t'i* (Controversial Questions of the Chinese Revolution), pp. 84 and 87.

68. *Ibid.*, p. 67.

69. *Ibid.*, p. 98.

70. *Ibid.*, p. 106.

71. *Ibid.*, p. 74.

72. *Ibid.*, p. 86.

73. *Ibid.*, p. 86.

74. *Ibid.*, p. 87.

75. *Hung-se Wu-t'ai* (The Red Stage), pp. 16–17.

76. See Bertram Wolfe, *Three Who Made a Revolution* (New York, 1948), pp. 288–291; also Trotsky, *The Permanent Revolution* (New York, 1931), and Trotsky, *Stalin* (London, 1947), Appendix p. 432.

77. From Trotsky's "Do Devyatago Yanvarya" (Before the Ninth of January), quoted by Wolfe, p. 290.

78. *Ibid.*, p. 290.

79. Mif, *Chin-chi Shih-chi-chung ti Chung-kuo Kung-ch'an-tang* (The Chinese Communist Party in Critical Days), p. 22.

80. Mao Tse-tung, "Hu-nan nung-min yün-tung kao-ch'a pao-kao" (A Report on an Investigation of the Agrarian Movement in Hunan), *Hsiang-tao chou-pao* (Guide Weekly), no. 191 (March 20, 1927). The passages quoted in the text are from the *Mao Tse-tung Hsüan-chi* (Selected Works of Mao Tse-tung) (1948), p. 19.

81. Snow, *Red Star Over China*, p. 160.

82. *Ibid.*, pp. 160–161.

83. "Hunan nung-min yün-tung kao-ch'a pao-kao" (A Report on an Investigation of the Agrarian Movement in Hunan) from *Mao Tse-tung Hsüan-chi* (Selected Works of Mao-Tse-tung), p. 19.

84. *Ibid.*, p. 22.

85. *Ibid.*, p. 25.

86. *Ibid.*, p. 24.

87. Lenin, *The Year 1919* in *Works*, XVI, 442; quoted in Trotsky, *The Third Internationale after Lenin* (New York, 1936), p. 226.

88. Snow, *Red Star Over China*, p. 162.

89. "Hunan nung-min yün-tung kao-ch'a pao-kao" (A Report on the Investigation of the Agrarian Movement in Hunan), p. 24.

90. *Chung-kuo Ko-ming Cheng-lun Wen-t'i* (Controversial Questions of the Chinese Revolution), p. 117.

V. *An Appraisal of Key Trends*

1. Quoted from Stalin's speech of April 5, 1927, in Isaacs' *The Tragedy of the Chinese Revolution*, p. 185.

2. *Ibid.*, p. 185.

3. Quoted in Trotsky's *Problems of the Chinese Revolution*, p. 292.

4. *Ibid.*, p. 41.

5. *Ibid.*, p. 53.

6. *Ibid.*, p. 131.

7. *Ibid.*, p. 54.

8. "Shōkaiseki no Kōho gunkangakkō kyōsanto ritō kankoku ensetsu" (An Address by Chiang Kai-shek at the Whampoa Officers' Academy Advising the Communist Party to Leave the Party), from Okubo, *Chūkyō Sanjūnen* (Thirty Years of Chinese Communism), pp. 64–65.

VI. *The New Line*

1. Stalin, "Krizis lyevogo Gomindana" (The Crisis in the Left Kuomintang), *Pravda* (July 26, 1927).

2. "An Abrupt Turn in the Chinese Revolution," *Inprecorr*, vol. VII, no. 41, p. 894.

3. "Theses on the Chinese Situation," *Inprecorr*, vol. VII, no. 11, p. 232.

4. Lenin, *Selected Works* (Moscow, 1947), I, 366.

5. Wolfe, *Three Who Made a Revolution*, p. 292.

6. Lenin, "Attitude of the Social Democrats Toward the Peasantry," *Selected Works*, I, 442.

7. Lenin, *Works*, vol. XI, part I, p. 79, quoted in Trotsky's *The Third Internationale After Lenin*, p. 221.

8. Stalin's speech at the Eighth Plenum of the ECCI, quoted in Isaacs, *The Tragedy of the Chinese Revolution*, p. 289.

9. "Resolutions on the International Situation," *Inprecorr*, vol. VII, no. 48, p. 1072 (August 18, 1927).

10. "Na krutom perevalye Kitaiskoi revolyutsii" (A Steep Pass in the Chinese Revolution), *Pravda* (July 10, 1927).

11. "Resolutions of the ECCI on the Present Situation of the Chinese Revolution," *Inprecorr*, vol. VII, no. 44 (July 28, 1927).

12. Ch'ü Ch'iu-pai's *Chinese Revolution*, p. 135, quoted in Isaacs' *Tragedy of the Chinese Revolution*, p. 349.

13. "Krizis lyevogo Gomindana" (The Crisis in the Left Kuomintang), *Pravda* (July 26, 1927).

14. *Problems of the Chinese Revolution*, p. 120.

15. "Report on Nanchang," *Inprecorr*, vol. VII, no. 48 (August 18, 1927); also *Shina Sobieto Undō no Kenkyū* (A Study of the Chinese Soviet Movement) (Tokyo, 1934), p. 137.

16. *Hung-se Wu-t'ai* (The Red Stage), pp. 12–24.

17. Isaacs, *Tragedy of the Chinese Revolution*, p. 343.

18. *Chung-kuo Kung-ch'an-tang Pa-yüeh Hui-i Hsüan-yen* (Manifesto of the August Conference of the Chinese Communist Party) (Moscow, 1927), p. 14.

19. "Hachi-shichi kaigi" (The August Seventh Conference), in Okubo, *Chūkyō Sanjūnen* (Thirty Years of Chinese Communism), p. 134.

20. *Ibid.*, p. 135.

21. *Chung-kuo Kung-ch'an-Tang Pa-yüeh Hui-i Hsüan-yen* (Manifesto of the August Conference of the Chinese Communist Party), p. 10.

22. *Ibid.*, p. 19.

23. *Ibid.*, p. 15.

24. Okubo, p. 133.

25. *Ibid.*, p. 134.

26. *Shina Kyōsantō no Gaikan* (A General Survey of the Chinese Communist Party) (Tokyo, 1929), p. 58.

VII. *The Ch'u Ch'iu-pai Leadership*

1. See Harold Isaacs, *Five Years of Kuomintang Reaction* (London, 1938).

2. "Chung-kuo Kung-ch'an-tang chien-ming-shih" (A Short History of the Chinese Communist Party), p. 10.

3. *Chung-kuo Kung-ch'an-tang Pa-yüeh Hui-i Hsüan-yen* (Manifesto of the August Conference of the Chinese Communist Party), p. 15.

4. Hua Kang, *Chung-kuo Ta Ko-ming-shih* (History of the Great Chinese Revolution), p. 365.

5. Snow, *Red Star Over China*, p. 167.

6. *Ibid.*, p. 167.

7. *Ibid.*, p. 169.
8. *Ibid.*, p. 167.
9. *Ibid.*, p. 167.
10. *Ibid.*, p. 167.
11. After the failure of Nanchang, the troops of Yeh T'ing and Ho Lung had attacked Swatow and Chao chow only to be defeated September 13.
12. *Chung-kuo Ta Ko-ming-shih* (The Great Chinese Revolution), p. 366.
13. Snow, *Red Star Over China*, p. 169.
14. *Chung-kuo Ta Ko-ming-shih* (The Great Chinese Revolution), p. 366.
15. Snow, *Red Star Over China*, p. 169.
16. See Chapter IV, note 53.
17. Johanson i Taube, *Soviety v Kitae* (Soviets in China) (Moscow, 1934), pp. 131–145.
18. "Noyabr'skii Plyenum Ts. K.K.K.P." (The November Plenum of the Central Committee of the CCP), in *Materialy po Kitaiskomu Voprosu* (Materials on the Chinese Question) (Moscow, 1928), no. 10, p. 7.
19. *Ibid.*, p. 6.
20. *Ibid.*, p. 9.
21. *Ibid.*, p. 1.
22. *Ibid.*, p. 20.
23. *Ibid.*, p. 9.
24. *Ibid.*, p. 7.
25. From Stalin's speech at the Eighth Plenum of the ECCI of May 1927, quoted in Trotsky's *The Third Internationale After Lenin*, p. 340.
26. Isaacs points out that "the Canton insurrection was made to coincide with the Fifteenth Congress of the Communist Party of the Soviet Union at which Stalin completed his conquest of the opposition" (*Tragedy of the Chinese Revolution*, p. 357).
27. *Hung-se Wu-t'ai* (The Red Stage), p. 40.
28. *Ibid.*, p. 38.
29. Trotsky, *Problems of the Chinese Revolution*, p. 128.
30. After his capture by the Kuomintang in 1935, Ch'ü Ch'iu-pai wrote a rather whimsical autobiographical work called *To-yü ti Hua* (Superfluous Words) in which he referred to himself in these terms. See Shinshi Teiichiro, Kushūhakuden (Biography of Ch'ü Ch'iu-pai), *Kaizō*, vol. XVIII, no. 8 (August 1936), p. 33.
31. Kushūhaku (Ch'ü Ch'iu-pai), *Chūgoku Kakumei* (The Chinese Revolution), a Japanese translation (Tokyo), p. 154.
32. *Ibid.*, p. 154.
33. *Ibid.*, p. 154.
34. *Ibid.*, pp. 154–155.
35. *Ibid.*, p. 156.

36. During the 1928–1930 period Ch'ü, who had assumed the Russian name Strakhov, was able to regain something of a reputation in Moscow and the International Communist movement. He never regained his power, however, in the Chinese Communist Party.

VIII. *A New Shift in Line*

1. The final decision not to coöperate with other political groups in China had already been taken at the Politburo meeting of the Chinese Communist Party held on September 19, 1927.

2. Trotsky, *Problems of the Chinese Revolution*, p. 144.

3. *Resolutions adoptées à la IXᵉ session plénière du C.E. de l'I.C.* (Resolutions Adopted at the Ninth Plenary Session of the ECCI) (Paris, 1928), p. 47.

4. *Ibid.*, p. 48.

5. *Ibid.*, p. 48.

6. *Ibid.*, p. 48.

7. *Ibid.*, p. 48.

8. *Ibid.*, p. 51.

9. "Cheng-chih chüeh-i-an" (Political Resolution) from the *Chung-kuo Kung-ch'an-tang ti-liu-tzu Ch'üan-Kuo Ta-hui I-chüeh-an* (Resolutions of the Sixth All-China Congress of the Chinese Communist Party) (Hoover Library), p. 25.

10. Johanson i Taube, *Soviety v Kitae* (Soviets in China), p. 6.

11. *Resolutions adoptées à la IXᵉ session*, p. 50.

12. *Ibid.*, p. 49.

13. "Cheng-chih I-chüeh-an," p. 40.

14. *Resolutions adoptées à la IXᵉ session*, p. 47.

15. *Ibid.*, p. 47.

16. *Ibid.*, p. 47.

17. Draft Program of the Sixth Comintern Congress, quoted in Trotsky's *The Third Internationale After Lenin*, p. 195.

18. *Thèses et resolutions du VIᵉ congrès de l'I.C.* (Theses and Resolutions of the Sixth Congress of the Comintern (Paris), p. 179.

19. Trotsky, *Problems of the Chinese Revolution*, p. 177.

20. *Ibid.*, p. 177.

21. *Ibid.*, p. 190.

22. *Ibid.*, p. 189.

23. *Ibid.*, p. 213.

24. The Sixth Congress of the Chinese Party was actually held one month before the Sixth Comintern Congress. The Comintern Congress Resolutions on China were actually based on the Resolutions of the Sixth Congress of the Chinese Communist Party.

25. *Hung-se Wu-t'ai* (The Red Stage), pp. 64–66.

26. *Ibid.*, p. 67.

27. Nakanishi Kō and Nishisato Tatsuo, *Bukan ni-okeru Kakumei to Hankakumei* (Revolution and Counterrevolution in Wuhan) (Tokyo, 1949), p. 152.

28. Snow, *Red Star Over China*, p. 171.

29. This theme runs, of course, throughout Marx's works. See in particular chap. xxxii of vol. I of *Capital* where Marx tersely describes the final process by which capitalism will be destroyed.

30. Lenin, "Die Entwicklung des Kapitalismus in Russland" (The Development of Capitalism in Russia), *Ausgewählte Werke* (Selected Works), I, 85–161.

31. Lenin, "Thèses sur la question agraire" (Theses on the Agrarian Question), *Oeuvres complètes*, XXV, 319.

32. "Arbeiterpartei und Bauernschaft" (The Workers Party and the Peasantry), *Ausgewählte Werke*, II, 242.

33. From Lenin's *Works*, vol. XI, part I, p. 198, quoted in Trotsky's *The Third Internationale After Lenin*, p. 220.

34. "Theses on the Chinese Situation," *Inprecorr*, vol. VII, no. 11, p. 231 (February 3, 1927).

35. Lenin, "The Agrarian Program of the Social Democrats," *Selected Works* (New York), III, 278.

36. Stalin's speech at the Eighth Plenum of the ECCI quoted in Trotsky's *The Third Internationale After Lenin*, p. 336.

37. *Chung-kuo Kung-ch'an-tang Pa-yüeh Hui-i Hsüan-yen* (Manifesto of the August Conference of the Chinese Communist Party), p. 19.

38. *Thèses et resolutions du VIe congrès de l'I.C.* (Theses and Resolutions of the Sixth Congress of the Comintern), p. 175.

39. *Ibid.*, p. 179.

40. *Ibid.*, p. 189.

41. *Ti-liu-tz'u Ta-hui kuan-yü T'u-ti Wen-t'i ti Chüeh-i-an* (Resolution of the Sixth Congress on the Land Problem) (Moscow, 1928), p. 7.

42. *Ibid.*, p. 7.

43. *Ibid.*, p. 10.

44. *Ibid.*, p. 14.

45. *Chung-kuo Kung-ch'an-tang Ti-liu-tz'u Tai-piao Ta-hui kuan-yü Nung-min Wen-t'i ti Chüeh-i-an* (The Resolution of the Sixth Congress of the CCP on the Peasant Problem) (Moscow, 1928).

46. *Ibid.*, p. 8.

47. *Ibid.*, p. 9.

48. *Ibid.*, p. 10.

49. "Cheng-chih chüeh-i-an" (Political Resolution), *Chung-kuo Kung-ch'an-tang Ti-liu-tz'u Ch'uan-Kuo Ta-hui I-chüeh-an* (Resolutions of the Sixth All-China Congress of the Chinese Communist Party), p. 39.

50. *Ibid.*, p. 39.

51. *Ibid.*, p. 45.

52. *Ibid.*, p. 49.

53. *Ibid.*, p. 51.

54. *Ibid.*, p. 53.

55. *Ibid.*, p. 232.

56. *Ibid.*, p. 116.

57. *Ibid.*, p. 51.

58. He had been a river boatman in his younger days and had held the post of Secretary of the Labor Federation in Hopeh at the time of the split between the Communist Party and the National Government.

IX. *The Li Li-san Leadership*

1. "Cheng-chih chüeh-i-an" (Political Resolution) in the *Chung-kuo Kun-ch'an-tang Ti-liu-tz'u Ch'uan-kuo Ta-hui I-chüeh-an* (Resolutions of the Sixth All-China Congress of the Chinese Communist Party), p. 40.

2. *Ibid.*, p. 51.

3. *Ti-liu-tz'u Ta-hui-hou ti Cheng-chih Kung-tso* (Political Activities After the Sixth Congress) (Shanghai, 1929), p. 8.

4. "Mu-ch'ien cheng-chih hsing-shih yü ch'ün-chung kung-tso" (Present Political Conditions and Mass Activities), p. 42.

5. Chou En-lai, *Mu-ch'ien Chung-kuo Tang Ti Tsu-chih Wen-t'i* (Organizational Problems of the Chinese Party at the Present Time) (Shanghai, 1929), p. 2.

6. Fang Fu-an, *Chinese Labour*, p. 97, quoted in Isaacs, *Tragedy of the Chinese Revolution*, p. 388.

7. *Ti-liu-tz'u Ta-hui-hou ti Cheng-chih Kung-tso* (Political Activities After the Sixth Congress), p. 21.

8. "Chung-yang T'ung-kao ti san-shih-hao" (C. C. Circular No. 30), work cited in note 7, p. 127.

9. *Ibid.*, p. 127.

10. "Chün-fa chang-cheng ti hsing-shih yü wo-men-tang ti jen-wu" (The Wars Among the Militarists and the Tasks of our Party), work cited in note 7, p. 185.

11. *Ibid.*, p. 193.

12. "Kung-ch'an Kuo-chi chih-hsing Wei-yüan-hui yü Chung-kuo Kung-ch'an-tang-shu" (Letters of the Executive Committee of the Communist Internationale to the Chinese Communist Party), work cited in note 7, p. 227.

13. *Ibid.*, p. 232. "Kemalist path" was used by Communists to designate a development similar to that which took place in Turkey under Kemal Atatürk.

14. *Ibid.*, p. 234.

15. "Fan-chün-fa chan-cheng-chung ti kung-tso fang-chen" (Our Policy on Activities Against the Wars Among the Militarists), pp. 220–221.

16. See Li Ang, *Hung-se Wu-t'ai* (The Red Stage), pp. 127–128; also, *Chung-Kuo Kung-ch'an tang Chung-yang Wei-yüan-hui K'uo-ta ti Ti-ssu-*

tz'u Ch'üan t'i Hui-i I-chüeh-an (The Resolutions of the Fourth Enlarged Plenum of the Central Committee of the CCP) (Shanghai, 1931), p. 2.

17. Chou En-lai, *Mu-ch'ien Chung-kuo Tang Ti-Tsu-chih Wen-t'i* (Organizational Problems of the Chinese Communist Party), p. 5.

18. *Ibid.*, p. 15.

19. See *Ti-liu-tz'ü Ta-hsui-hou ti Cheng-chih Kung-tso* (Political Activities After the Sixth Congress), pp. 133–137.

20. See Isaacs, *Tragedy of the Chinese Revolution*, p. 341.

21. *Chung-kung Chung-yang Ti-erh-tz'u Ch'uan-ti Hui-i Ts'ai-liao* (Materials of the Second Plenum of the Central Committee of the CCP) (Shanghai, 1929), p. 126.

22. *Ibid.*, p. 129.

23. *Ibid.*, p. 129.

24. *Ibid.*, p. 77.

25. *Ibid.*, p. 29.

26. *Ibid.*, p. 129.

27. *Ibid.*, p. 134.

28. "Lun Kuo-min-tang kai-tsu-p'ai ho Chung-kuo Kung-ch'an-tang ti jen-wu" (Concerning the Kuomintang Reorganizationists and the Tasks of the CCP), *Hung-ch'i* (Red Flag), no. 16 (February 15, 1930), p. 9.

29. *Ibid.*, p. 10.

30. *Ibid.*, p. 11.

31. *Ibid.*, p. 11.

32. "Kōgun no hatten katei ni-tsuite Shūonrai no hōkoku" (Chou En-lai's Report on the Development of the Red Army), in Okubo, *Chūkyō Sanjūnen* (Thirty Years of Chinese Communism), p. 143.

33. Snow, *Red Star Over China*, p. 179.

34. Tang Shin-she, "Comrade Mao Tze-dung," *Inprecorr*, vol. X, no. 14 (March 20, 1930).

35. Trotsky, *Problems of the Chinese Revolution*, p. 302.

36. *Shih-li-p'ai* in Chinese. See Li Ang, *Hung-se-Wu-t'ai* (The Red Stage), p. 127; also, *Shina Sobieto Undō no Kenkyū* (A Study of the Chinese Soviet Movement), p. 130.

37. *Hung-ch'i* (Red Flag), no. 16 (February 15, 1930), p. 11.

38. "Kao Ch'üan-t'i T'ung-chih-shu" (A Letter to all Comrades), in *Ti-liu-tz'u Ta-hui-hou ti Cheng-chih Kung-tso* (Political Activities After the Nineteenth Congress), p. 52.

39. Snow, *Red Star Over China*, p. 174.

40. "Chün-pei chien-li ko-ming cheng-ch'üan yü wu-ch'an chieh-chi ti ling-tao" (Preparing To Set Up a Revolutionary Regime and the Hegemony of the Proletariat), *Hung-ch'i* (Red Flag), no. 88 (March 29, 1930).

41. *Ibid.*, p. 2.

42. "Tsen-yang chün-pei to-ch'ü i-sheng yü chi-sheng cheng-ch'üan ti-sheng-li ti t'iao-chien" (Conditions for Preparing the Victory of a Regime in One or Several Provinces), *Hung-ch'i*, no. 90 (April 5, 1930).

43. "Kuan-yü wu-ch'an chieh-chi ling-tao ti wen-t'i" (The Problem of Proletarian Hegemony), *Hung-ch'i*, no. 104 (May 24, 1930).

44. Pavel Mif, "Navstrechu gryadushchim revolyutsionnym buryam v Kitae" (Toward Coming Revolutionary Storms in China), *Pravda* (April 28, 1930).

45. Ivin, "The Partisan Movement," *Inprecorr*, vol. X, no. 24, p. 431 (May 1930).

46. *Shina Kyosanto Undoshi* (History of the Chinese Communist Movement) (Tokyo, 1931), p. 314.

47. *Ibid.*, p. 323.

48. "Ch'üan-kuo ti-i-tz'u Su-wei-ai chü-yü Tai-piao Ta-hui Hsüan-chüan kang-yao" (A Summary of the Declaration of the All-China Conference of Delegates from the Soviet Areas), *Hung-ch'i*, no. 112 (June 21, 1930).

49. "Hsin ti ko-ming kao-ch'ao yü i-sheng huo chi-sheng shou-hsien sheng-li" (A New Revolutionary Wave and an Initial Victory in One or Several Provinces); "I-ch'ien chiu-pai san-shih-nien liu-yüeh shih-i-jih cheng-chih-chü hui-i t'ung-kuo mu-ch'ien cheng-chih jen-wu ti chüeh-i" (Resolution on Our Present Political Tasks Passed by the Politburo Meeting of June 11, 1930), *Hung-ch'i*, no. 121 (July 19, 1930).

50. *Ibid.*, p. 3.

51. *Ibid.*, p. 3.

52. *Ibid.*, p. 3.

53. *Ibid.*, p. 1.

54. *Ibid.*, p. 1.

55. "Resolution on the Chinese Question by the Political Secretariat of the ECCI, July 23, 1930," quoted in Isaacs, *Tragedy of the Chinese Revolution*, p. 403.

X. *Changsha and The "Li Li-san Line"*

1. "The Occupation of Changsha by the Chinese Red Army," *Inprecorr*, vol. X, no. 36 (August 7, 1930).

2. "The Soviet Revolution and the War of the Generals in China," *Inprecorr*, vol. X, no. 38 (August 21, 1930).

3. "Na preddveriya novoi revolyutsionii v Kitae" (On the Eve of a New Revolution in China), *Kommunisticheskii Internatsional* (August 10, 1930).

4. "Letter of Ch'en Tu-hsiu to the Central Committee" (August 1929), in Appendix of Ch'ü Ch'iu-pai's *Chung-kuo Ch'ü-hsiao-chu-i ho Chi-hui-chu-i* (Liquidationism and Opportunism in China) (Moscow, 1930), Appendix, p. 44.

5. *Ibid.*, p. 44.

6. *Wo-men ti Cheng-chih I-chien-shu* (A Statement of our Political Views) (Shanghai, 1929).

7. *Ibid.*, p. 16.

8. *Ibid.*, p. 18.

9. *Ibid.*, p. 20.

10. *Ibid.*, p. 20.

11. *Ibid.*, p. 23.

12. *Ibid.*, p. 20.

13. *Hung-ch'i*, no. 121, p. 4 (July 19, 1930).

14. *Shino Sobieto Undō no Kenkyū* (A Study of the Chinese Soviet Movement), p. 126.

15. *Liu-ngo-p'ai* in Chinese. *Ibid.*, p. 126, also Li Ang, *Hung-se Wu-t'ai* (The Red Stage), p. 133.

16. *Ibid.*, p. 133.

17. Mif was appointed director of the Sun Yat-sen Academy after Radek's removal. See Li Ang, *Hung-se Wu-t'ai*, pp. 138–140.

18. *Ibid.*, p. 139.

19. *Wu-chuang Pao-tung* (Armed Uprisings) (Shanghai, 1929).

20. *Ibid.*, p. 12.

21. *Ibid.*, p. 113.

22. *Ibid.*, p. 12.

23. *Ibid.*, p. 159.

24. "Mu-ch'ien chün-fa chan-cheng yü tang ti jen-wu" (The Present Wars Among the Militarists and the Party's Tasks), *Pu'rh-se-wei-k'o* (Bolshevik), vol. III, no. 4, p. 95 (May 15, 1930).

25. *Ibid.*, p. 103.

26. Ozuka Reizo, "Chung-kuo Kung-ch'an-tang chih hsien-shih" (The Present Situation in the Chinese Communist Party), translated from the Japanese, *Kuo-wen Chou-pao*, vol. VIII, no. 29, p. 3 (July 27, 1931).

27. See *International Press Correspondence* for the 1929–1930 period. Many of Ch'ü's contributions appear under his Russian pseudonym, Strakhov.

28. Ch'en Tu-hsiu, *Wo-men ti Cheng-chih I-chien-shu* (A Statement of Our Political Views), p. 23.

29. *Hung-se Wu-t'ai* (The Red Stage), p. 129.

30. Chou En-lai, *Shao-shan Pao-kao-San-chung Ch'üan-hui Ts'ai-liao* (The Report of Chou En-lai; Materials of the Third Plenum of the Central Committee) (Hoover Library), p. 4.

31. *Ibid.*, pp. 1–4.

32. *Ibid.*, p. 1; also Isaacs, *Tragedy of the Chinese Revolution*, p. 402.

33. *Shao-shan Pao-kao* (The Report of Chou En-lai), p. 3.

34. *Ibid.*, p. 1.

35. *Ibid.*, p. 6.

36. *Ibid.*, p. 8.

37. *Ibid.*, p. 4.

38. *Ibid.*, p. 4.

39. *Ibid.*, p. 8.

40. *Ibid.*, p. 8.

41. "Wei-ta ti Chung-kung ti-san-tz'u Chung-yang Ch'uan-t'i-hui" (The Great Third Plenum of the Central Committee of the CCP), *Hung-ch'i*, no. 48 (October 4, 1930).

42. *Ti-ssu-tz'u Ch'üan-t'i Hui-i I-chüeh-an* (Resolutions of the Fourth Plenum), p. 4.

43. See contents of the November 16 letter of the ECCI as outlined in Ozuka's "Chung-kuo Kung-ch'an-tang chih hsien-shih" (The Present Situation in the Chinese Communist Party), *Kuo-wen Chou-pao*, vol. VIII, no. 29, p. 2 (July 27, 1931).

44. For contents of this letter see article referred to in note 43; also, Isaacs, *Tragedy of the Chinese Revolution*, pp. 408–409, and Chung-kuo Kung-ch'an-tang Chung-yang Wei-yüan-hui kao T'ung-chih-shu (A Letter of the Central Committee of the Chinese Communist Party to Our Party Comrades) (Hoover Library, microfilm).

45. *A Report to the Oriental Bureau of the Comintern* (Hoover Library), p. 4.

46. Van Min (Wang Ming), "Bor'ba s lilisyanovshchinoi v Kitaiskoi Kompartii" (The Struggle With Li Li-sanism in the Chinese Communist Party), *Revolutsionnyi Vostok* (The Revolutionary East), nos. 3–4 (1932), p. 146.

47. Van Min, p. 148.

48. *Ibid.*, p. 148.

49. *Ibid.*, p. 148.

50. Chou En-lai, p. 1.

51. *Die Kommunistische International vor dem VIIten Weltkongress* (The Communist International Before the Seventh Congress) (Moscow, 1935), p. 428.

52. D. Manuilsky, *The Revolutionary Crisis Is Maturing* (New York, 1933), p. 15.

53. Ozuka, p. 2.

54. "Cheng-chih chüeh-i-an" (Political Resolution), in *Chung-kuo Kung-ch'an-tang Ti-liu-tz'u Ch'uan-kuo Ta-hui-i I-chüeh-an* (Resolutions of the Sixth All-China Congress of the CCP), p. 40.

55. *Kung-ch'an-tang Chung-yang Wei-yüan-hui Kao T'ung-chih-shu* (A Letter of the Central Committee of the Chinese Communist Party to Our Party Comrades), p. 9.

56. Lozovsky, "Help to the Labour Movement in China," *Inprecorr*, vol. VIII, no. 38, p. 691 (July 19, 1928).

57. Ozuka, p. 2.

58. See Chapter IX.

59. *A Report to the Oriental Bureau of the Comintern*, p. 5.

60. Van Min, p. 152.

61. Mif, "Na poroge novogo revolyutsionnogo pod'ema v Kitae" (On the Threshold of a New Revolutionary Upsurge in China), *Pravda* (September 25, 1929), p. 11.

62. *Chung-kuo Kung-ch'an-tang Chung-yang Wei-yüan-hui Kao T'ung-chih-shu* (Letter of the Central Committee of the CCP to Our Comrades), p. 13.

63. *A Report to the Oriental Bureau of the Comintern*, p. 10.

64. "Kitaiskaya revolyutsiya i niekapitalisticheskii put' razvitiya" (The Chinese Revolution and the Non-capitalist Path of Development), *Problemy Kitaya* (Problems of China) (1931), quoted in *Soviety v Kitae*, p. 497.

65. Manuilsky, *The Revolutionary Crisis Is Maturing*, p. 54.

66. See Chapter IX, note 47.

67. *Ti-ssu-tz'u Ch'üan-t'i Hui-i I-chüeh-an* (Resolutions of the Fourth Plenum), p. 1.

XI. *The Wang Ming Leadership*

1. Li Ang, *Hung-se Wu-t'ai* (The Red Stage), p. 154.

2. Ho Meng-hsiung, *Ho Meng-hsiung I-chien-shu* (A Statement of Views by Ho Meng-hsiung) (Shanghai, 1931), pp. 1–2.

3. *Ibid.*, p. 4.

4. *Ibid.*, p. 6.

5. Ozuka, "Chung-kuo Kung-ch'an-tang chih hsien-shih" (The Present Situation of the Chinese Communist Party), *Kuo-wen Chou-pao*, vol. VIII, no. 29, p. 5.

6. Van Min, "Bor'ba s lilisyanovshchinoi v Kitaiskoi Kompartii" (The Struggle With Li Li-sanism in the Chinese Communist Party), p. 158. After the Fourth Plenum, Ch'ü was forced to denounce his own "cowardly rotten opportunism"; see Isaacs, *Tragedy of the Chinese Revolution*, p. 407.

7. Ozuka, p. 6.

8. Isaacs, *Tragedy of the Chinese Revolution*, p. 407.

9. *Ti-ssu-tz'u Ch'üan-t'i Hui-i I-chüeh-an* (Resolutions of the Fourth Plenum), p. 2.

10. *Fei-ch'ang Wei-yüan-hui* in Chinese. See *Shina Sobieto Undō no Kenkyū* (A Study of the Chinese Soviet Movement), p. 126; also, Wo Wen, "Ch'uan Kung-tang Fei-ch'ang Wei-yüan-hui" (An Account of the Communist Party Emergency Committee), in *Hsien-tai Shih-liao* (Materials on Modern History) (Shanghai, 1934), III, 266.

11. Isaacs, *Tragedy of the Chinese Revolution*, p. 407; also Li Ang, *Hung-se Wu-t'ai* (The Red Stage), pp. 140–141.

12. Wo Wen, "Ch'uan Kung-tang Fei-ch'ang Wei-yüan-hui" (An Account of the Communist Party Emergency Committee), pp. 266–270.

13. "Hai-tsung kung-tso-chung ti yu-ch'ing chi-hui-chu-i" (Right Opportunism in the Activities of the General Federation of Maritime Workers), *Hung-ch'i Chou-pao* (The Red Flag Weekly), no. 25, p. 21 (December 2, 1931).

14. *Ibid.*, p. 23.
15. Ozuka, p. 6.
16. Van Min, p. 152.
17. Actually, nothing new was to be added until the Seventh Comintern Congress of July 1935.
18. Ozuka, p. 3; also *Chung-kuo Kung-ch'an-tang Chung-yang Kao T'ung-chih-shu* (Letter of the Central Committee of the CCP to Our Comrades), p. 13.
19. *Ibid.*, p. 13.
20. *Ibid.*, p. 13.
21. *Ti-ssu-tz'u Chiüan-t'i Hui-i I-chüeh-an* (Resolutions of the Fourth Plenum), p. 2.
22. *Ibid.*, p. 2.
23. *Chung-kuo Kung-ch'an-tang Chung-yang Kao T'ung-chih-shu* (A Letter of the Central Committee of the CCP to Our Comrades), p. 13.
24. Mif, "Grazhdanskaya voina i bor'ba za Soviety v Kitae" (The Civil War and the Struggle for Soviets in China), *Bol'shevik*, no. 13, p. 72 (July 15, 1931).
25. *Ibid.*, p. 76.
26. Kuchumov, "The Struggle for the Bolshevization of the Communist Party of China," *Communist International* (March 1931), p. 162.
27. Yolk, "Novaya pobieda Kitaiskikh Sovietov" (A New Victory of the Chinese Soviets), *Pravda* (November 4, 1931).
28. See Trotsky, *The Third Internationale After Lenin*, p. 329.

XII. *The Triumph of Mao Tse-tung*

1. Hatano Kanichi, *Sekishoku Shina no Kyūmei* (A Study of Red China) (Tokyo, 1941), pp. 49–50.
2. Snow, *Red Star Over China*, p. 173.
3. *Ibid.*, p. 168.
4. *Ibid.*, p. 172.
5. *Shina Sobieto Undō no Kenkyū* (A Study of the Chinese Soviet Movement), p. 126; also, Ch'eng Sheng-ch'ang "Fu-t'ien shih-pien yü tang nei-pu fen-hua" (The Fut'ien Incident and the Internal Divisions in the Party), *Hsien-tai Shih-liao* (Materials on Modern History), III, 265. The Chinese expressions used are *Tang-ch'üan-p'ai* and *Chün-ch'üan-p'ai*.
6. "Chung-kuo Kung-ch'an-tang Hung-chün ti-ssu-chün ti-chiu-tz'u tai-piao ta-hui chüeh-i-an" (Resolutions of the Ninth Conference of the Fourth Army of the Red Army of the CCP) *Mao Tse-tung Hsüan-chi* (Selected Works of Mao Tse-tung), p. 547.
7. *Ibid.*, p. 547.
8. *Ibid.*, p. 547.
9. Snow, *Red Star Over China*, p. 174.
10. Li Ang, *Hung-se Wu-t'ai* (The Red Stage), p. 152.

11. K'o Ch'eng, "Mao Tse-tung ti chuan-heng-lu" (A Record of Mao Tse-tung's Tyranny), *Hsien-tai Shih-liao* (Materials on Modern History), III, 256.

12. Snow, p. 182.

13. *Ibid.*, p. 182.

14. Hatano, *Sekishoku Shina no Kyūmei* (A Study of Red China), p. 206.

15. *Ibid.*, pp. 206–207.

16. *Ibid.*, pp. 206–207.

17. *Ibid.*, p. 207.

18. Ch'eng Sheng-ch'ang, p. 267.

19. Snow, p. 182.

20. K'o Ch'eng, p. 152.

21. *Ti-ssu-tz'u Ch'uan-t'i I-chüeh-an* (Resolutions of the Fourth Plenum), p. 1.

22. Johanson i Taube, *Soviety v Kitae* (Soviets in China), p. 246.

23. Li Ang, p. 152.

24. Johanson i Taube, pp. 314–317.

25. The First All-China Congress of Soviets met at Juichin on November 7, 1931.

26. See Chapter IV, p. 73.

27. Snow, p. 169.

28. *Ibid.*, p. 171.

29. "Ch'ing-kang-shan Ch'ien-wei tui-Chung-yang ti pao-kao" (A Report from the Chingkanshan Front Committee to the Central Committee), *Mao Tse-tung Hsüan-chi* (Selected Works of Mao Tse-tung), p. 542.

30. *Resolutions adoptées à la IXe session plenière du C.E. de l'I.C.* (Resolutions Adopted at the Ninth Plenary Session of the ECCI), p. 51.

31. Snow, p. 171.

32. Li Li-san had participated as a consultant at the Ninth Plenum of the ECCI and had played a dominant role at the Sixth Congress of the CCP.

33. Snow, p. 178.

34. "Hsin ti ko-ming kao-ch'ao yü i-sheng huo chi-sheng shou-hsien sheng-li" (A new Revolutionary Wave and an Initial Victory in One or Several Provinces), *Hung-ch'i*, no. 121, p. 3 (July 19, 1930).

35. Snow, p. 179.

36. Ch'en Tu-hsiu, *Wo-men ti I-chien-shu* (A Statement of Our Views), p. 23.

37. Hatano, "Shūonraiden" (Biography of Chou En-lai), *Kaizo*, vol. XIX, no. 7 (1937), p. 89.

38. *Soviety v Kitae* (Soviets in China), p. 255.

39. *Ibid.*, p. 269.

40. *Ibid.*, p. 269.

41. *Hung-se Wu-t'ai* (The Red Stage), p. 126.

42. Snow, p. 180.

43. *Ibid.*, p. 179.

44. *Ibid.*, p. 179.

45. K'o Ch'eng, "Mao Tse-tung ti chuan-heng-lu" (A Record of Mao Tse-tung's Tyranny), p. 256.

46. Sinani, "The Red Army of the Chinese Revolution," *Communist Internationale* (October 1931), p. 527.

47. Isaacs, *The Tragedy of the Chinese Revolution*, p. 405.

48. *Ibid.*, p. 406.

49. *Hung-se Wu-t'ai* (The Red Stage), p. 154.

50. Snow, p. 415.

51. *Hung-se Wu-t'ai* (The Red Stage), p. 156.

52. *Ibid.*, p. 143.

53. *Ibid.*, p. 143.

54. *Shina ni-okeru Kyōsan Undō* (The Communist Movement in China) (Tokyo, 1933), p. 158.

55. See Johanson i Taube, *Soviety v Kitae* (Soviets in China), pp. 417–456.

56. Wang I-shih, *K'ang-chan i-ch'ien ti Chung-kuo Kung-ch'an-tang* (The Chinese Communist Party Before the War of Resistance) (Chungking, 1942), p. 70.

57. *Hung-se Wu-t'ai* (The Red Stage), p. 156.

58. *Ibid.*, p. 155.

59. *Ibid.*, p. 156.

60. *Ibid.*, p. 157.

61. Wang I-shih, p. 70; also Chin Tung-p'ing, *Yen-an Chien-wen-lu* A Record of an Inspection Trip to Yenan) (Chungking, 1945), p. 1.

62. Li Ang, p. 159.

63. Hatano, "Shūonraiden" (Biography of Chou En-lai), p. 90.

64. Li Ang, p. 159.

65. Hatano, *Sekishoku Shina no Kyūmei* (A Study of Red China), p. 229.

66. *Die Kommunistische International vor dem VIIten Weltkongress* (The Communist International Before the Seventh Congress), p. 280.

67. Ypsilon in his *Pattern for World Revolution*, p. 425, claims that Mao Tse-tung had accompanied Li Li-san to Moscow where he received the blessing of Stalin. This account is unsupported by any other source seen, either pro- or anti-Communist. There is little reason to suppose that Mao Tse-tung would have kept such a fact secret. As has been pointed out, Mao has been extremely eager to create the impression that his power is legitimate in terms of the Marxist-Leninist-Stalinist tradition. If Stalin had conferred upon him the mantle of power he would have been proud to proclaim this fact.

68. Li Ang, p. 157.

XIII. *Essential Features of the Maoist Strategy*

1. "Ch'ing-Kang-shan Ch'ien-wei Chung-yang ti pao-kao" (A Report of the Chingkanshan Front Committee to the Central Committee), p. 516.
2. *Ibid.*, p. 542.
3. *Ibid.*, p. 516.
4. *Ibid.*, p. 516.
5. Snow, p. 180.
6. George Lukacs, *Lenin, Eine Studie über den Zusammenhang seiner Gedanken* (Lenin, a Study of the Structure of his Thought), p. 23.
7. *Ibid.*, p. 24.
8. *Shao-shan Pao-kao* (Report of Chou En-lai), p. 7.
9. Trotsky, *Problems of the Chinese Revolution*, p. 158.
10. *International Press Correspondence*, vol. X, no. 51, p. 1063 (November 13, 1930).
11. Trotsky, *Problems of the Chinese Revolution*, p. 239.
12. Nym Wales, *Inside Red China* (New York, 1939), p. 221.
13. Lenin, "Thèses sur la question agraire" (Theses on the Agrarian Question), *Oeuvres complètes*, XXV, 319.
14. See *Soviety v Kitae* (Soviets in China), pp. 425–432.
15. "Wei kung-hui hui-yüan wen-t'i kei ko-Su-chü kung-hui hsin" (A Letter to Union Branches in All the Soviet Areas Concerning the Problem of Union Members), *Hung-ch'i Chou-pao*, no. 52, p. 53 (November 15, 1932).
16. See, for example, chapters vi and xxvii of Marx's *Capital*, vol. I.
17. "Wei kung-hui hui-yüan wen-t'i kei ko-Su-chü kung-hui hsin," p. 35.
18. *Ibid.*, p. 36.
19. *Ibid.*, p. 35.
20. *Ibid.*, p. 36.
21. *Soviety v Kitae* (Soviets in China), p. 92.
22. *Ibid.*, p. 106.
23. Lenin, "Sur les questions coloniales et nationales," *Oeuvres complètes*, XXV, 420.
24. Stalin, "The Revolution in China and the Tasks of the Communist International," *Communist International*, vol. V (June 30, 1927).
25. *Soviety v Kitae*, p. 95.
26. *Tragedy of the Chinese Revolution*, p. 404.
27. *Inside Red China*, p. 335.
28. See Chapter VIII, note 39.
29. The recent history of Eastern Europe would suggest that the latter part of this formula is not necessarily an essential, permanent element. The Communist Party has in these countries shown its complete willingness to attain power by such means as the control of the Ministry of the Interior. In China, however, the original formula was applied in full.

A BIBLIOGRAPHY OF PRIMARY SOURCES

Books

1. *Ajia Mondai Kōza*[1] (Lectures on Problems of Asia) Seijigunjihen[2] (Political Military Section), vol. II, Sogansha[3] (Tokyo, 1940). pp. 524.

2. Ch'en Shao-yü[1] (Wang Ming),[2] *Wu-chuang Pao-tung*[3] (Armed Uprisings) (Shanghai, 1929). pp. 160. Hoover Library, Chinese Coll. HX388C959.

3. Ch'en Tu-hsiu,[1] *Kao Ch'üan-tang T'ung-chih Shu*[2] (A Letter to All Our Party Comrades) (Shanghai, 1929). pp. 25. Hoover Library, Chinese Coll. HX388C519.

4. *Ch'en Tu-hsiu P'ing-lun*[1] (Discussions Concerning Ch'en Tu-hsiu), Pei-p'ing Tung-ya Shu-chü[2] (Peiping, 1933). pp. 256.

5. Ch'en Tu-hsiu, *Tu-hsiu Wen-ts'un*[1] (Collected Works of Ch'en Tu-hsiu), Oriental Book Co. (Shanghai, 1922), 3 vols. pp. 662.

6. Ch'en Tu-hsiu, *Wo-men ti Cheng-chih I-chien-shu*[1] (A Statement of Our Political Views) (Shanghai, 1929). pp. 46. Hoover Library, Chinese Coll. HX388C516.

7. Ch'en Tuan-chih,[1] *Wu-ssu Yün-tung chih Shih ti P'ing-chia*[2] (An Historical Evaluation of the May Fourth Movement), Sheng-huo[3] (Shanghai, 1935). pp. 390.

8. Chin Tung-p'ing,[1] *Yen-an Chien-wen-lu*[2] (A Record of an Inspection Trip to Yenan), Tu-li Ch'u-pan-she[3] (Chungking, 1945). pp. 164.

9. Chou En-lai,[1] *Mu-ch'ien Chung-kuo Tang ti Tsu-chih Wen-t'i*[2] (Organizational Problems of the Party in China at the Present Time) (Shanghai, 1929). pp. 44. Hoover Library, Chinese Coll. HX388C539.

10. Chou En-lai, *Shao-shan Pao-Kao San-chung Ch'uan-hui Ts'ai-liao*[1] (Report of Shao-shan [Chou En-lai] Materials on the Third Plenum of the Central Committee) (1929). pp. 44. Hoover Library, Chinese Coll. HX388C539.

11. Ch'ü Ch'iu-pai[1] (Kushuhaku), *Chūgoku Kakumei*[2] (The Chinese Revolution), a Japanese translation from Chinese. pp. 340. Library of Congress.

12. Ch'ü Ch'iu-pai, *Chung-kuo Ch'ü-hsiao-chu-i ho Chi-hui-chu-i*[1] (Liquidationism and Opportunism in China), Kommunisticheskaya Universita Trudyashchikhsya Kitaia Im. Sun Yat-sena (The Communist University of the Toilers of China in the Name of Sun Yat-sen) (Moscow, 1929). pp. 50.

13. Ch'ü Ch'iu-pai, *Chung-kuo Ko-ming chih Cheng-lun Wen-t'i*[1] (Controversial Questions of the Chinese Revolution) (Shanghai, 1927). pp. 222. Hoover Library, microfilm.

14. Ch'ü Ch'iu-pai, *Chung-kuo Ko-ming yü Kung-ch'an-tang*[1] (The Chinese Revolution and the Communist Party) (1928). pp. 298. Hoover Library, Chinese Coll. HX388C561.

15. Chu-Hsin-fan,[1] *Chung-kuo Ko-ming yü Chung-kuo She-hui Ko-Chieh-chi*[2] (The Chinese Revolution and the Various Classes of Chinese Society), Hsin Sheng-ming Shu-chü[3] (Shanghai, 1930). pp. 364.

16. *Chung-kung Chung-yang Ti-erh-tz'u Ch'üan-t'i Hui-i Ts'ai-liao*[1] (Materials of the Second Plenum of the Central Committee of the Chinese Communist Party), K.U.T.K. (Sun Yat-sen University) (Moscow, 1929). pp. 137. Library of Congress.

17. *Chung-kuo Ko-ming Wen-t'i Lun-wen-chi*[1] (A Collection of Articles on Problems of the Chinese Revolution), Hsin-Ch'ing-nien-she[2] (Shanghai, 1927). pp. 544. Hoover Library, Chinese Coll. HX-388C518.

18. *Chung-kuo Kung-ch'an-tang Chung-yang Wei-yüan-hui K'uo-ta ti Ti-ssu-tz'u Ch'uan-t'i Hui-i I-chüeh-an*[1] (The Resolution of the Fourth Enlarged Plenum of the Central Committee of the Chinese Communist Party) (Shanghai, 1931). pp. 5. Hoover Library, Chinese Coll. HX384.31.1931 A.I.

19. *Chung-kuo Kung-ch'an-tang Pa-yüeh Hui-i Hsüan-yen*[1] (Manifesto of the August Conference of the Chinese Communist Party), K.U.T.K. (Sun Yat-sen University) (Moscow, 1927). pp. 50. Library of Congress.

20. *Chung-kuo Kung-ch'an-tang Ti-liu-tz'u Ch'üan-kuo Ta-hui Chüeh-i-an*[1] (The Resolutions of the Sixth All-China Congress of the Chinese Communist Party). pp. 272. Hoover Library, Chinese Coll. HX388C588.

21. *Chung-kuo Kung-ch'an-tang Ti-liu Tai-piao Ta-hui Kuan-yü Nung-min Wen-t'i ti Chüeh-i-an*[1] (The Resolution of the Sixth Congress of the Chinese Communist Party on the Peasant Problem), K.U.T.K. (Sun Yat-sen University) (Moscow, 1928). pp. 11. Library of Congress.

22. "The Declaration of the Chinese Communist Party on the Political Situation," translated by Leo Steiner from *Novyi Vostok* (The New East) (1922), no. 2. pp. 600–612.

23. Dewey, John, *Letters from China and Japan*, E. P. Dutton (New York, 1921).

24. *The Fourth Congress of the Communist International* (London, 1922). pp. 291.

25. Hatano, Kanichi,[1] *Sekishoku Shina no Kyūmei*[2] (A Study of Red China), Daito Shuppansha[3] (Tokyo, 1941). pp. 384.

26. Ho Meng-hsiung,[1] *Ho Meng-hsiung I-chien-shu*[2] (A Statement of the Views of Ho Meng-hsiung) (1931?). pp. 8. Hoover Library, Chinese Coll. HX384A4464.

27. *Hsien-tai Shih-liao*[1] (Material on Modern History), Hai-t'ien Ch'u-pan-she[2] (Shanghai, 1934). 3 vols. Hoover Library, Chinese Coll. DS775.H873.

28. Hua Kang,[1] *Chung-kuo Ta Ko-ming-shih*[2] (A History of the Great Chinese Revolution), Ch'un-keng Shu-t'ien[3] (Shanghai, 1932). pp. 561.

29. Isaacs, Harold, *Five Years of Kuomintang Reaction*, Forum Publishing Co. (Shanghai, 1932).

30. Isaacs, Harold, *The Tragedy of the Chinese Revolution*, Sacker and Warburg (London, 1938). pp. 502.

31. Johanson i Taube, *Soviety v Kitae* (Soviets in China), translated from German, Partiinoe Izdatyel'stvo (Moscow, 1934). pp. 518.

32. *Die Kommunistische International vor dem VIIten Weltkongress* (The Communist International Before the Seventh World Congress), Verlagsgenossenschaft Auslandischer Arbeiter (Moscow, 1935). pp. 718.

33. Kuo Chan-po,[1] *Chin Wu-shih-nien Chung-kuo Ssu-hsiang-shih*[2] (An Intellectual History of China in the Last Fifty Years), Jen-wen Shu-tien[3] (Peiping, 1935). pp. 432.

34. Lenin, V., *Ausgewählte Werke* (Selected Works), Marx-Engels-Lenin Institut (Moscow, 1937). 12 vols.

35. Lenin, V., *Imperialism, the Highest Stage of Capitalism*, International Publishers (New York, 1939).

36. Lenin, V., *Oeuvres Complètes*, Editions Sociales Internationales (Paris, 1935). 25 vols.

37. Lenin, V., *Sämtliche Werke*, Verlag für Literatur und Weltpolitik (Vienna, Berlin, 1929). 25 vols.

38. Lenin, V., *Selected Works*, Foreign Language Publishing House, (Moscow, 1947). 2 vols.

39. Lenin, V., *Selected Works*, International Publishers (New York). 12 vols.

40. Li Ang,[1] *Hung-se Wu-t'ai*[2] (The Red Stage), Sheng-li Ch'u-pan-she[3] (Chungking, 1942). pp. 184.

41. Li Li-san,[1] *Kung-ch'an Kuo-chi Tui Chung-kuo Ko-ming Chüeh-i-an*[2] (Resolutions of the Communist International on the Chinese Revolution), with a preface by Li entitled "Chung-kuo Ko-ming ti Chiao-hsün"[3] (The Lessons of the Chinese Revolution). Hoover Library, microfilm.

42. Lukacs, György, *Lenin, Eine Studie über den Zusammenhang seiner Gedanken* (Lenin, A Study of the Structure of His Thought), Malik Verlag (Vienna, 1924). pp. 77.

43. Mandalian, *Wei shen-mo Chung-kuo Kung-ch'an-tang ti Ling-tao P'o-ch'an*[1] (Why Did the Leadership of the Chinese Communist Party Fail?), translated from the Russian, K.U.T.K. (Sun Yat-sen University) (Moscow, 1927). pp. 13. Library of Congress.

44. Manuilsky, D., *The Revolutionary Crisis is Maturing*, International Publishers (New York, 1933). pp. 68. A speech at the Seventeenth Congress of the CPSU.

45. Mao Tse-tung,[1] *Mao Tse-tung Hsüan-chi*[2] (Selected Writings of Mao Tse-tung), Tung-pei Shu-tien[3] (1948). pp. 999. The latest edition of Mao's writings.

46. Marx, Karl, *Capital*, Modern Library, Random House (New York, 1906), vol. I.

47. Marx, Karl, *A Contribution to the Critique of Political Economy*, International Library Publishing Co. (New York, 1904). pp. 314.

48. Mif, Pavel, *Chin-chi Shih-chi-chung ti Chung-kuo Kung-ch'an-tang*[1] (The Chinese Communist Party in Critical Days), translated from the Russian (Moscow, 1928). pp. 79. Library of Congress.

49. Nakanishi Kō[1] and Nishisato Tatsuo,[2] *Bukan ni okeru Kakumei to Hankakumei*[3] (Revolution and Counterrevolution at Wuhan), Minshū Hyōronsha[4] (Tokyo, 1949). pp. 217. Hoover Library.

50. Nakanishi Kō, *Chūgoku Kyōsantoshi*[1] (A History of the Chinese Communist Party), Hakutosha[2] (Tokyo, 1949). pp. 271.

51. Nakanishi Kō and Nishisato Tatsuo, *Chugoku Kyosanto to Minzoku Toitsu Sensen*[1] (The Chinese Communist Party and the National United Front), Taigado[2] (Toyko, 1946). pp. 154.

52. Obikawa Tsunetada,[1] *Shina Seiji Soshiki no Kenkyu*[2] (A Study of China's Political Organization), Keiseisha[3] (Tokyo, 1933). pp. 1051.

53. Okubo, Yasushi,[1] *Chūkyō Sanjūnen*[2] (Thirty Years of Chinese Communism), Nyūsusha[3] (Tokyo, 1949). pp. 382. A collection of important documents.

54. Pasvolsky, Leo, *Russia in the Far East*, Macmillan (New York, 1922). pp. 181.

55. Plekhanov, George, *Fundamental Problems of Marxism*, International Publishers (New York, 1930). pp. 145.

56. *Resolutions adoptées à la IXᵉ session plénière du C.E. de l'I.C.* (Resolutions Adopted at the Ninth Plenum of the ECCI), Bureau d'Editions (Paris, 1928). pp. 56.

57. *Report to the Oriental Bureau of the Comintern* (translated at Hoover Library). pp. 25. Contains Li Li-san's recantation.

58. Roy Manabendra, *Revolution and Counterrevolution in China*, Renaissance Publishing Co. (Calcutta, 1948). pp. 478.

59. *Saikin Shina Nenkan*[1] (The New China Yearbook), Toa Dobunkai[2] (Tokyo, 1935). pp. 1703.

60. *The Seventh Congress of the Communist International*, Foreign Language Publishing House (Moscow, 1939). pp. 595.

61. *Shih-shih P'ing-lun Hui-k'an Ti-i-chi*[1] (Compilation No. 1 of Articles on Current Affairs) (Shanghai, 1931). pp. 58. Hoover Library, Chinese Coll. HX388K94.

62. Shih Ts'un-t'ung[1] and Yün Tai-ying,[2] *Chung-kuo Ko-ming ti Li-lun Wen-t'i*[3] (Theoretical Problems of the Chinese Revolution) and *Shih Ts'un-tung tui-yü Chung-kuo Ko-ming ti Li-lun*[4] (Shih Ts'un-tung's Theory of the Chinese Revolution), K.U.T.K. (Sun Yat-sen University) (Moscow, 1929). pp. 90. Library of Congress.

63. *Shina Kyōsantō no Gaikan*[1] (A General Survey of the Chinese Communist Party) (Tokyo, 1929). Library of Congress.

64. *Shina Kyōsantō Undōshi*[1] (A History of the Chinese Communist Movement), Sambo Hombu[2] (The General Staff) (Tokyo, 1931). pp. 382. Library of Congress.

65. *Shina Sobieto Undō no Kenkyū*[1] (A Study of the Chinese Soviet Movement), Tōa Keizai Chōsakyoku[2] (Tokyo, 1934). pp. 459. Hoover Library, Japanese Coll. HX387T627.

66. Shub, David, *Lenin, A Biography*, Doubleday (Garden City, 1948). pp. 438.

67. Smedley, Agnes, *China's Red Army Marches*, Vanguard Press (New York, 1934). pp. 315.

68. Snow, Edgar, *Red Star Over China*, Modern Library, Random House (New York, 1938). pp. 529.

69. Strong, Anna Louise, *China's Millions*, Coward-McCann (New York, 1928). pp. 413.

70. *Su-lien Yin-mou Wen-cheng Hui-pien*[1] (A Collection of Documents on the Soviet Conspiracy) (Peking, 1928). 2 vols. Hoover Library, Chinese Coll. DS775K16. The documents seized in the Soviet Embassy by Chang Tso-lin.

71. Tai Chi-t'ao,[1] *Sun-wen-chu-i chih Che-hsüeh chih Chi-ch'u*[2] (The Philosophic Foundations of Sun Yat-senism) (Shanghai, 1925). pp. 60.

72. *T'an-ho Kung-ch'an-tang Liang Ta-yao-an*[1] (Two Proposals for the Impeachment of the Communist Party), subtitle *Chung-kuo Kuo-min-tang Kuang-tung Chih-pu T'an-ho Kung-ch'an-tang Yüan-wen chi Tsung-li chih P'i-shih*[2] (Original Text of the Proposal of the Kwangtung Branch of the Kuomintang for the Impeachment of the Communist Party, annotated by Dr. Sun Yat-sen) (Shanghai, 1923). pp. 30.

73. Tang Leang-Li, *The Inner History of the Chinese Revolution*, Routledge and Sons Ltd. (London, 1930). pp. 365.

74. Teng Chung-hsia,[1] *Chung-kuo Chih-kung Yün-tung Chien-shih*[2] (A Short History of the Chinese Labor Movement), Chieh-fang-she (Yenan, 1943). pp. 287.

75. *Thèses et resolutions du VIᵉ congrès de l'I.C.* (Theses and Resolutions of the Sixth Comintern Congress), Bureau d'Editions (Paris). pp. 230.

76. *Ti-liu-tz'ü T'u-ti Wen-t'i ti Chüeh-i-an*[1] (Resolution of the Sixth Congress on the Land Question), K.U.T.K. (Sun Yat-sen University), Library of Congress (Moscow, 1928). pp. 23.

77. Ti-liu-tz'u Ta-hui-hou ti Cheng-chih Kung-tso[1] (Political Activities After the Sixth Congress), Shanghai Min-chih Shu-chü[2] (Shanghai, 1929). pp. 282. Hoover Library. An extremely significant collection of party circulars.

78. Trotsky, Leon, *The Permanent Revolution*, Pioneer Publishers (New York, 1931). pp. 157.

79. Trotsky, Leon, *Problems of the Chinese Revolution*, Pioneer Publishers (New York, 1932). pp. 432.

80. Trotsky, Leon, *Stalin*, Hollis and Carter (London, 1947). pp. 516.

81. Trotsky, Leon, *The Third International After Lenin*, Pioneer Publishers (New York, 1936). pp. 357.

82. Wales, Nym, *Inside Red China*, Doubleday, Doran (New York, 1939). pp. 356.

83. Wang I-shih,[1] *K'ang-chan i-ch'ien ti Chung-kuo Kung-ch'an-tang*[2] (The Chinese Communist Party Before the War of Resistance), Sheng-li Ch'u-pan-she[3] (Chungking, 1942). pp. 100.

84. Wolfe, Bertram, *Three Who Made a Revolution*, Dial Press (New York, 1948). pp. 661.

85. Yakhontoff, Victor, *The Chinese Soviets*, Coward-McCann (New York, 1934). pp. 296.

86. Ypsilon (pseudonym), *Pattern for World Revolution*, Ziff-Davis (New York, 1947). pp. 479.

Periodicals and Newspapers

87. *Bol'shevik*, Izdatyel'stvo Pravda (Moscow, 1921–). Russian Research Center, microfilm.

88. *Chien-she*[1] (Reconstruction), a monthly, Chien-she Yüeh-K'an-she[2] (Shanghai, 1919–1920), vols. I–II. Yenching Institute Library.

89. *Chūō Kōron*[1] (Central Review), a monthly, Chuo Koronsha[2] (Tokyo, 1912–). Yenching Institute Library.

90. *The Communist International*, Workers Library Publishers (New York, 1924–1938). Widener Library.

91. *Hsiang-tao Chou-pao*[1] (Guide Weekly) (Shanghai, 1925–1927), nos. 150–171, 184–186. Library of Congress, microfilm. Organ of the Chinese Communist Party.

92. *Hsin Ch'ing-nien*[1] (Youth), Shanghai Ya-tung T'u-shu-kuan Ch'iu-i Shu-she[2] (Shanghai, Peking, 1915–1921). 7 vols. Yenching Institute Library.

93. *Hung-ch'i*[1] (The Red Flag). Hoover Library. Chinese Coll. HX384A1936. Scattered issues from 1929 to 1931. A party organ.

94. *Hung-chi Chou-pao*[1] (The Red Flag Weekly). Hoover Library, Chinese Coll. HX384A1936. Scattered issues from 1931 to 1934. A party organ.

95. *International Press Correspondence* (Moscow, 1925–1935). 10 vols. Organ of the Executive Committee of the Communist International. Widener Library.

96. *Kaizō*,[1] Kaizōsha[2] (Tokyo, 1932–). Yenching Institute Library.

97. *Kommunisticheskii Internatsional*, weekly organ, Ispolnitel'nogo Komityeta Kommunisticheskogo Internatsionala (Moscow, 1920–). Russian Research Center, microfilm.

98. *Kuo Wen Chou-pao*,[1] weekly, Kuo-wen Chou-pao-she[2] (Tientsin, 1931). Yenching Institute Library.

99. *Materialy po Kitaiskomu Voprosu* (Materials on the Chinese Question), K.U.T.K. (Sun Yat-sen University) (Moscow, 1927–1928), nos. 9–14. Widener Library.

100. *Pravda* (Moscow, 1918–). Russian Research Center, microfilm.

101. *Revolyutsionnyi Vostok* (The Revolutionary East), Nauchno-, isslyedovatyel'skaya Assotsiatsiya po Izucheniyu Natsional'nykh I Kolonialnykh Problem (The Scientific Association for the Study of National and Colonial Problems) (Moscow, 1931–1933). Scattered issues 1931–1933. Chinese Library, Harvard University.

102. *Pu'rh-se-wei-k'o*[1] (Bolshevik) (Shanghai, Juichin). Scattered issues, 1930–1932. Hoover Library, Chinese Coll. HX384A1976.

Chinese names and titles followed by small reference numbers in the Bibliography are rendered in their original form on the following two pages. In title no. 10, the character for *Kao* was inadvertently omitted.

NOTES TO BIBLIOGRAPHY

1. (1)アジア 問題講座 (2)政治軍事篇 (3)創元社
2. (1)陳韶玉 (2)王明 (3)武裝暴動
3. (1)陳獨秀 (2)告全黨同志書
4. (1)陳獨秀評論 (2)北平東亞書局
5. (1)獨秀文存
6. (1)我們的政治意見書
7. (1)陳端志 (2)五四運動之史的評價 (3)生活
8. (1)金東平 (2)延安見聞錄 (3)獨立出版社
9. (1)周恩來 (2)目前中國黨的組織問題
10. (1)少山報.中三全會材料
11. (1)瞿秋白 (2)中國革命
12. (1)中國取消主義和機會主義
13. (1)中國革命之爭論問題
14. (1)中國革命與共產黨
15. (1)朱新繁 (2)中國革命與中國社會各階級 (3)新生命書局
16. (1)中共中央第二次全體會議材料
17. (1)中國革命問題論文集 (2)新青年社
18. (1)中國共產黨中央委員會擴大的第四次全體會議

19. (1)中國共產黨八月會議宣言
20. (1)中國共產黨第六次全國大會決議案
21. (1)中國共產黨第六 代表大會關於農民問題的決議案
25. (1)波多野乾一 (2)赤色支那の究明 (3)大東出版社
26. (1)何孟雄 (2)何孟雄意見書
27. (1)現代史料 (2)海天出版社
28. (1)華崗 (2)中國大革命史 (3)春耕書店
33. (1)郭湛波 (2)近五十年中國思想史 (3)人文書店
40. (1)李昂 (2)紅色舞台 (3)勝利出版社
41. (1)李立三 (2)共產國際對中國革命決議案 (3)中國革命的教訓
43. (1)為什么中國共產黨的領導破產
45. (1)毛澤東 (2)毛澤東選集 (3)東北書店
48. (1)緊急時期中的中國共產黨
49. (1)中西功 (2)西里 龍夫 (3)武漢に於ける革命と反革命 (4)民主評論社

50. (1)中國共產黨史 (2)白都社

51. (1)中國共產黨と民族統一戰線 (2)大雅堂

52. (1)及川恒忠 (2)支那政治組織の研究 (3)啓成社

53. (1)大久保泰 (2)中共三十年 (3)ニューズ社

59. (1)最近支那年鑑 (2)東亞同文會

61. (1)時事評論彙刊第一集

62. (1)施存統 (2)惲代英 (3)中國革命的理論問題 (4)施存統對於中國革命的理論

63. (1)支那共產黨の概觀

64. (1)支那共產黨運動史 (2)參謀本部

65. (1)支那ソヴィート運動の研究 (2)東亞經濟調査局

70. (1)蘇聯陰謀文證彙編

71. (1)戴季陶 (2)孫文主義之哲學之基礎

72. (1)彈劾共產黨兩大要案 (2)中國國民黨廣東支部彈劾共產黨原文及總理之批釋

74. (1)鄧中夏 (2)中國職工運動簡史

76. (1)第六次土地問題的決議案

77. (1)第六次大會後的政治工作 (2)上海民志書局

83. (1)王一士 (2)抗戰以前的中國共產黨 (3)勝利出版社

88. (1)建設 (2)建設月刊社

89. (1)中央公論 (2)中央公論社

91. (1)嚮導週報

92. (1)新青年 (2)亞東圖書館求益書社

93. (1)紅旗

94. (1)紅旗週報

96. (1)改造 (2)改造社

98. (1)國聞週報 (2)國聞週報社

102. (1)布爾塞維克

INDEX

Adventurism, Li Li-san attacked for, 159–160

Agrarian question, policy of Chinese Communist Party, 65–68; Mao's report on, in Hunan, 73–78, 84; in August Seventh Conference, 95, 121

All-China Conference of the Soviets, First, 185, 194

All-China Labor Conference, First, 36

All-China Labor Federation, 53, 126

"Analysis of the Different Classes of Chinese Society" (Mao Tse-tung), 74

Anarchism, in China, 31, 33

Anhwei, partisan groups in, 173

Anti-Bolshevik faction, in Soviet areas, 174, 177, 181, 182

Armed Uprisings (Wang Ming), 149–150

August Seventh Conference, 93–96, 97, 98–99

Autumn harvest uprisings, 99–102, 104

Backward areas, potentialities of, in world revolution, 7–8, 28, 30, 37; Trotsky's views on, 82

Basic Problems of the Chinese Revolution (P'eng Shu-chih), 68–69

"Basis for the Realization of Democracy, The" (Ch'en Tu-hsiu), 19

Bolsheviks. *See* October Revolution

Borodin, Mikhail, influence on Sun Yat-sen, 44; organization of Kuomintang, 50, 79, 80, 81, 83; in organization of Whampoa academy, 51; on armed peasants, 54; tension with Ch'en Tu-hsiu, 55; and March Twentieth incident, 56; agreement with Chiang, 56; and northern expedition, 57

Boxer Rebellion, Ch'en Tu-hsiu on, 14–15

Browder, Earl, 81

Buddhism, influence of, 9; in Li's philosophy, 10, 11; in Boxer Rebellion, 15

Bukharin, Nikolai, 104; on Kuomintang-Communist alliance, 55, 65, 71; at Seventh Plenum of ECCI, 69; on bourgeois revolution, 73; position on peasantry, 78; on Chinese Party

leadership, 87; on revolutionary surge in China, 110, 111

Cadets, 43

Canton, Ch'en Tu-hsiu at, 34

Canton Commune, 105–107, 111, 196

Central Committee, financial dependence on Soviet areas, 184; growing insecurity of, 185; removal to Juichin, 185–186. *See also* Communist Party, Chinese

Centralism, opposition to, in Chihli, 107–108

Chang Chi, attacks Kuomintang-Communist alliance, 51

Chang Fa-k'uei, 80; in Nanchang uprising, 90, 93; conflict with Li Chi-shen, 106

Chang Hsüeh-liang, attempts seizure of Chinese Eastern Railroad, 145–146

Chang Kuo-t'ao, 68, 107; in Society for the Study of Marxism, 16; conversion to Marxism-Leninism, 25, 26; in Li's Peking group, 34; in early Communist Party, 38; on Politburo, 73; position on urban proletariat, 78; rise of, in party, 93

Chang T'ai-lei, protests Canton uprising, 106

Chang Tso-lin, 83

Chang Tung-sun, on China's misery, 28

Chang Wen-t'ien (Lo Fu), 186; member of Returned Student Clique, 148

Changsha, abortive strikes in, 99; attack on, 141, 144–145, 151, 153, 158–159, 181–183

Ch'en Ch'iung-ming, warlord of Kwangtung, 34, 54

Ch'en Kung-po, at First Party Congress, 34

Ch'en Sheng-ch'ang, on Fut'ien incident, 176

Ch'en Tu-hsiu, 35, 161, 192; intellectual development of, 8–10, 12–13, 15; article on Von Ketteler Monument, 14–15; and Society for the Study of Marxism, 16; in May Fourth Movement, 17–19; influence of Dewey on, 19–20, 22–23;

in bid for power, 156; opposition to
Returned Student Clique, 164–166;
expulsion from party, 166; influence
in labor unions, 166–167
Lo I-nung, 60
Lominadze, Comintern delegate to
Chinese Party, 93, 103, 105, 113
Losovsky, on workers' and peasants'
movements, 159
Lukacs, George, on activity of Com-
munist Party, 191

Madyar, on Chinese society, 123
Manchester liberalism, 9
Mandalian, 81; on Kuomintang-Communist alliance, 53, 54, 60–61; on
Chinese Communist Party, 64
Manuilsky, D., on struggle around
China, 158; on Chinese revolution,
162, 192, 193, 194
*Manifesto of the August Seventh Con-
ference*, 93–95
Mao Tse-tung, 84; in Society for the
Study of Marxism, 16; conversion
to Marxism-Leninism, 25, 26; activities in Hunan province, 34, 35;
appreciation of Leninism, 35; organizational activities, 65; report on
agrarian movement in Hunan, 73–
78, 84; and formula of revolutionary elite, 85; in autumn harvest uprisings, 100–102, 104; takes refuge
in Chingkanshan mountains, 102–
103, 108; adherence to Marxist-
Leninist-Stalinist tradition, 116–
117; Moscow background of Communist development, 122, 123–124,
126, 136; in emergence of Red
Army, 135; autobiography, 172;
rise to preëminence, 172–178; relations to organs of party authority,
178–181; relations to Li Li-san
leadership, 181–183; assumes control of Chinese Communist Movement, 185; role of Moscow in leadership of, 187–188; strategy of,
189–191; and Marxist-Leninist
dogma, 191–199; and party line,
199–201; as faithful Stalinist, 201–
204
March Twentieth incident, Chiang's
coup d'état, 54–56
Maring, 31; interview with Sun Yat-
sen, 38; and Kuomintang-Communist alliance, 39, 40–41, 43, 44
Maritime union, 166–167
Marx, Karl, 37

Marxism, neglect of, in China prior to
1919, 7–8; concept of morality, 23;
attitude toward peasantry, 117. *See
also* Society for the Study of Marxism
Marxism-Leninism, philosophies of Li
Ta-chao and Ch'en Tu-hsiu, 8–13;
influence of October Revolution, 12,
13–16; appeal of, to Chinese intelligentsia, 22, 85; problems of, 28;
concept of political parties, 43;
Maoist strategy and, 191–199;
abiding elements of, 201–204
Mass movement, Chinese Communist
control of, 52, 53–54
"Material Change and Ethical
Change" (Li Ta-chao), 23
May Fourth Movement, 8; rise of
nationalism, 17–18; influence of
Russell and Dewey, 19; in rise of
Chinese proletariat, 25; in Shang-
hai, 31
May Thirtieth incident (1925), 52–
53, 107
Mensheviks, 43
Mif, Pavel, 61, 81, 164; on Ch'en Tu-
hsiu, 64; on Fifth Party Congress
(1927), 68; on Soviet movement in
China, 139–140; appointed Comin-
tern Delegate to China, 148–149,
151; seeks to unseat Li Li-san, 154,
155, 156, 159; on economic struggle
of Chinese proletariat, 160–161; and
Wang Ming leadership, 165–166; in
Fourth Plenum, 169–170
Militarists, Chinese, 56–57
Mill, John Stuart, 7
Molotov, V. M., 157
Montesquieu, Charles de, 7
Morality, Marxian and Confucian, 23–
24
"My Views on Marxism," (Li Ta-
chao), 16–17

Nakanishi, on Maoist development of
Chinese Communism, 116
Nanchang, 182; uprising at, 90, 92–
93, 104
Nanking, 182; breaks control of labor
unions, 97; Central Committee ac-
tivities in, 129
Narodniks, 76, 89, 117
Nationalism, of student generation of
1919, 17–18; bourgeois, Soviet em-
phasis on, in Asia, 38; Sun's and
Ch'en's views of, 42; effect of north-

Russian Research Center Studies

* Out of print.
† Publications of the Harvard Project on the Soviet Social System.
‡ Published jointly with the Center for International Affairs, Harvard University.